The Secret Language
of Financial Reports

The Secret Language of Financial Reports

The Back Stories That Can Enhance Your Investment Decisions

Mark E. Haskins

Darden Graduate School of Business

University of Virginia

New York   Chicago   San Francisco   Lisbon
London   Madrid   Mexico City   Milan   New Delhi
San Juan   Seoul   Singapore   Sydney   Toronto

1 2 3 4 5 6 7 8 9 0   DOC/DOC   0 9 8 7

ISBN 978-0-07-154553-2
MHID 0-07-154553-0

This book is printed on acid-free paper.

This book is dedicated to my son, Greg, and,
to my daughter, Meredith. I love you both.

Contents

Secret #5

It's as Simple as 1-2-3
It's all about ins and outs; ups and downs!

Secret #6

It's Old News
Is it relevant, reliable, neither, or both?

Secret #7

It's Full of Choices
What's your pleasure?

Secret #8

It's Imprecise
Give it your best guess!

Secret #9

It's Incomplete
Something is missing

Secret #10

It's Blessed (Most of the Time)
Of controls and certifications

Secret #11

It's Important
Perfect? No! Useful? Yes!

Secret #12

Secret #13

Secret #14

Foreword

After the United States' stock market collapse in 1929, there was enormous pressure on the government to act. Congress held hearings and considered a variety of new regulations to prevent the stock market abuses that had contributed to the depth of the depression. One of the critical questions, in that emotion charged time, was what role the government should play in the regulation of the stock market. The regulation that prevailed determined that investment decisions should be left to the individual investors, as it had been in the past—but with a big difference. Companies who wanted to sell their stock to the public would be required to provide full, public disclosure about their financial affairs. A government agency was given the responsibility to establish the minimum standards for that public disclosure, but that agency was to be specifically precluded from expressing any opinion as to the suitability of the stock for any investor. That agency was the Securities and Exchange Commission (SEC).

That full-disclosure approach, adopted in the Securities Acts of 1933 and 1934, was entirely consistent with the Western world's long established notion of individual responsibility, whereby investors should be free to make their own decisions, to benefit from their own wisdom, and suffer from their own mistakes. It was also consistent with an emerging notion of corporate accountability, whereby every company that raised money from investors, no matter how large, had a duty to explain what was done with those funds.

The SEC has the primary responsibility for establishing full disclosure standards, but has long delegated financial reporting issues to private-sector standard-setting bodies; today, in the United States, it is the Financial Accounting Standards Board (FASB). Together, the SEC and the FASB have agreed that the financial statements and footnotes included in each company's annual and quarterly reports would be at the heart of full disclosure. As a result, companies have the ability (and the obligation) to tell their story in full. As investors, we have the opportunity (and the obligation) to dig into the full disclosure packages offered by companies and look for nuggets. That search can be fulfilling and rewarding. Mark Haskins' *The Secret Language of Financial Reports* can help demystify the words and the practices that underlie the annual reports that companies provide as they complete their side of the full disclosure process.

As Haskins points out, that core set of financial statements includes a balance sheet (where does the company stand today, financially) an income statement (what were the results of the company's operations during the last period) and a statement of cash flows (where did the company's cash come from during the period and where did it go). Those statements are supported by footnotes that provide further information, not readily quantifiable in the financial statements themselves. Those statements, and those additional footnote disclosures, are required by SEC rules and regulations and by Generally Accepted Accounting Principles (GAAP).

In this day of the Internet, investors have a wide variety of sources from which to gather information about stocks they are considering. Most every publicly traded company has a website and one of the windows on the site will be "investor information." In that window, the company provides access to their most recent annual and quarterly reports. Most companies also mail those reports to registered shareholders as well, but a few have insisted that shareholders download quarterly reports on their own. Very soon the SEC will have available a system called XBRL. With that system, a potential investor will be able to download financial statements from a set of companies and do comparative analysis of all of the companies in that set. XBRL has the potential to dramatically impact the traditional approach to investment analysis; but it will still depend on the core financial statements filed with the annual report. XBRL will make it much easier to do an intelligent analysis of a company's annual report, but it will be incumbent on the XBRL user to understand the conventions underlying the preparation of the financial statements themselves.

In addition to formal, published annual and quarterly reports, most companies make information available to the investment community through press releases, presentations to analyst meetings, and conference calls with interested parties. The SEC enacted Regulation FD, which says that if important information is provided to one interested party it must be available to all interested parties. In some respects, the Regulation FD depends on the financial press for dissemination of information. A CEO may meet with an analyst one-on-one, but if any important information comes from that meeting, it must then be available, as in a press release, before it can be acted on. Although these informal means of disseminating information about a company are important to a company's efforts to tell its story, it is also important to note that all of that information is subject to cross analysis—proof, if you will—by reference to the company's annual and quarterly reports filed in the normal, formal manner. Any information provided in a conference call or a CEO speech will be anchored in, and confirmed by, the data in the annual report.

Preparing an annual report for public dissemination is a challenging, mind-expanding experience—there are almost always fascinating decisions to make. If the report contains good news it will be pleasant work, but if the report has to present bad news (e.g., sales are down and we lost money for the first time in 10 years) it will be heavy going. Our financial reporting system asks management to prepare its own annual report—reporting on its stewardship of the investors' funds. Because we know that it is human nature to want to delay reporting bad news, most companies make sure that their financial reporting processes are subject to a set of rigorous safeguards. Still, even with safeguards, we have seen too many instances of fraudulent financial reporting. Some annual report readers managed to avoid investing in companies whose financial statements were fraudulent. In retrospect it seems clear that they carefully analyzed the results reported in the company's annual reports and asked themselves logical questions. Not all frauds can be uncovered by outside investors, but a careful study of the annual report is always the first line of defense.

Robert J. Sack
Emeritus Professor, Darden Graduate School, UVA
Former Chief Accountant Enforcement Division, SEC
Former Partner, Touche Ross & Company

Preface

One day soon, you'll likely need to read a corporate annual report. Why? There are many possible reasons: Maybe you are heading off to business school. Perhaps you'll want to evaluate an investment in a publicly traded company. Perhaps a current or prospective employer will share year-end information about its financial performance. During negotiations with a major vendor or customer, you may receive that firm's annual report as part of a package about its business situation. You are a newly promoted, nonfinancial manager and now participate in management meetings where your company's financial picture and performance are discussed. An annual report may cross your desk for any of these reasons and many others. Now be honest: Last time you received a corporate annual report, did you . . .

1. Throw it away immediately?
2. Skim a few paragraphs, glance at the pictures, notice that several pages were filled with numbers, and *then* throw it away?
3. Look at its financial statements and wonder how precise, complete, and relevant they really were?
4. Notice the footnotes to those financial statements, but discount them as trivial—being merely footnotes?
5. Vow never to read an annual report again?

If you answered "yes" to any of the questions above, you are not alone. A popular magazine once called annual reports "the million books that no one reads." That's a pity. There are some great stories in these reports.

I've been a professor for more than 25 years. I teach the fundamentals of corporate annual reports to nonfinancial business executives and MBA students with no business background. Many people need a basic understanding of corporate annual reports. But few possess it. They find these documents daunting, even impenetrable. They recoil from their financial jargon. Some try to plow through a corporate annual report, but make it only halfway, reaching incomplete or erroneous conclusions about the company and then giving up. In recognition of this tendency, this book is for you. Its goal is to help you navigate the primary parts of an annual report, understand its context and constructs, recognize what it does and does not communicate, and never again have to answer yes to any of the questions above.

This book views legally prepared annual reports as a form of financial storytelling. We'll cut through the complexity, mystery, and jargon to provide a clear view of what such a story does and does not convey. In so doing, this book explains the basic elements of annual reports in simple ways, using diagrams, analogies, and examples. It offers some suggestions to develop insight into a company's performance and condition. It sheds light on the forces at work behind the scenes in producing annual reports. It also discusses the lack of precision, timeliness, completeness, and relevancy inherent in parts of an annual report's financial statements. All of this is done to foster a comprehensive appreciation for the context in which annual reports are crafted and to gain a more complete, better informed understanding of their purpose and contents.

This is not a typical book on accounting or finance. It clearly deals with the financial reporting practices contained in more traditional accounting primers but it does so much more succinctly and with an emphasis on the larger business settings, trade-offs, and concerns within which those practices exist. Thus, this book is an important prerequisite for other books devoted to financial statement analysis techniques.

This book is organized around 14 fundamental secrets found in corporate annual reports. Each is used as a window into the fundamental, practical, and less widely recognized attributes of the topic. The overarching point is this: Financial statements and corporate annual reports are important man-made artifacts. They're developed in response to a demand for information in the financial marketplace. As a result, they can best be understood in the context of the purposes, preferences, systems, compromises, and shortcomings behind their construction. These are the "secrets" revealed in this book:

1. There's a Corporate Financial Trilogy: *How many financial stories does a company really tell?*
2. It's Storytelling: *With characters, plot, and action*
3. It's a Language: *What do those new words mean?*
4. There's a Trilogy within the Trilogy: *The BS, the IS, and the SCF*
5. It's as Simple as 1-2-3: *It's all about ins and outs, ups and downs*
6. It's Old News: *Is it relevant, reliable, neither, or both?*
7. It's Full of Choices: *What's your pleasure?*
8. It's Imprecise: *Give it your best guess*
9. It's Incomplete: *Something is missing*
10. It's Blessed (Most of the Time): *Of controls and certifications*
11. It's Important: *Perfect? No! Useful? Yes!*
12. It's a Global Challenge: *Can't we all just get along?*
13. It's Political: *Let's make a deal*
14. It's Not Always as Simple as 1-2-3: *Four issues for the experts*

Throughout this book, my goal is to help you learn about financial reporting in as interesting, honest, and engaging a way as possible. In the spirit of facilitating your mastery and enjoyment of what you read, each "secret" begins with a set of key questions that set the stage for that chapter's content. Each chapter concludes with three recurring sections. One is a brief summary of chapter takeaways under the heading, "The Inside Scoop" Next, there is a section titled "Practical Application," in which you're led through an application of those takeaways to a financial report–related scenario. Each chapter also looks forward to the one that follows with a teaser entitled "In Anticipation of the Next Secret."

If you were to attend one of my seminars, you'd likely hear me ask a student at some point, "Please explain that for Grandma, who was a bright, witty woman, but never went to business school." With that question, I'd be asking for simple language and clear, intuitive explanations. In that spirit, and in the pages that follow, my goal is to make annual reports real, understandable, and meaningful to those who might not otherwise have believed that possible. That's the litmus test for this book. So here's to you, Grandma. You're an inspiration.

Mark Haskins
Charlottesville, VA

Acknowledgments

This book has been in my head for nearly a decade. It is now on paper as the result of a number of wonderful people. I want to thank Kathy Kane and Debbie Quarles of the Darden School, University of Virginia. They are excellent assistants and caring colleagues. A special thanks goes to Dianne Wheeler, my editor at McGraw-Hill. Her professionalism is outstanding, her enthusiasm contagious, and her kind heart refreshing. My gratitude is also extended to Lorna Brown of McGraw-Hill. She has been a friendly face at my office door for many years and helped launch this book. I want to thank Marc Goldstein of Impact LLC and Amy Lemley of the Darden School for their excellent editing skills. The book benefitted greatly from their practiced eye and narrative suggestions. It is important to also thank Debbie Masi and James Cappio at Westchester Book Group for their attention to detail and for shepherding the book through production so smoothly. Moreover, this is a better book because of the objective and frank critiques of numerous other professionals along the way. Last, I want to thank my Heavenly Father for His grace.

The Secret Language
of Financial Reports

Secret #1

There's a Corporate Financial Trilogy

How many financial stories does a company really tell?

The questions behind Secret #1:

- What are the three financial stories that a company prepares every year?
- How do these differ from one another?
- Can we financially reconcile the three stories?
- Do we have access to all three?
- Can we comfortably rely on just one of them?

All great performers customize their portrayal of a theme to meet the needs of their audience. Politicians emphasize different issues in the Rust Belt than they do in the Sunbelt. Musicians interpret their songs in one way at nightclubs, and in quite another at arenas. When reciting *The Iliad* and *The Odyssey*, the poet Homer is said to have revised his epics to honor his hosts on a given night. Even you or I may relate the events of our lives in one way to our parents, in another to our spouses, and in quite another to our children. All three versions will be truthful. But they may differ dramatically in emphasis. Each may include some details and omit others.

When a company tells its financial story, it follows a similar dynamic. Each year, corporations report their financial results via a trilogy—in three different ways, addressing the needs of different audiences and pursuing different goals.

Corporate Audiences

There are several constituencies to which a company must regularly provide financial information. One key audience includes current and future shareholders and lenders. A second is the tax authorities. A third includes the company's own managers, who make myriad ongoing strategic and operating decisions. Companies generate three sets of financially oriented books, one for each audience, resulting in three slightly different versions of their financial story for a given time period. If a company does work for the federal government, as defense contractors do, or if it operates in a regulated industry, as utilities do, it may keep additional sets of books for those audiences.

Now you may say, "Aha! I knew it! There should only be one financial story!" But before you call the Attorney General, please let me assure you: multiple sets of books are a good and necessary thing. By way of analogy, consider your checkbook register and your income tax return.

Insider's Note

Companies prepare at least three financial stories—one for external constituencies (e.g., lenders and shareholders), one for its managers, and one for the tax authorities.

Your checkbook, assuming it is up to date, offers a window into your daily finances. Its balance tells you how much you can spend today on food, clothing, travel, and entertainment. You wouldn't use a tax return to run such household finances or monitor cash on hand. And yet, your tax return does represent one version of a year's financial activities. It is connected in many ways to the financial picture that emerges from all the ins and outs of your checkbook. But it's not identical with the register.

Note that I said "connected to," not "identical with." As we all know, there are items on our tax returns that don't appear in our checkbooks. These include the standard deduction that we're allowed to take, the child tax credit, and deductions for other dependents. You'll never find these in a checkbook. And yet, they're a real part of each year's financial story as told to the tax authorities.

Similarly, if you were to estimate the net increase in your personal wealth this year, you'd include certain items that don't appear in either your checkbook or tax return. For example, you'd measure any appreciation in the value of your home, as well as depreciation of your cars. Thus, even in our personal lives, we have at least three ways to compose our financial results for a given year.

A Framework for Corporate Financial Stories

Let's consider the corporate financial trilogy in more detail. Each component—the external constituent, the internal managerial, and the tax books—differs from the others along six dimensions:

- Target audience
- Reports produced
- Goals and objectives
- The authority governing those reports
- The guidance through which that authority codifies its instructions
- Time frame

> ### Insider's Note
> *A company's three sets of books have different target audiences, objectives, and governing authorities.*

The External Constituent Financial Books

Current and prospective shareholders comprise a key audience for corporations, as they seek to understand the financial health and performance of the companies in which they're holding or contemplating an investment. Current and prospective lenders take a similar interest, as financial results determine a company's ability to service its debt. Naturally, any organization seeking to acquire a company will review its financial books with particular care. A company's major suppliers, customers, and partners will also review its financial books, seeking to evaluate the risks and rewards of their relationship with it. (Any former supplier to Enron or WorldCom can attest to the importance of those risks—if it is still in business.)

In these financial books, the primary company-generated story is presented in the annual report. Suffice it to say that annual reports consist of numerous elements, including a balance sheet, income statement, statement of cash flows, and other financial tabulations. Annual reports also contain explanatory financial statement footnotes, along with certifications from managers and auditors about the company's proper use of financial reporting conventions and the effectiveness of the company's controls over the financial reporting process.

The objectives of an annual report are fourfold. First, an annual report must be constructed and composed of information that complies with all applicable financial reporting regulations. Second, it must strive to faithfully represent the actual financial condition of the company as of the reporting date, as well as its financial performance for the year then ended. Third, it must provide information that is useful for external readers' decision making. That is, its content must be sufficiently relevant and reliable to serve as the basis for ascertaining, at a minimum, whether the company is financially sound. Fourth, and let's be honest here, most companies will legally seek in their annual reports to report more rather than less income.

> **Insider's Note**
>
> *The objectives of the external constituent financial books include:*
>
> - *Providing decision-useful insights to readers,*
> - *Faithfully reflecting a company's financial circumstances,*
> - *Maximizing net income, and*
> - *Complying with GAAP.*

In the United States, Congress holds the ultimate authority over the corporate mandate to provide quarterly and annual reports to the public. That body can and has passed laws requiring companies to report in certain ways and at certain times. The Securities Exchange Act of 1934 and the Sarbanes-Oxley Act of 2002 (SOX) establish the underpinnings for the current financial reporting environment in the United States. While Congress has the authority to promulgate specific financial reporting rules, however, it has empowered the Securities and Exchange Commission (SEC) to perform much of this role. The SEC, in turn, has authorized the private-sector Financial Accounting Standards Board (FASB) to issue detailed guidelines on specific line items in financial statements, as well as on the disclosures made in associated footnotes. Even so, the SEC has retained its primary authority to issue financial reporting rules of its own, such as Regulation Fair Disclosure (Regulation FD), and to enforce reporting requirements outlined by the FASB.

Splashing through this alphabet soup, it may be useful to think of the U.S. Congress as maintaining an interest in financial reporting from the overarching perspective of national public policy. This body then delegates to the SEC the slightly narrower responsibility of overseeing corporate financial reports, the mutual fund industry, the investment banking industry, and other elements of the financial markets. The SEC, in turn, relies on the FASB, established in the early 1970s, to study, devise, and publish specific financial reporting rules and regulations. Thus, in the United States, we can envision the flow of ever-more-specific financial reporting authority as a funnel (see Figure 1.1).

The FASB provides detailed guidance in the form of official Statements of Financial Accounting Standards (SFASs), which carry the full force and authority of the legislative body at the top of the funnel. It has issued over 150 such pronouncements to date. The collective body of these pronouncements, and a few others from additional U.S. entities, is known as Generally Accepted Accounting Principles (GAAP, pronounced "gap").

Globally, the International Accounting Standards Board (IASB)—a body similar to the FASB—issues guidelines called International Financial Reporting Standards (IFRS). These comprise a body of GAAP intended to

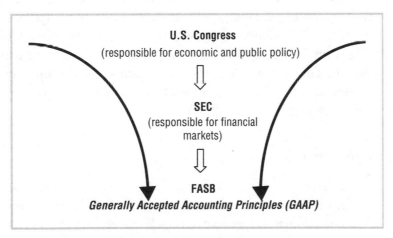

Figure 1.1 The Source of Financial Reporting Authority

serve as a worldwide approach to financial reporting and annual reports. Currently, U.S. companies are not required to adopt IFRS. Nor have they done so. (We'll discuss the IASB later in this book.)

In the chapters to come, we'll highlight some of the major elements of U.S. GAAP, noting what is and is not required or allowed. By contrast, we will *not* discuss creative accounting practices. These can be abbreviated as CrAP, a wonderfully descriptive term, pronounced just as you might expect. Unfortunately, CrAP exists. For those corporate executives using CrAP, it can lead to mug shots, prison ID numbers, and a second career making license plates.

With regard to the timing of financial information published for shareholders, lenders, and others in the public domain, there are three points to note. First, companies may end their financial (i.e., fiscal) year on any date they please. Most choose December 31. Others pick June 30 or January 31. Firms generally select a year-end date that coincides with a customary lull in operations. The Boston Celtics basketball team, for example, uses June 30, shortly after the NBA championship series. Retailers often pick January 31, just after the holiday spike in their operating activities. Regardless of the date it chooses, a company must publish its annual report within 60 days after its fiscal year end.

Second, once a company establishes its fiscal year-end, that date dictates the conclusion of its financial quarters. These end at three-month intervals within its fiscal year. Quarterly reports, presenting abbreviated versions of the company's balance sheet, income statement, and statement of cash flows, must be published within 40 days after each quarter-end.

Third, the SEC requires companies to make public—through real-time filings with the agency throughout the year—information related to any financial event viewed as important to investors. Such events may include a correction of a prior year's financial statement or the departure of a key company executive.

The Internal Managerial Books

Think of the dashboard of a car. It features many sources of information, each intended to help the driver operate the vehicle well. These include the fuel gauge, odometer, speedometer, tachometer, and thermostat, all of which provide a continuous flow of information. The driver also receives operational feedback from many other sources, some of which are not widely appreciated. There is, for example, the recurrent clicking associated with turn signals, letting the driver know that a blinker is engaged and working. There is also the annoying but vitally important squeal generated by a mechanism near the brakes, which is designed to rub against metal for just that purpose when they wear down—but before they fail.

Corporate managers receive information on their businesses from a similarly diverse range of measurement and monitoring sources. Imagine that you're a Wal-Mart store manager, a Ford factory supervisor, a Merck district sales manager, or a Mary Kay unit director. As such, you receive information about your sphere of responsibility and about the activities you must perform to do your job well. You need fairly frequent information on how your people are doing, how your operations are running, and how well your resources are being used. You need a dashboardlike array of indicators, metrics, and sensors to help you take timely action on a wide range of issues. These issues might include any of the following:

- The goods on aisle #7 aren't moving.
- Quality defects hit an unacceptable level in last night's production run.
- Sales have picked up along the beltway but declined in the city center.
- Neither Lucy nor Sue has placed an inventory replenishment order for six weeks. Kathy has, but she did it wrong.

As suggested by these examples, the audience for a company's managerial books and reports encompasses a broad range of internal decision makers.

There is no officially mandated set of managerial reports, common across all companies. There are certainly reports on common issues, including product cost sheets, factory production reports, and sales force activity logs, but their format and focus are customized to the needs of the manager using them. Nevertheless, these reports share certain general hallmarks. They're highly current—in some instances, real time. They're specific to a person, product, business segment, or locale, and to a relatively short span of time. Their content and form evolve as managers seek new insights.

The objective of managerial reports is quite simple: to provide insights for managing the business better. At a basic level, businesses compete on three primary dimensions—time, quality, and cost. As a result, managerial reports are frequently designed to provide actionable insights on these dimensions.

No governmental body has the authority to dictate the types of internal managerial reports that must be created. To be sure, numerous industry associations, authors, and other experts promulgate their own notions on how best to accumulate and report the critical data for running a business. But their authority derives solely from their prestige, track record, and powers of persuasion.

Experts provide guidance in many forms. Most prevalent, perhaps, are the "best practices" studies that are frequently published. Typically, such studies focus on companies that have enjoyed significant, positive accomplishments in a certain aspect of their business endeavors. These companies might have performed remarkable turnarounds, smoothly integrated newly acquired companies, attained stellar sales growth, or successfully slashed costs. From their experiences, the author of a best-practices study will derive insights into the actions that others should take, the information they should monitor, and the reports they should compile in order to optimize their own performance.

The timing of managerial reports can be summarized in a single word: Now. Most managers need the most current information possible to help them make operational decisions. They require key reports frequently. Weekly and even daily reports have long been the norm in many businesses. With the ease and prevalence of modern desktop computing, many management reports are generated continuously or on demand.

The Tax Books

The content of a company's tax books can be highly detailed and complex. We're all familiar with the effort involved in completing our individual tax returns. A company may have to endure this ordeal for operations in 22 municipalities in 12 American states, and for cross-border transactions involving 15 nations. Moreover, it may need to take all of these geographies into consideration for purposes not only of income taxes, but also of real estate taxes, property taxes, sales taxes, payroll taxes, pollution taxes, and more. As corporate tax audits are not uncommon, the audience for a firm's tax books may include not only the relevant government agency, but also the individual tax auditor who may call one day with the words we all dread to hear: "Hello, I'm with the IRS . . ."

The federal income tax report filed by U.S. companies is Form 1120. It has a look similar to the Form 1040 used by individuals. The instructions for completing it are precise and specific. That's not to say there aren't choices and judgments to be made in filing corporate returns. There are. Those choices must be made, however, in the context of instructional verbiage that's best measured in pounds, not pages.

In this book, when taxes are mentioned, we'll be referring to U.S. federal income taxes. From that perspective, and from the vantage point of the executives managing a company, the objectives undergirding the filing of a tax return can be viewed as twofold—to minimize reported taxable income and to comply with all applicable tax laws. This raises an interesting point: as you'll recall, one of the objectives of the external constituent financial books was to *maximize* reported earnings. Thus, for the very same year, a company may seek to minimize reported income in one set of books, while maximizing it in another.

> ## Insider's Note
>
> *The objectives of the tax books are to minimize the taxes a company pays while adhering to all pertinent tax laws.*

Now you may be thinking: "Uh-oh. No wonder the IRS makes those calls." But rest assured, done properly, this is legal. It's even ethical and prudent. As noted above, a company's financial and tax books relate different but equally true versions of the same financial story. Within the rules that pertain to these books, different conventions are used to craft their stories.

As the FASB issues guidance on corporate financial reporting, deriving its authority from the SEC and Congress, the Internal Revenue Service (IRS) issues and enforces federal income tax regulations, under the auspices of the U.S. Treasury Department, which, in turn, reports to Congress. And, as Mark Twain has been quoted as saying: "No man's property is safe while Congress is in session."[1] In the United States, under this chain of command, the IRS receives, reviews, and audits corporate tax returns. It also investigates violations, pursues tax evaders, and seeks remedies. It's a busy agency. In Brazil, the equivalent agency is the Secretaria da Receita Federal (SRF); in New Zealand, the Inland Revenue Department (IRD). No matter the country, the authority granted the relevant agency is rooted in national law.

The law that establishes a country's federal tax agency seldom prescribes the specifics of the taxes levied. Rather, the tax rules enumerating these details are generally the composite result, modified over time, of other tax-focused statutes, agency rulings, case law, and interpretations issued by various nongovernmental parties. Under the circumstances, we need hardly wonder why even Albert Einstein is reputed to have quipped,

	External Constituent Books	Tax Books	Managerial Books
Audience	Current and prospective shareholders and lenders, customers, suppliers, partners, and acquirers	IRS	Company managers
Reports	Annual report with a balance sheet, income statement, and statement of cash flows	Form 1120	Forecasts, budgets, cost sheets, and other reports deemed useful by company
Objectives	• Decision-useful information • Compliance with GAAP • Faithful representation of financial condition and performance • Legally maximize reported earnings	Legally minimize or defer tax liability	Provide information on costs, quality, competitiveness, and progress toward goals
Authority	U.S. Congress, SEC, and FASB	U.S. Congress, Treasury Dept., and IRS	Company policy and practices
Guidance	GAAP in the form of Statements of Financial Accounting Standards	U. S. Tax Code	Managerial judgment
Timing	Annually and quarterly	Annually, perhaps quarterly	As needed

Figure 1.2 The Three Sets of Books for Public Companies

"The hardest thing in the world to understand is income tax."[2] Nonetheless, corporate management must understand it. Tax violations have legal consequences, including jail time.

A U.S. company must file its Form 1120 by the fifteenth day of the third month following the end of its chosen tax year. Under certain conditions, it must also make quarterly filings and payments. With regard to timing, one interesting federal income tax notion differs markedly between U.S. companies and individuals: if a company has a loss on its tax books in a given year, it can use this to offset prior years' taxable earnings and receive a refund of taxes paid. Furthermore, if this loss exceeds all earnings in the years to which it can be retroactively applied, the remainder can be used to offset taxable earnings over a stipulated number of future years. Clearly, the U.S. government has chosen a public policy that subsidizes corporate losses. (Point that out to your friends at a cocktail party around April 15, and watch the sparks fly.)

Figure 1.2 summarizes the six dimensions along which the three sets of books can vary, in tabular form.

Reconciling the Books

All the variations outlined in Figure 1.2 beg a question: if there are three sets of books for the same company, reporting results for the same year, and they don't all say the same thing at the same time, are they reconcilable? The answer is: Yes.

The reason is simple. Once a business transaction has been executed by a company, none of the reporting conventions used to depict it can change its factual existence or details. Thus, each of a company's three financial books reports information on the same set of events. Their differences, with some exceptions, relate primarily to the timing under which reporting conventions are applied. Consequently, differences in reported results among these books are numerically reconcilable at any point in time. Consider the following two examples.

Reconciliation of External Constituent and Tax Books

The reconciliation between a company's external constituent and tax books will focus primarily on differences in the timing of deductions reported on its tax return versus the income statement in its annual report. Remember that the tax code sets its own guidelines for allowable deductions, and one of its major objectives is the furtherance of national economic public policy. On the other hand, the FASB's objective in its financial statement guidelines is to generate a fair representation of a company's performance for shareholders and other interested external parties. These two objectives are not quite the same. Therefore, how and when certain deductions are reported in the two reports can—and do—differ.

As a brief example, let's look at the deductions pertaining to the cost of a company's office building. Assume the building is purchased today for $10 million. The U.S. Congress wishes to spur investments in such long-lived assets because it believes these stimulate the economy and foster faith in the economic future of the country. Therefore, under the tax code, it may allow the company to depreciate the cost of this building over a life of 20 years. (Disclaimer: Taxpayer beware. Please consult a tax specialist before using anything in this example in your own tax reporting.) Consequently, $500,000 ($10 million ÷ 20 years) would be deducted on the company's Form 1120 in each of the next 20 years, reducing taxable earnings by that amount. For purposes of the annual report's income statement, however, GAAP stipulates that the life of the building should approximate its actual usefulness as corporate offices. A reasonable estimate of that might be 25 years. Therefore, in its financial books, the company deducts only $400,000 per year ($10 million ÷ 25 years) from earnings for the building.

Let's assume that the building is occupied and used by the company as intended for the next 25 years. As you can see, there will be $100,000 more in depreciation deducted for this building on the company's tax return than on its annual report income statement in each of the first 20 years of the building's financial life. In each of years 21 through 25, however, the company will deduct $400,000 more for this building on its financial income statement than on its tax return. Because both books have focused on the very same $10 million building, no matter what the life assigned to it, the company will deduct only the original cost of $10 million in both its tax returns *and* its annual reports. The only difference is that on the tax books, this will be a 20-year process, while on the external constituent annual report books, it will take 25 years.

At any given time during the life of the building, the total difference in depreciation between the two books can be ascertained. As of the end of year 16, for example, $1.6 million ($100,000 × 16 years) more depreciation will have been deducted on tax returns than in annual report income statements. As of the end of year 22, however, only $1.2 million ([$100,000 × 20 years] − [$400,000 × 2 years]) more depreciation will have been deducted on tax returns than in annual report income statements. At the end of year 25, the total deduction differential must be—and will be—zero.

Here's an important related point. A company's taxable earnings on Form 1120 represent the basis for taxes to be paid to the government in any given year. By contrast, the earnings shown on its annual report income statement are used to calculate a GAAP-based tax expense figure, which is then deducted from income on that statement. As seen in the example above, those figures can differ at any point in time due to something as simple as assigning different lives to a building for different books. Thus, during the 25 years of this building's financial life, the accumulated difference in the amount of taxes owed and/or paid (per tax returns) versus tax expense (per income statements) can also be reconciled and tracked as an item identified as "deferred taxes" in an annual report.

> ### Insider's Note
>
> *The external constituent and tax stories are reconciled for us by a company reporting and detailing an item called "deferred taxes" in its annual report.*

Reconciliation of Managerial and External Constituent Books

Have you ever prepared a budget? Perhaps you've done this for school, or a vacation, or to build a house. Such budgets are a type of managerial report used to oversee a project or the activities of a certain time period. At the end of the project or period, if time permits, we might tally actual financial results and compare them to the budgeted figures. The differences between the two are often called "variances."

At the corporate level, the financial performance depicted in a company's annual report represents the aggregated results of a year's worth of individual projects and activities, each of which has its own budget. As noted earlier, the annual report does not depict the myriad details comprising all those projects and undertakings. Behind the aggregate results, however, lie a host of details that companies *do* monitor and reconcile to their financial plans. In reviewing these, managers generally want to know where results differed from plan, by how much, and why. This final point is perhaps the most crucial for managing the business better. Was a variance the result of poor assumptions, erroneous planning, or weak execution? Detailed variance reviews are intended to improve a firm's planning capabilities, which should in turn yield wiser strategies, more productive operations, and—ultimately—more predictable and attractive financial results for owners. Then, as in many stories, everyone lives happily ever after.

The Inside Scoop

Every year, companies prepare a financially oriented trilogy—one installment for an external audience, another for tax authorities, and a third for internal managers. Not only is the audience different for each of these, so too are the specific reports, their objectives and timing, and the authorities and guidance that direct their preparation. Despite these differences among financially oriented corporate books, all relate to the same set of business events. A company's activities are what they are. Subsequent reporting doesn't change them. So it is the audience served, and the objectives relating to that audience, which generate the need for differing books. Each of a company's three constituencies—external, managerial, and tax authorities—maintains a slightly different focus, requiring different information, all related to the same events.

Practical Application

Unless you're a corporate insider, you likely don't have access to all three of a company's financially oriented books. You can see only the version leading to its annual report. I'm in the same position—outside, looking in.

Nevertheless, we can anticipate certain tendencies with regard to a company's books. By surfacing those tendencies, we can enhance our understanding of the pressures, needs, and desires faced by corporate managers when they make financial reporting decisions.

For example, when planning for a corporate operating expenditure, all other things being equal and stable, do you think managers will prefer to deduct that expenditure this year or next in their (1) corporate tax return, (2) annual report income statement, or (3) departmental budget? Generally, managers prefer to deduct an expenditure in *this* year's tax return and *next* year's income statement. Why? Well, by deducting it in the tax return, they can reduce taxable earnings, which in turn will reduce the firm's near-term tax obligation, preserving cash. In contrast, by deducting it in this year's income statement, managers will reduce earnings reported to shareholders. And shareholders generally prefer their companies to have more, not less, income now. As to the budget, the answer is "it depends." If a departmental manager is in a favorable position vis-à-vis budget (i.e., if expenditures to date are running lower than planned), he or she may prefer to count an expenditure against this year's budget. If expenditures are running higher than planned, the reverse may be true.

A second question: Given the opportunity to close a sale in December versus January, at a company with a December 31 year-end, in which month will a manager prefer to record that sale for purposes of (1) the company's tax return, (2) its annual report income statement, and (3) its budget? In general, the manager will prefer to record the sale in *next* year's tax return, but *this* year's income statement. As to the budget, this again will depend on whether the manager is running ahead of or behind plan.

A general pattern can be extracted from these preferences. For tax return purposes, managers want to legally delay the recording of sales and hurry the recording of deductions. For annual report income statement purposes, they generally want just the opposite. With regard to internal managerial records, particularly the budget, preferences often depend on where actual financial results fall in relation to forecasts at the relevant point in time. Such tendencies will be worth bearing in mind as we explore some of the nuances of financial reporting in subsequent chapters.

In Anticipation of the Next Secret

From here on, we'll concentrate on that version of the corporate story portrayed by a company in its external constituent annual report. Of course this begs the question: what recurring parts appear in an annual report story?

Secret #2

It's Storytelling

With characters, plot, and action

The questions behind Secret #2:

- At the most fundamental level, what is an annual report?
- Do all annual reports have similar parts? If so, what are they?
- How are financial data typically conveyed in an annual report?
- What time perspective does an annual report embrace?
- Why do annual reports change over time?

Have you ever gotten lost in an exciting book? Or enjoyed the recollections of grandparents? A well-told story can bring Technicolor to an otherwise black-and-white world. It draws people together. It conveys history, values, feelings, insights, cautions, anticipations, information, traditions, and wisdom. It triggers emotions. It opens perspectives. It fosters expectations. And stories are everywhere. We tell them ourselves, and invite others to relate them to us: "How was your day?" "Where did you go on vacation?" "You'll never believe what I did last night!" By sharing stories, we get to know each other better.

In the business world, executives frequently seek to present their companies' stories to external constituencies. They do this for many reasons:

- To promote their firms' products and services
- To build a reputation for strong management and success
- To raise money from banks and investors
- To explain challenges and goals
- To place their performance in context, and ensure that it's understood
- To publicize their contributions to the greater good of their markets and communities

Companies use a variety of vehicles to tell their stories to external constituencies, including press releases, advertisements, brochures, speeches, documentaries, and financial annual reports. The last of these, the annual report, will be our focus.

External Corporate Annual Reports Are Performance Stories

Let's pretend it's a beautiful day and your boss has dropped by your office. After a bit of chitchat, she gets right to the point: "As you know, it's time for your annual review. I think you're doing an awesome job. And headquarters needs a written appraisal to justify the 30% raise I'm requesting for you. Would you mind writing that?"

Trying not to stammer, you agree to give it a shot.

"Great," your boss says. "Keep it short and sweet. But don't be shy."

Now I don't know about you, but if I were allowed to write my own performance appraisal, I might find some pretty nice things to say. Terms like "world class" might come to mind. Or "record-setting performance," "employee of choice," and "well positioned for continued stellar results." And of course: "Has an uncanny ability to delight every constituency." Are these exaggerations? That depends on who you ask. I'll swear by every word, which is only natural. We all like to think the best of ourselves. We emphasize our strengths, not our weaknesses. As Garrison Keillor describes the children of Lake Wobegon, we all like to believe we're above average.

In a financial annual report, a corporation presents its own yearly performance review. It tells readers about its results, its positioning vis-à-vis competitors, and its prospects for the future. As in our fictitious scenario above, corporate executives themselves write their firm's annual report. They enjoy a fair amount of discretion (more than you might think) in what they say and how they say it. And they generally focus on the positive. By contrast with the scenario above, however, companies do face some checks and balances as they craft their annual reports. We'll address these in a later chapter. As we begin our exploration of annual reports, please recognize the perspective from which they're written: they're fundamentally autobiographical performance stories. This doesn't negate their usefulness. Nor does it cast their authors in an unbridled, self-serving role. But it does

> **Insider's Note**
>
> *Corporate annual reports are autobiographical performance stories. As such, the conventions used to craft those stories are important to understand.*

suggest that we should read annual reports with a modicum of healthy skepticism regarding what is and is not said, as well as the way in which it's presented. We should also complement our reading of these reports with information from other sources.

Parts of an Annual Report

The CEO's Letter

The winter holiday season brings many joys and blessings. Among my personal favorites are the family letters that friends sometimes mass-produce and bulk mail. Yes, these can be corny. But any one of them will tell us some important things:

- Overall, what kind of year did our friend have? Was it "full of fun and surprises?" "Steady as she goes?" "Troubled by disappointments?"
- What were the big events of the year? Perhaps Melinda got married. Or Steve moved to California. Or Bill dropped out of college to start a business. ("We worry, but wish him well.")
- What are our friend's key values? Is he or she blessed with close friends, a caring family, and a religious community that makes a difference? Or is it all about cars and real estate?

- Finally, what are our friend's hopes and expectations for the coming year? Does he or she plan to retire? Or travel? Or build a lake house?

Corporate annual reports also begin with a friendly letter—in this case, from the company's president and/or Chief Executive Officer (CEO). In two to four pages, this executive provides an overview of the firm's experience of the year. By contrast with our friend's holiday note, however, this letter has an added dimension: its author aims to build or buttress confidence in the company, its strategies, and the competence of management. The CEO also seeks to instill the belief that the company has shareholders' interests in mind.[1] Toward that end, the author pays careful attention to the tone of the letter, and presents a well-calculated blend of good and slightly less good news—the latter being needed for the sake of credibility.

Insider's Note

Annual reports consist of seven parts. The first is a letter from the CEO that summarizes the most recently completed year. The second is a narrative overview of the company's major business units.

Corporate Review of Operations

Over the years, some holiday letters from distant friends have probably prompted you to call them for a chat. Those letters have led us to want to know more about what friends were doing, how they were feeling, and where they were focusing their time and energy. During one such call, a friend might describe his son's new business—his products, customers, challenges, and growth strategies, as well as the splash he'd made in the local market.

Here again, companies do the same in their annual reports. This is commonly called a "Corporate Review of Operations." Assuming a reader has more interest in the company than can be satisfied by the CEO's letter, the operations review generally follows this letter and provides elaborating detail on each of the major business segments of the company. PepsiCo, for example, discusses its Frito-Lay results separately from its beverage business and talks about the potential of overseas markets. The review of operations also provides information concerning the size, location, and performance of each business unit, as well as important corporate initiatives in such areas as research and development, organizational restructuring, employee training, and the purchase or sale of other companies. In essence, this annual report section provides more detail and context about the year, much like a phone call following up on a holiday letter from a friend.

Management's Discussion and Analysis

What if your friend had launched a business venture, and you'd invested in it? Money *would* be an appropriate point of discussion, even if only for a moment. You might ask about it. Your friend, in turn, might report that funds were running low, but that he'd refinanced his mortgage and hired a part-time sales person, and now revenues were picking up. He might relate worries about new competitors or an unreliable distributor. He'd share this information, of course, in the spirit of assuring you that your investment was still secure, and that business prospects were positive. There were simply a few operational issues to be addressed.

By law, corporate annual reports must include a section titled "Management's Discussion and Analysis" (MD&A). Here, management must discuss its business results as if the reader were eavesdropping on a management meeting. In other words, the issues and concerns of significance to management must be presented in the MD&A, along with an analysis of their real or anticipated financial effect on the business. The MD&A should be a "heart to heart" conversation with the company's owners. Therefore, the MD&A tends to be a bit more detailed and revealing than the CEO's cordial opening letter.

It usually follows the context-setting operations overview section of the annual report. It includes a range of content, both financial and non-financial; generally historical, but with a bit of prospective information. It covers management's view of what happened and why. In the MD&A, a company must also provide multiyear comparative financial data concerning various issues, including major sources and uses of cash, sales and expense trends, debt strategies and levels, significant contractual obligations, major customers, critical accounting choices, and material risks and uncertainties.

Clearly, for those interested in the financial facets of a company, the MD&A is important. It conveys a rich context for the detailed financial data that must be presented later. It also provides a glimpse into management's explanations, disappointments, worries, anticipations, and sense of accomplishment. We don't have to agree with what they say. We may not like what they say. We may wonder why they said one thing and not another. But the thoughts piqued by an MD&A can provide an important context for delving into the rest of the annual report.

Financial Statements: Where the Action Is

Consider again the scenario in which you've invested in a friend's business. Your friend's holiday letter and phone call may satisfy you that he's been a good steward of your funds. They may even persuade you that a substantial return on your investment is imminent. But what if your "friend" is really more of an acquaintance? Or what if he lives far away, making it impossible for you to visit and see that all is in order? Or what if another friend has offered you an even better financial opportunity, tempting you to withdraw cash from your current investment? In any of these cases, you may need more information than you've received so far to determine whether to leave your money where it is. Indeed, you might ask to see your friend's financial records—the tax returns, checkbook, and bank statements—pertaining to your investment. Your purpose in doing so will be twofold:

- First, you want to see a broader spectrum of financial data, from which you can craft your own view of the business's strengths and weaknesses, rather than relying on the narrative story presented by your friend.
- Second, you want to see these data in formats that are not only familiar, but also comparable in form and content to those provided by your other friend in making *his* request for your investment.

The same is true in corporate annual reports. Companies are required to provide information about their year-end resources and debts, as well as a summary of their annual sales, expenses, and cash inflows and outflows. To enhance the ease with which one company's information can be compared with another's, financial-reporting regulations dictate standard formats for presenting these data. Required financial statements include:

- The income statement, which outlines a firm's sales and expenses
- The balance sheet, which depicts the company's resources and debts
- The statement of cash flows, which communicates the sources and uses of the company's cash

All of these statements are near the MD&A section of the annual report and—like a bank statement, check register, or personal tax return—each has a uniform look. This commonality of format and focus exists throughout the United States, and for the most part around the world.

Financial Statement Footnotes: Elaborations and Explanations

By now, if you've perused the bank statements, tax returns, and checkbook register pertaining to your friend's business, you have a pretty good idea of its financial status. But even so, you may want more information. Yes, your friend wrote a check for $10,000 with the notation, "tractor." But you'd like to know: Was that a new or used tractor? Was it a lawn or farm tractor? Did it come with or without attachments? Was it ready to use or did it need major repairs? How long does your friend expect it to last? Did it carry a warranty? Any number of such questions may arise, because all you've seen so far is an expenditure notation for a tractor. You haven't seen the tractor, nor do you plan to fly out and inspect it. After all, it's just a tractor! It was, however, a major expenditure at a time when your friend's business wasn't flourishing. Consequently, you want further detail to help you understand the expenditure more fully.

The easiest way for your friend to convey this information might be to provide a brief narrative explanation, accompanying the tractor's listing in the checkbook register. Over the years, if you request such details, your friend may learn to anticipate the types of items for which you want extensive, specific explanations. In fact, your friend may ultimately deliver his checkbook with an array of narrative explanations, coded to relevant line items, so that you can easily find the details you want.

Corporate annual reports are no different. Anticipating the details that readers are likely to want, pertaining to various financial statement line items and data, annual reports contain a host of explanatory financial statement footnotes. These serve a range of needs:

- They explain how the reported financial amounts were calculated. This is especially true of the first footnote, which summarizes a company's significant financial reporting practices.
- They provide additional detail concerning the components of items aggregated in the three primary financial statements.
- They outline the time frames pertinent to certain long-lived assets, such as tractors, and multiyear obligations, such as leases.
- They discuss significant uncertainties surrounding the business, its resources, obligations, and prospects.

The footnotes are an integral part of a company's overall financial story. They add valuable elaboration to the line items presented in the financial statements.

In subsequent chapters, we'll discuss some of the information that footnotes do and do not present. Now, however, please attend to one caution: Footnotes may look boring—and even off-putting—in their small font, single-color format, and dry prose style. They are, however, critical to understanding a company's financial results and condition, and to anticipating its prospects. In reviewing any firm's annual report, we're most interested in obtaining as complete a financial story as possible. The financial statement footnotes contribute immensely to that end.

Auditor's Report: Can I Get An "Amen" Here?

Perhaps you've trusted friends in the past with some of your money, and been hurt. Now you want the most objective information you can get on your friend's use of the money you've invested in his business. You might even want a third-party affirmation of his business situation. If it were possible, you might ask his bank to mail the statements for his business account directly to you, ensuring that they couldn't be doctored. One morning, without prior notification, you might even visit his business to observe the nature and extent of its resources, and to get a feel for its activities.

Of course, if you did any of these things, your friendship would likely end. But you'd gain added information, indicating whether the financial story your friend told you was honest and comprehensive in all significant ways. The reality is clear: You can't stay with your friend all year, observing his daily spending and decision-making, and the aggressiveness with which he pursues sales. Consequently, you must rely on periodic reports. The trustworthiness of those reports is enhanced, however, when an objective third party helps establish their reliability.

Precisely the same situation exists in the corporate world. Absentee constituents rely on periodic financial reports from the companies they are interested in. In doing so, they look for the added informa-tion contained in a short report from a key third party. That party, the external auditor, serves as the eyes and ears of those who are interested in the company, but are not directly involved in running it. Auditors scrutinize, corroborate, and interpret evidence pertaining to the fairness of a company's financial statements and the controls in place to prevent misreporting of financial data. Without conscientious, skilled auditors,

> **Insider's Note**
>
> *The last two parts of an annual report are certifications regarding the fairness of the financial data presented in the financial statements and footnotes. One certification is from an outside auditor and one is from a company's own CEO and CFO.*

however, who knows what fictions might be published in annual report stories? Thank goodness for auditors! Their report appears near the financial statements.

Management's Report

So far, in reviewing your friend's business, you've received the following materials: (1) a somewhat generic holiday letter about the year, (2) additional information, pertaining to your friend's major activities and those of his family, (3) a self-authored, comparative, multiyear financial narrative, containing a bit of explanation and interpretation, (4) three detailed financial statements, with accompanying elaborations, and (5) a third-party attestation to the veracity of his financial disclosures. Is that enough to render judgment on your friend's use of your money, and your prospects of getting it back with an attractive return? Yes, but . . . you want one more thing. You want a letter from your friend that says something like:

> **Dear Mark:**
> **I have taken every reasonable precaution to make sure your money is used well, is completely accounted for, and will be paid back to you when and as agreed.**
> **Your friend,**
> **Jim**

Such an all-encompassing statement of conscientiousness and trustworthiness from the person to whom you have entrusted your money can be reassuring—and therefore important.

In the corporate world, similar statements are included in every annual report. In fact, there are two of them:

- One declares that management is responsible for the financial statements and footnotes found in the annual report and for establishing sound controls over the process by which they were crafted.
- The second states management's opinion as to whether those controls are working.

These statements may be made separately or combined in a single document. In either event, they're displayed close to the external auditor's report, and signed by the company's chief executive and chief financial officers. In essence, they represent the CEO and CFO's personal assurance that you can trust the story they've told you. (And in this post-Enron era, such assurances are backed by regulatory teeth.)

Pies, Bars, and Numbers

Pictures, narratives, graphs, data tables, and pie charts offer powerful means to convey and embellish a story. Corporate annual reports use them all, reinforcing their key messages in multiple ways. In so doing, they follow the old principle: "Tell them what you are going to tell them. Tell them. And then tell them what you told them." In that spirit, an annual report may provide a narrative description of research and development activities, embellished with photos from the lab. It may present geographical financial results in both a data table and a pie chart. It may outline comparative financial figures over time, both textually and in a longitudinal graph. Because different people learn best through different media—through images, written words, conversation, and other means—annual reports use multiple channels to tell their story. Yes, it's redundant, but even this repetition can be a learning mode.

Companies use an even broader range of media to tell their financial stories *outside* their annual reports. On its Web site, a company may post an audio replay of its executives' financial presentation to Wall Street analysts. It may offer the PowerPoint™ slides used in this presentation. The company may issue press releases to newspapers, describing financial results. Its executives may appear on televised business news shows. One or more of those executives may even write books about their leadership philosophy or their strategies for success.

All of these materials—gripping as they may be—must be viewed with a critical eye. Outside its required annual or quarterly reports, a firm's recital of its performance may not have been audited. That's not to say that its managers would willfully provide misleading information. It's simply best to rely on audited financial data.

Past, Present, or Future?

Do you like historical novels? Perhaps you prefer science fiction, thrillers, or contemporary autobiographies. If your taste runs toward the latter, corporate annual reports may be for you. Annual reports are autobiographical, in that they're performance stories told by a company's own management—with guidance from regulators and some verification by auditors. They're contemporary, in that they focus on the most recent year's results, accompanied by comparative data from two prior years, with perhaps a brief look forward in the MD&A.

Corporate archives and Web sites offer prior years' annual reports, perhaps all the way back to the company's founding. It's unlikely, however, that these archived reports will be very useful. There are several reasons for this:

- Since the time of these past reports, the company may have undertaken numerous business mergers and divestitures.
- The company has likely introduced and abandoned multiple products.
- Financial reporting conventions have changed.

Consequently, though annual reports from many years past may be available, they're not likely to convey much meaningful information for today.

Please note that annual reports do not present—nor are companies required to present—financial projections. Readers of annual reports might take great interest in such future-oriented information. As public documents, however, annual reports don't reveal it. There are multiple reasons for this: First, such materials would be of special interest to a company's competitors, and companies are generally not required to disclose information that might undermine their competitive position. Second, budgets and projections are subject to uncontrollable factors, which can make actual results quite different from those anticipated. Because regulators generally prefer that investors and lenders make their investment decisions on the basis of documented, achieved performance rather than promised or projected performance, annual reports are limited to financial data for the current and two prior years.

> **Insider's Note**
>
> *The financial data presented in an annual report is generally limited to the current year and two prior years. Companies are not required to provide any financial projections.*

That's not a bad thing. The primary purpose of the story presented in an annual report is to enable readers to make their own projections about a company's future prospects—that is, to guess at the sequel before it's written. That's the essence of affiliating with a company via investing, lending, contracting, acquiring, or partnering: we strive to predict the future based on the past, in concert with our own forward-looking assumptions. This latter point is important. Our *assumptions* fuel any projections we make about a company's future performance. Of course, few of us study companies, industries, or economies closely enough to make truly well-founded assumptions about the future; thus, the rise of professional financial analysts whom we pay for their projections, counsel, and insights.

By contrast with many of the best-selling stories we read and enjoy, a corporate annual report has no ending. We don't know if everyone lives happily ever after. Each annual report is just one chapter in the life of a company whose accomplishments and longevity won't be known until they've come and gone. We can't know how many such chapters there will be, or how the story will eventually end. We only know the twists and turns of this year's chapter and those of prior years. We make projections about the company's success, failure, or mediocrity—or pay others to make those for us. We listen for clues in the speeches of company executives, and look for them in news releases. But we must remember that those words emanate from the most optimistic, vested voices. Based on the information available, and on our own thinking, we conclude that a company is strong, weak, promising, or in decline. Was that a valid conclusion? We can't know until the future arrives.

The Basic Rule of Supply and Demand

An interviewer once asked a popular novelist, "What's the formula for a successful book?" The novelist's answer, here paraphrased, was elegantly simple: "You create likeable characters, get them in trouble, and then get them out again." As I think about this novelist's books, which I love, that's a fine description of what he does really well.

Corporate annual reports also follow a formula. They include recurring parts. They present three primary financial statements, each adhering to a prescribed template. They follow a standard outline for details provided in the MD&A and financial statement footnotes. They include required statements from external auditors, indicating a level of confidence in the information communicated by management through much of the report. All of this begs a question: Where does this formula come from? Who decides what information should be presented? The answer is simple: Past investors and lenders.

Over the years, investors and lenders have collectively needed, wanted, and demanded certain information in exchange for their capital. If companies needed money from these third parties, they had no choice but to provide that information. As business progressed through the stock market crash of the 1920s, the post–World War II industrial boom, the rise of the investor class, the inflation of the 1970s, the emergence of global financial markets, the tech boom of the 1990s, and the bust and corporate scandals of the turn of the century, investors have continually fine-tuned the information they require to the needs of their times. As the collective demand for a certain type of information grows louder, this captures the attention of regulators, leading to new laws and regulations, which change the financial-reporting landscape.

Now, I'd love to know the financial details of Boeing's sales forecasts, Nike's budgets, and Google's upcoming innovations. But these companies would rather not tell me, because that would place the information in the public domain—making it available to competitors. Yes, in the end, regulators could make a firm divulge any and all information they felt the public should know. But they're sensitive to companies' competitive positions, and generally refrain from requiring companies to publish competitively damaging information. Still, as new technologies make it easier to obtain information, and as new avenues provide access to previously protected data, companies' willingness to supply that information evolves.

Thus, the content of any year's annual report represents the convergence of investors' demand for information—as voiced by regulators—and companies' willingness and ability to supply it. Two quick examples will illustrate this point. The statement of cash flows now required of all publicly traded companies in the United States was not a required part of annual reports up into the 1970s. Investors and creditors wanted it. They made the case for it. Regulators agreed. Professionals deliberated on an appropriate format. And the statement is now required. By contrast, in the mid-1970s, U.S. companies *were* required to present certain inflation-adjusted financial disclosures in the footnotes to their annual reports. Over time, however, as U.S. inflation cooled, investors and creditors began to find these disclosures extraneous. They stopped asking for them. And eventually, corporations stopped presenting them in annual reports—with the blessing of regulators.

Insider's Note

The format and content of annual reports evolves over time as regulators' demands for more or different information evolves and as companies' willingness and ability to supply information evolves.

The Inside Scoop

Companies communicate their financial stories in their annual reports. It is useful to think of those annual reports as contemporary, autobiographical performance stories. Those reports follow a generally consistent template. This includes the following main sections:

1. A brief letter from the CEO, touching on the high points of the year
2. A narrative and pictorial overview of the company's businesses and operations
3. A required management discussion and analysis (MD&A) of key financial aspects of the company
4. Three particularly important financial statements—the balance sheet, income statement, and statement of cash flows
5. Elaborating footnotes to the financial statements
6. An auditor's report on the financial statements
7. A concluding letter from key executives, attesting to the reliability of their financial controls and financial statements

Annual reports use words, pictures, charts, and numbers to convey past and present information. Very little, if any, future-oriented information is provided in annual reports. As the marketplace for financial information changes over time, reflecting the evolution of readers' demands and companies' willingness to supply information, the content of annual reports changes, too.

Practical Application

Think of a large, publicly traded company in which you're interested. Go to its Web site and find its latest annual report. For example, I just went to www.pepsico.com, where I clicked first on "investors," then on "annual reports," and then on the icon for Pepsico's latest PDF-formatted annual report. If you have a hard copy of an annual report, that would also be an excellent document to use at this juncture.

Skim the report, and locate the seven annual report sections discussed in this chapter. Did you find them? Keep looking; they're there. If not, try a different report. The first one may have been an abbreviated, summary report. As you skim each of the sections in a full annual report, note the following points to get an overall sense of the company.

- The CEO's letter is welcoming, presents some of the year's highlights, and may allude to one or two challenges. Take note of its content and assess its tone. Is it glowingly positive? Boldly optimistic? Brutally frank? Consistently equivocating?

- The review of operations is full of pictures, charts, graphs, and data tables, all serving to convey information about the company's products, operations, and personnel, as well as financial highlights of its major business sectors. Take note of the company's product lines and geographic markets, and the relative size of the items in each of these categories. Is the product portfolio fresh or aging? Are most of the company's sales made in domestic markets or overseas?

- The MD&A will probably be 5 to 15 pages long. Note, in particular, the existence of two subsections—one discussing the company's critical accounting policies (more on these later), and another addressing the firm's business risks. Do any of the risks surprise you? Do they seem generic or company-specific?

- Next, you should see the three key financial statements, noted above. (You may ignore a fourth statement, concerning owner's equity, as it's generally viewed as far less important than the others.) For now, please earmark these—we'll discuss them at length in chapters to come.

- Immediately after the financial statements, you'll find a number of pages titled "Notes to Consolidated Financial Statements," or words to that effect. Skim the headings on those pages, noting the array of topics discussed. In later chapters we'll decipher a few of the more significant footnote topics. At this juncture, simply note that the footnotes provide additional details and explanations pertaining to a number of the line items in the financial statements.

- Did you find the auditors' report and management's report? Skim these, taking particular note of their mention of the three key financial statements and the company's internal controls over the financial reporting function. Are the concluding comments favorable? They should be.

This overview approach can be used to begin the process of delving into an annual report story.

In Anticipation of the Next Secret

Annual report storytelling uses its own unique language. Before we go any further, let's clarify what some of those mysterious words mean.

Secret #3

It's a Language

What do those new words mean?

The questions behind Secret #3:

- What are the crucial terms for beginning to understand the story presented in corporate annual reports?
- What do those terms mean?
- Are they part of an international language of business?

I recently attended a dinner party with business executives from eight different countries. The conversation that night was exhilarating. It moved from first-hand accounts of movements for political freedom, to the challenges of employing a largely illiterate work force, to the pressures of negotiating a transaction while the military stands just outside a company's walls. The executives shared insights and recounted vivid stories that added texture and tone to aspects of the world I'd previously known only through the evening news.

Although English was a second or third language for all of these executives, they used it to discuss business with a fluency and precision born of years of practice and study. External financial reporting is like that. There is a universal aspect to the conventions, guidelines, and terminology used to describe a company's resources, obligations, profits, losses, and cash flows. In this chapter, we'll focus on some of the most fundamental, most important terminology used by companies to tell their financial stories in annual reports.

Lost in the Wider World

Imagine four different journeys—and four very different experiences of your destinations based on a varied familiarity with the local language.

Scenario 1   Throughout college, the highways called you. And so, the summer after graduation, you packed a knapsack and made a cross-country trek, visiting states you'd never seen before. You knew no one in any of these places. But of course you knew the language. You could read and understand all the maps and signs. You never had a bit of trouble getting information and directions from the locals. You were able to immerse yourself fully in every setting.

Scenario 2   For your honeymoon, you went to France. Neither you nor your spouse were very good in French. But you'd studied the language in school. So you could read the signs. You could even converse at a basic level. You did reasonably well without a guide, finding most destinations on your own. And when lost, you could always ask for directions from the local citizens, many of whom knew a bit of English.

Scenario 3   You always wanted to visit Japan. And so, when you learned of a tour group heading for Tokyo, you signed up. The fact that you didn't know the language, or even the alphabet, didn't deter you. Your group was well chaperoned, with a Japanese translator and guide, whose sole task was to take care of you and members of your group.

Scenario 4   Finally, business took you to the Ukraine. You attended a week-long round of meetings in Kiev, rarely leaving offices and hotels. When these were over, however, you decided to stay for an extra couple of days, hoping to travel on your own and take in a few sights. But it was hard. All the shop names and street signs were in an unfamiliar alphabet. You couldn't read the map. You had no host or guide. You knew none of the language. The moment you left the hotel, all you could do was gulp, venture forth, and try to remember all the landmarks you could, hoping to retrace your steps at the end of the day. Ultimately, you got lost anyway. And while you did see a few sights, you also missed a great deal, and misinterpreted much of what you saw.

These four scenarios typify the orientations of most readers of corporate annual reports: (1) very literate and comfortable with the report's basic information, even if it pertains to an unknown company, (2) modestly literate and able to puzzle out a few pertinent details, (3) clueless and reliant on a well-informed guide, and (4) trying hard, but utterly lost. Simply by reading this book you've demonstrated a desire for an annual-report journey aimed for category 1 or 2. That's great! Let's go.

The Vocabulary of Financial Reports

Accounting is many things to many people. To some, it's just a bunch of numbers running around, looking for an argument. To others, it's economics without the assumptions. But for our purposes, let's define *accounting* as the conventions and processes used to collect, codify, and communicate data pertaining to the financial affairs of a company. The processes pertain to what most would call *bookkeeping*. The conventions pertain to a discipline that we'll call *financial reporting*, and that involves the guidelines, formats, and disclosures needed to craft a universally recognizable, largely standardized set of annual report financial communications.

At this stage, there are a dozen fundamental terms that you need to understand. You can learn these terms through the following personal analogies, corporate examples, and succinct definitions.

1. **Assets**   *Personal analogy* → Your car, titled in your name, from which you expect to receive transportation benefits for several years.

Corporate examples→Buildings, investments in other companies, and merchandise to be sold to customers.

Definition

The tangible and intangible resources owned by an organization, which are expected to provide it with future identifiable benefits.

2. **Liabilities**   *Personal analogy* → The obligation remaining on the loan you took out to buy your car.

Corporate examples → Obligations remaining on loans, taxes owed but not yet paid, monies owed to suppliers for materials received, and workers' earned retirement benefits.

Definition

The monetary value of an organization's obligations to others for goods or services received or to fulfill commitments made.

3. **Equity**   *Personal analogy* → If your house is worth $300,000, and the mortgage amount you still owe is $160,000, then your equity in the house is $140,000 ($300,000 − $160,000 = $140,000).

Corporate example → Those who purchase the stock of a company become owners of that company. Thus, if a company's total assets equal $15 billion, and its total liabilities are $1 billion, then its owners possess an aggregate recorded equity in the company of $14 billion ($15 billion − $1 billion = $14 billion).

Definition

The owners' financial claims on an organization's assets.

4. Entity   *Personal analogy* → Let's say you work for IBM and, in your spare time, you own and manage an ice cream shop. Let's also say I want to buy the shop. In that case, in evaluating this deal, the ice cream shop is the distinct, relevant entity. I'd only be interested in *its* financial results and performance. I'd have no claim on, or access to the details of, your status as an IBM employee.

Corporate example → Microsoft Corporation must publish an annual report that pertains to the finances of the legal organization known as—what else?—Microsoft. That report does not include the personal finances of any Microsoft employee or stockholder, except to the extent that these bear directly and materially on the finances of the corporate entity.

Definition

The organization for which an annual report is prepared, separate and apart from the owners and employees of that organization.

5. Value   *Personal analogy* → Let's say you paid $5,000 for a Ford Mustang convertible in 1966 and now wish to sell it. If buyers and sellers today are striking deals for such a car at a price of $20,000, then that is its value: $20,000, not the $5,000 you originally paid for it.

Corporate example → Let's say you own 100 shares of Google stock. You may determine their value at any time by calling a stockbroker or checking the Web, looking for the stock price of the latest trade. Almost certainly, these figures will be different from the price you paid for it in the distant past. The same will be true for virtually any asset a company owns. As we'll see later, annual reports tend to focus on historical prices paid for assets, not their value.

Definition

The monetary price that would be paid for an item today in a transaction between an unrelated and willing buyer and seller. The word "value" is often used interchangeably with such terms as "fair value," "current value," or "market value."

6. Cost

Personal analogy → The cost of your new house is equal to the cash you presented as a down payment, plus the amount of the mortgage you took out to complete the purchase.

Corporate example → When United Airlines buys a jet from Boeing, its cost for that asset is the sum paid and/or financed for that purchase. Boeing's cost for the same asset may be calculated as the sum of its costs for component parts, wages for the factory workers who built it, and other expenditures related and required to produce that plane.

Definition

The monetary amount ascribed to the resources given up, and/or the obligation incurred, to acquire or make an asset.

7. Expense

Personal analogy → The amount of cash you pay a lawn service this month for cutting your grass is an expense of running your household. Other such expenses are represented by your phone and electric bills.

Corporate example → As United Airlines operates its planes, a fraction of the economic usefulness of each plane is deemed to have been used up in the delivery of flight services. Consequently, a fraction of that plane's recorded purchase cost is reported as an expense associated with its use, along with the fuel used, and the flight crew's wages.

Definition

The monetary cost of a service or benefit received, or of "using up" all or part of an asset, in the course of producing and delivering goods or services.

8. Revenue

Personal analogy → While the fees you pay for lawnmowing represent an expense to your household, these sums constitute revenues for your lawn services vendor.

Corporate example → When United Airlines flies a passenger from one point to another, the amount paid by the passenger for that service becomes revenue for the airline. (Note: This sum does not become "revenue" until the flight is made. Until then, a passenger's prepayment for a ticket generates a liability for the airline—services owed.)

Definition

The monetary amount accruing to a seller in exchange for goods and/or services delivered to a customer. "Revenue" is often used interchangeably with "sales" and "top line" since it is the first item reported in an income statement.

9. Account

Personal analogy → Let's say you purchased two airline tickets this morning. You also wrote the monthly check for your mortgage. And you bought groceries at a butcher shop, farm stand, dairy, and supermarket. Each of these three different types of transactions would warrant its own account—i.e., travel, mortgage, and food. Multiple instances of a transaction type might be recorded within a single account—for example, purchases from the butcher, farm stand, dairy, and supermarket would all appear under "food."

Corporate example → Companies engage in thousands, if not millions, of transactions each year. The financial effects of similar transactions are aggregated into descriptive categories, such as revenue, wage expense, and inventory.

Definition

A financial statement line item in which the financial effects of similar business transactions are aggregated.

10. Net Income

Personal analogy → Let's say your niece made 10 sales at her lemonade stand, at $1 per sale, generating total revenues of $10. Let's say she incurred $3 in expenses for lemons, cups, and water. Her net income then was $7, a fantastic rate. Time to franchise!

Corporate example → Microsoft has historically been very profitable. That is, its yearly income statement has consistently shown aggregate revenues far in excess of expenses, yielding substantial net income. Compare this to the early years of many dot-com companies, where expenses exceeded revenues. The importance of net income may be seen in the vast number of these firms that have disappeared. Remember the Pets.com sock puppet, for example? It is now only a memory.

Definition

The difference between an organization's aggregate revenues and aggregate expenses for a stated period of time, generally one year or one calendar quarter. "Net income" is often used interchangeably with "earnings," "profit," and the "bottom line." When aggregate expenses exceed aggregate revenues, the term *net loss* is used.

11.	**Capital**	*Personal analogy* → Let's say you gave your niece seed money to open her lemonade stand. In that case, one might say, you provided her business with capital. Let's also say she used some of this money (or some of her sales proceeds) to buy a juicer that she plans to use for many years. This purchase is a capital expenditure.

Corporate example → In business, the term "capital" is used in several different contexts. A company's "capital structure," for example, refers to the proportion of its assets financed by owners' versus creditors' money. A "capital expenditure," on the other hand, is the monetary amount invested in an asset that's expected to provide long-term economic usefulness to the company. The amounts involved in such expenditures are often substantial, both for individual assets and in the aggregate. In one recent year, for example, Norfolk Southern Railroad's capital expenditures for new locomotives, coal cars, bridge replacements, and rail lines exceeded $1 billion.

Definition

In a business context alone, the term "capital" has at least three meanings. (Sorry!) It may refer to the "owners' equity" in a company. In other instances, it may refer to an organization's total portfolio of assets. On still other occasions, it may relate to the cash expended or obligations incurred for one or more long-term assets. The context in which this term is used will dictate its meaning.

12.	**Debit/ Credit**	*Personal analogy* → A store gives you a credit when you return that holiday tie your uncle gave you. In essence, the store increases its liability to you, which allows you to come in later and acquire some

merchandise for which you will not have to pay, at least to the extent of the store credit.

Corporate example → When Ford Motor Company records a sales transaction, it credits (increases) its revenue account. When Sears buys another parcel of ground on which it will build a store, it debits (increases) its land asset account. When Coca-Cola makes a mortgage payment on an office building it owns, it debits (decreases) its mortgage payable liability account.

Definition

Debits are another term for the monetary *increases* made to an asset account or to an expense account as well as the monetary *decreases* made to a liability account or to an owners' equity account. Credits are just the opposite of debits.

✦ **News Flash** ✦ *Even though many accounting books use these two terms, we will not . . . hallelujah! They can be confusing and they are superfluous to the topic of annual reports and to understanding financial reporting. Instead, we will use the simpler, just as accurate, and more intuitive terminology of "increase" or "decrease." They are presented here just so you will know them in case a colleague peppers his/her financial discussion with them.*

Esperanto

In the late nineteenth century, L. L. Zamenhof, a Polish ophthalmologist, invented an easy, flexible new language, hoping it might be adopted universally to foster international communications, understanding, and peace. Leveraging similarities among western Indo-European languages, Dr. Zamenhof built his language, Esperanto, on the fundamentals of

Slavic, Romance, and Germanic tongues. Seeking to make his new language easy to learn and use, he established phonetic spellings. He eliminated grammatical nuances unique to specific tongues. He standardized the suffixes that could be used to expand or alter words' meanings.

Today, more than a century after its invention, in a tribute to people's eagerness for world communications and understanding, Esperanto is still in use. Thousands can speak the tongue. Esperanto associations are sprinkled around the globe, hosting conferences and publishing books and periodicals. But Esperanto has never become the universal language of Dr. Zamenhof's dreams.

Consider, however, the possibility that financial reporting has become such a universal language[1]—at least in the business world. Yes, some words used in annual reports do differ among nations. The American word "inventory" becomes "stocks" in the United Kingdom. Nonetheless, the concepts, rules, and objectives of financial reporting are fairly uniform across the world of corporate annual reports. Almost universally, these reports are intended to serve the informational needs of shareholders and to facilitate the fairness of the financial markets. Balance sheets, cash flow statements, and income statements the world over are broadly similar in terms of the items depicted, the principles governing disclosures, and even the format of their presentations.

> ### Insider's Note
>
> *To a large extent, annual-report terminology and conventions function as a shared, global business language.*

Recently, the world has seen a remarkable convergence in the basic conventions of financial reporting. Many attribute this to the rise of global financial markets and the spread of information technology. These forces enable investors to buy shares of Rolls Royce on the London Exchange with a single call to their brokers in Cincinnati or Poughkeepsie. They enable securities analysts in Denver to access online information about companies based in Milan or Kyoto. As technology and globalization have significantly integrated the world's financial markets, the language of annual reports has become something of an Esperanto for the financial community—and for those who take an interest in it.

The Inside Scoop

Because annual reports use a unique language, this chapter has simply explained some of that language. The following key terms were defined, analogized, and exemplified in the corporate setting:

- Assets
- Liabilities
- Equity
- Entity
- Value
- Cost

- Expense
- Revenue
- Account
- Net Income
- Capital
- Debit/Credit

The language of annual reports is universal. The reports of most of the world's largest publicly owned companies are published in English and, more importantly, use very similar vocabulary. They follow many of the same conventions and formats. Indeed, the language of annual reports is the Esperanto of the financial community.

Practical Application

To exemplify bringing the terms defined in this chapter to life, let's focus on four of them—assets, liabilities, revenues, and expenses. These are perhaps the most fundamental words used in telling financial stories. Let's consider some of the line items reported in the recent financial statements of certain well-known companies under headings of these terms. These line items represent a robust, and quite common, array of the assets, liabilities, revenues, and expenses reported by most companies.

Excerpts from the **asset** *section in a balance sheet from Nike, Inc.— manufacturer of various athletic items*
    Cash and equivalents
    Short-term investments
    Accounts receivable
    Inventories
    Prepaid expenses

Property, plant, and equipment
Identifiable intangible assets

Excerpts from the **liability** *section in a balance sheet from William Wrigley Jr. Company—manufacturer of chewing gum*
Accounts payable
Accrued liabilities
Interest payable
Dividends payable
Income and other taxes payable
Current portion of long-term debt
Long-term debt

Excerpts from the **revenue** *section in an income statement from United Technologies Company—manufacturer of elevators and jet engines*
Product sales
Service sales
Financing revenues
Other income

Excerpts from the **expense** *section in an income statement from E. I. du Pont de Nemours and Company—manufacturer of various Teflon®, Corian®, and Kevlar® products*
Cost of goods sold
Selling, general, and administrative expenses
Amortization of intangible expenses
Research and development expenses
Interest expense
Provision for income taxes

These accounts raise a question: in general, how can we interpret the specific line items in corporate annual reports without a reference book devoting a page to each? I'd offer three simple suggestions. First, always place a line item in the context of the financial statement category within which it's listed by the company. Second, strive for a literal interpretation of its descriptive label. Third, a line item in a corporate financial statement will generally aggregate a number of smaller, more specific, related items. We can bring it to life by considering its likely component parts.

This process is good news, as it demonstrates the role of contextual understanding, literal interpretation, and common sense in grasping the nature of items in financial statements. For example, in this chapter, we learned that an "asset" is a corporate resource—something that a company owns, and from which it expects to derive future value. Consequently, if Nike lists "accounts receivable" as an asset, we can surmise that it represents monetary amounts receivable *by* Nike—that is, collectible by Nike from someone else. This is correct. Who are the parties most likely to owe Nike this money? Customers. And there are thousands of them.

We can follow a similar process to interpret the "research and development expense" reported by DuPont. Relying on the two-pronged definition of "expense," we can surmise that part of this line item pertains to the "using up" of laboratory facilities. Another part may represent the dollar amount of wages paid to DuPont scientists. Taking this a step further, we can anticipate that DuPont has scores of labs, thousands of scientists, and dozens of large databases on special computer systems. All of these smaller, more specific items have likely been aggregated into the one line item that DuPont reports as research and development expense.

Wrigley reports a line item as "income and other taxes payable." Before reading further, take a moment to use our three-step process to bring that item to life. What is its context? It's a liability. What does that mean? It represents a dollar amount owed by Wrigley to outside parties. What sort of parties? Taxing agencies. And which might those be? They are likely to be a host of bodies at the local, state, and federal levels, administering such levies as property, income, real estate, payroll, sales, and excise taxes.

In Anticipation of the Next Secret

Like a three-piece suit, the financial-statements section of an annual report comes in a three-part ensemble. Next, we'll discuss what each part is, and why we can't wear the jacket without the slacks.

Secret #4

There's a Trilogy within the Trilogy

The BS, the IS, and the SCF

The questions behind Secret #4:

- Whose activities are covered in an annual report?
- What is the essence of a balance sheet (BS) and what does one look like?
- What is the essence of an income statement (IS) and what does one look like?
- What is the essence of a statement of cash flows (SCF) and what does one look like?

In Chapter 1 we established the existence of a corporate financial trilogy. There is one set of financial books for corporate inside managers, another for tax authorities, and a third for external constituents such as shareholders and lenders. In Chapter 2 we zeroed in on the corporate annual report as the primary vehicle by which companies tell their financial story to external constituencies. There, we noted that just as each installment in an author's series of engrossing novels often follows a general pattern, so too, do annual reports. Specifically, and in part, every corporate annual report contains a financial statement trilogy—a balance sheet (BS), an income statement (IS), and a statement of cash flows (SCF).[1] This trilogy employs much of the language of Chapter 3. Moreover, each part of that trilogy embraces certain conventions and story lines that render each unique and informative. With curiosity and care, let's delve more deeply into this financial statement trilogy.

A Question of Entities: Whose Annual Report Is It Anyway?

Before reviewing the three financial statements in a firm's annual report, we must address one basic question: what entity is described in that report? Now you may smile and answer, "The company, of course." And you'd be right—to an extent. But defining that company may require some guidance, as many corporations own shares of stock in other corporations. Thus, we must understand the circumstances under which the operations of one company are integrated into the annual report of another.

Consider these possibilities. If General Motors (GM) owns 1% of the shares of Car Seats, Inc. (a fictitious but not far-fetched idea for a company), should Car Seats' financial results be integrated into the GM financial statements? What if GM owns 10% of Car Seats? Or 50%? Or 100%? The answer is that if GM owns more than 50% of the shares of Car Seats, Inc. stock in the public domain—that is, more than 50% of Car Seats' "outstanding" stock—then GM must consolidate Car Seats' operations with its own in its annual report. For the moment, we may think of this "consolidation" as literally adding the two organizations together to create a single financial reporting entity, even as they remain distinct legal entities, each with their own products, managers, facilities, and histories.

As a result of such consolidations, the entity portrayed in an annual report consists of the focal company, plus all others over which it has control. For annual report purposes, one company is assumed to "control" another if it owns more than 50% of its outstanding shares of stock. Since stock, particularly "common stock," represents ownership, the holders of that stock need a means to exercise their ownership. This is achieved through voting rights. That is, stockholders have a right to elect their company's board of directors. Those directors, in turn, hire and oversee the firm's top executives. Generally, in these elections, each share of common stock gives its owner the right to cast one vote. Thus, if there are 2 million shares of Car Seats, Inc. stock in the public domain, and GM owns 1,000,001 of them, the presumption is that GM has the power to elect a majority of Car Seats, Inc.'s board of directors, enabling it to govern Car Seats, Inc. with GM's interests in mind.

Many annual reports include not only the focal company, but also 10, 20, or even 100 other companies in which the focal company holds a majority stock interest. From year to year, GM, Microsoft, and other companies may acquire some new majority stock positions, while divesting others. Consequently, the financial reporting entity known as GM or Microsoft is actually an evolving, ever-changing organization. Readers of annual reports take a keen interest in these changes, and companies often provide information about them. Sadly, however, in some annual reports this information is rather sparse.

> ## Insider's Note
>
> *A single corporate annual report presents the financial results of the main, focal company combined with the results of all the other companies that it has control over via (most often) a majority stock position in them.*

The Balance Sheet: A Snapshot in Time

My son is fully grown. He's tall and muscular, with close-cropped hair and three tattoos. He's an independent—very independent—and hard-working young man. But on an office shelf, I keep an eight by ten photo of him from the summer when he was 12 years old. That image captures a distinct moment in time—a summer of braces, curly hair, skinny arms, and long, lazy afternoons by the pool. It was a summer of boyish pranks, lost shoes, and outrageous adventures that often ended with him covered in mud. Such moments don't last. But photos do. And if I ever want to recall my son during the summer before he entered his teens, I need only look at that photo.

Balance sheets are, similarly, a snapshot in time. They depict a company's assets (A), liabilities (L), and owners' equity (OE) as of midnight on the last day of its financial year. More precisely, a balance sheet reports the assets owned by a company and the extent to

> ## Insider's Note
>
> *A corporate balance sheet presents assets (A), liabilities (L), and owners' equity (OE) as of a moment in time and, $A = L + OE$.*

which those assets have been financed by creditors and owners. In short, a balance sheet depicts the following fundamental relationship:

$$\text{Assets owned} = \text{Liabilities owed} + \text{Owners' equity}$$
$$A = L + OE$$

At a more personal level, I expect you'll find that this very same relationship holds true for your car or home. Your car, for example, is yours to drive as you wish—within the law. It is your asset. You may have financed it, however, with a down payment (your "OE") and a loan (your "L"). The same pattern applies to the broad portfolios of assets held by General Electric, IBM, and other companies. Their reported assets will be matched by the sum of their liabilities and owners' equity (see Figure 4.1).

In gaining familiarity with balance sheets, bear in mind three key concepts related to them: completeness, reported monetary amounts, and disclosure. On the surface, each of these concepts seems quite straightforward, and to a large extent they are. But there is also a problematic aspect to each that we will briefly mention here and discuss in greater detail later.

With regard to completeness, corporate managers and their external auditors work hard to ensure that all items that *should* be reported on a company's balance sheet are there. Rookie auditors often spend New Years Eves in clients' far-flung warehouses, for example, making sure clients' inventory asset records accurately reflect inventory items physically on hand. (Talk about a "New Year's Rockin' Eve"!) Similarly, auditors mail hundreds of letters to clients' customers, asking them to verify the sums they owed at year-end for goods or services delivered, but for which they'd not yet paid. In this way, auditors ensure the completeness of their clients' accounts receivable reported-asset amount. Similarly, to validate a year-end accounts payable amount, auditors look at the bills paid by a corporate client during the month immediately following year end, and determine if these applied to obligations incurred prior to that date. If so, they must be included in that year-end balance sheet liability.

Scan the Car Seats, Inc. balance sheet again (see Figure 4.1). Can you think of an asset that doesn't appear there, and that won't be listed on any balance sheet? If you guessed the employees, you're correct. While firms regularly declare, "our employees are our most important asset," those personnel aren't reflected in the asset section of any company's balance sheet. This

Car Seats, Inc.[2]
Consolidated Balance Sheets
as of December 31

Assets	This year	Last year
Current assets		
Cash and equivalents	$ 25,710	$ 22,120
Receivables (net of allowances)	276,590	287,780
Inventories	248,500	236,500
Other current assets	42,200	52,800
Total current assets	593,000	599,200
Property, plant and equipment		
(net of accumulated depreciation)	204,360	208,500
Goodwill	32,000	43,330
Investments	66,000	70,160
Other long-term assets	79,340	68,110
Total assets	**$ 974,700**	**$ 989,300**
Liabilities and owners' equity		
Current liabilities		
Short-term debt	$ 7,900	$ 33,640
Current portion of long-term debt	4,100	5,880
Accounts payable	84,350	88,620
Accrued expenses and other current liabilities	125,700	133,350
Total current liabilities	222,050	261,490
Long-term debt	210,740	192,900
Deferred income taxes	5,090	13,970
Other long-term liabilities	47,600	32,770
Total liabilities	485,480	501,130
Owners' equity		
Common shares ($1 par value)	50,220	51,100
Capital in excess of par value	222,120	227,350
Retained earnings	225,880	208,720
Other	(9,000)	1,000
Total owners' equity	489,220	488,170
Total liabilities and owners' equity	**$ 974,700**	**$ 989,300**

Figure 4.1 Example of a Typical Balance Sheet

illustrates a key point: A corporate balance sheet must report completely those items that it's required to report. These are generally the tangible and intangible assets that it has purchased (or made) and now owns, along with the legally binding debts that it owes. But this does not necessarily include all the company's resources, rights, and obligations. In a later chapter, we'll discuss the *incompleteness* of balance sheets in more detail.

Some of the items that fail to appear on a balance sheet do so because of an unresolved debate about the monetary amount at which they should be reported. As established earlier, resources and obligations are initially listed on a balance sheet at their historical cost. This amount has the benefit of being objectively determinable. It's based on a clear transaction event. Of course, companies can and do adjust these historical figures over time. In subsequent chapters, we'll discuss some of these adjustments. At present, it's important to note that all balance sheet items are initially reported at their historical cost. Items without an objectively measurable historical cost generally do not find their way onto a balance sheet.

Financial statement footnotes are important. They are not prosaically captivating or pictorially inviting. The disclosures therein, however, provide explanations and data that help to clarify and detail the balance sheet items captured in a year-end snapshot. You can count on the footnotes to provide information about how the reported balance sheet monetary amounts were determined, as well as the subcomponents of various line item aggregations, and any significant reductions made to items' reported amounts due to unusual or unfortunate circumstances.

The Income Statement:
For a *Period* of Time

A growing number of people are discovering and enjoying the game of lacrosse. It is a fast-paced, physical sport demanding a range of skills. As one dad shared with me on the sidelines as we watched an exciting game, "If they'd had this sport at my school when I was growing up, I never would have played baseball." For some of us, it's that cool. Well, my son was pretty good in high school, and he hoped to play college lacrosse. But this raised a challenge: how could we get college coaches to spot a player at a small high school not known as a hotbed of the sport? The partial answer: during my son's junior year, I videotaped all his games. In essence, I turned the camcorder on when the season began and turned it off when it ended, recording one complete year of his performance. We offered those videotapes to the college coaches that we met and liked.

A corporate income statement may be compared to a videotape. On the first day of a company's financial year, managers metaphorically load a blank tape into the corporate camcorder. They focus the camera on their firm's revenue and expense events, and allow it to run for 365

days. Then they turn it off. They edit the tape, package it for public consumption, and so produce their company's annual income statement. That financial statement, unlike a balance sheet, pertains to a *period* of time, not a *point* in time.

Figure 4.2 presents the income statement for Car Seats, Inc. It is fairly typical. While it consists of only a few line items, don't let its brevity lead you to discount its significance. Each of those items represents an aggregation of components. More importantly, the Net Income figure at its end is a key performance metric.

In crafting an income statement, the fundamental reporting issue is "revenue recognition." That is, when is a sale truly a sale, warranting inclusion in a particular period's income statement? The general answer is: when a company's earnings process is complete. Of course, this point differs among companies. A company like Car Seats, Inc., for example, in a very straightforward manner, fully earns its revenue from a simple, ordinary sale when it delivers car seats to a customer like Wal-Mart.

Note that it does not earn this revenue when it receives an order, or when it manufactures or ships a seat, or when it bills a customer, or even when it receives payment. The company earns its revenue when it delivers a product to a customer. Many companies have gotten into trouble by playing fast and loose with revenue recognition practices. In response, regulators have published increasingly detailed guidelines in this area—though they're always just a little behind the creative sales arrangements engineered by some companies seeking to record revenue sooner rather than later.

	This year	Last year	Two years ago
Car Seats, Inc.			
Consolidated Income Statements			
for the Years Ended December 31			
Sales	$1,961,620	$1,883,330	$2,200,120
Cost of goods sold	1,623,410	1,506,450	1,682,660
Gross profit	338,210	376,880	517,460
Selling, general and administrative	299,506	346,870	380,720
Write-down of intangible assets	—	5,440	—
Operating income	38,704	24,570	136,740
Interest expense	8,220	9,310	9,770
Other income (net)	100	1,990	3,180
Income from continuing operations before income taxes	30,584	17,250	130,150
Income tax expense	14,334	18,290	48,400
Income (loss) from continuing operations	16,250	(1,040)	81,750
Income (loss) from discontinued operations (net of taxes)	2,910	220	(660)
Net income (loss)	**$ 19,160**	**($ 820)**	**$ 81,090**
Net income (loss) per basic share	$2.55	($ .11)	$ 11.18

Figure 4.2 Example of a Typical Income Statement

The Statement of Cash Flows: For a Period of Time—Part 2

Cash is the lifeblood of a business—as it is for our personal finances. If you doubt this, ask my daughter. For the past two pay periods, her boss has forgotten to turn in her time sheets. As a result, she hasn't been paid. From the perspective of her personal income statement (not that she has one), she's earned two paychecks. That is, from the point of view of GAAP-based accounting, she's done the work and could report those wages as earned. Her employer acknowledges that she's owed the money. Her boss promises she'll be paid. She could, if she wished, draft a personal balance sheet with an asset line item titled "wages receivable" in the amount of her back pay.

But try taking *that* to the coffee shop to buy a cappuccino. Somehow, it just doesn't compare to cash.

This highlights the difference between income statement revenues and cash inflows. Under accrual accounting for income statements, just as revenues are recognized when earned, expenses must be recognized when incurred—that is, when a resource is used or expended. The recognition of an expense may differ in time, however, from the moment when a company pays for it. Income statement revenues and expenses, all reported for a particular period of time on the accrual basis, are important. It's also important to report cash inflows and outflows for the same period of time. Of special importance, though, is that the cash flow impact of an event can differ in timing, sometimes markedly, from the income statement impact of the very same event.

In the United States and, increasingly, around the world, companies use a standard format to report their cash flows for a year. This format divides those flows into three categories: cash flows from operating (CFFO), cash flows from investing (CFFI), and cash flows from financing (CFFF) activities. In this way, the statement of cash flows depicts the net difference between a company's beginning- and end-of-year cash balances as a result of its operating, investing, and financing activities over the course of the year. By way of example, observe the Car Seats, Inc. statement of cash flows in Figure 4.3.

> ### Insider's Note
>
> *In short, a statement of cash flows reports the sources and uses of a company's cash for a specific time period. By convention, the cash flows are reported in one of three categories: cash flows from operations, cash flows from investing, and cash flows from financing activities.*

CFFO: Cash Flows From Operating Activities

Figure 4.3 portrays three main features of the statement of cash flows' CFFO section. Let's introduce each at a conceptual level. The first is that it begins with the net income figure from the company's income statement. Ultimately, the statement of cash flows ends with the figure in the balance sheet's *cash account at year end*. These starting and ending points are important. The statement of cash flows explicitly connects the income statement's accrual-based earnings to the balance sheet's cash asset. It reports and highlights the ways in which a company's earnings

Car Seats, Inc.

Consolidated Statement of Cash Flows

for the Years Ended December 31

	This year	Last year	Two years ago
Cash flows from operating activities			
Net income (loss)	$ 19,160	($ 820)	$ 81,090
Adjustments to reconcile net income (loss) to net cash provided by operating activities			
Write-down of intangibles	—	5,440	—
Gain on sale of discontinued business (net of taxes)	(550)	(730)	—
Depreciation	20,230	27,110	31,700
(Increase) decrease in net receivables	11,190	(7,660)	(16,500)
(Increase) decrease in inventories	(12,000)	(12,800)	(18,270)
Increase (decrease) in payables	(4,270)	10,998	6,900
Increase (decrease) in deferred tax liab.	(8,880)	(9,740)	8,000
Change in other current assets and liab.	2,950	(3,060)	(9,300)
Total adjustments	8,670	9,558	2,530
Net cash provided by operating activities	**27,830**	**8,738**	**83,620**
Cash flows from investing activities			
Proceeds from disposal of assets	1,320	8,360	3,110
Proceeds from sale of discontinued business	16,040	8,970	—
Purchases of additional property	(17,410)	(11,630)	(15,220)
(Increase) decrease in other long-term assets	(11,230)	1,880	(8,560)
Net cash (used for) provided from investing activities	**(11,280)**	**7,580**	**(20,670)**
Cash flows from financing activities			
Proceeds from debt	24,320	2,010	3,330
Payments on debt	(34,000)	(19,990)	(26,760)
Repurchase of stock	(6,110)	(9,220)	—
Dividends paid	(2,000)	(2,250)	(4,340)
Increase (decrease) in other long-term liabilities and shareholders' equity	4,830	1,222	(4,250)
Net cash used for financing activities	**(12,960)**	**(28,228)**	**(32,020)**
Change in cash and equivalents	3,590	(11,910)	30,930
Cash and equivalents at beginning of the year	22,120	34,030	3,100
Cash and equivalents at end of year	**$ 25,710**	**$22,120**	**$ 34,030**

Figure 4.3 Example of a Typical Statement of Cash Flows

focus differs from its cash ins and outs. By presenting the data to reconcile a company's net income to its ending cash balance, the statement of cash flows also depicts how a company obtained and deployed its cash.

Moving on to the second feature of the CFFO section, please note the specific items listed to convert accrual-based net income to a measure of cash generated by operations. Depreciation, for example, was deducted as an expense on the income statement. Here, however, it's added back. The reason: while depreciation is a legitimate expense of doing business, it does not consume cash. When a company acquires an asset, such as a truck, it may write a check for that purpose, using cash. If it then depreciates that truck over a three-year economic life, it recognizes the "using up" of the asset by deducting a portion of its cost each year as a depreciation expense on its income statement. This, however, does *not* use cash.

To move from the accrual basis of net income to the cash perspective of the statement of cash flows, depreciation expense must be added back. You'll notice that Car Seats, Inc. has done so—to the tune of $20,230 this year. It has done the same with other noncash expenses, such as the write-down of intangibles ($5,440 last year). Similarly, if there were noncash revenues included in the net income figure, they must be *subtracted* on the statement of cash flows. Remember, the purpose of the CFFO section is to recast accrual-based net income as a cash-based measure of operating performance.

The third major component of the CFFO section concerns the various accounts through which a company runs most of its daily operating transactions. Take "accounts receivable" as an example. Many corporate sales—especially to frequent or favored customers—are made on credit terms. That is, they don't generate immediate cash. If you or I went to Home Depot, bought a ladder, and asked the cashier to put it on our tab, that would be a credit sale. At the end of the month, Home Depot would send us a bill for all of our purchases that month, including the ladder, and we'd pay for it then. I don't know about you, but I do not have that arrangement with Home Depot—maybe I'll ask.

Corporations often do make sales to other companies on a credit basis, however. Home Depot, to continue the example, might tell a large home builder: "We value your business so highly that we'll let you take 30 days to pay for the materials we sell you." From the perspective of Home Depot, once it delivers materials to a builder, it's made a sale and may book the resulting revenue on its income statement—even though it won't receive cash for it for another 30 days.

As a large corporation, Home Depot likely makes millions of such transactions each year, generating millions of accounts receivable—that is, customers' promises to pay. During the course of a year, most of these will be collected, including many booked toward the end of the prior year. Consequently, the amount by which Home Depot's total accounts receivable changes from the beginning to the end of a year will reflect the amount by which that year's recorded sales differ from cash collections on credit sales. Thus, Home Depot's statement of cash flows will include a CFFO line item that adjusts accrual-based net income to reflect the net change in accounts receivable during the year.

Let's look into this a bit further—it's an important concept. Assume the following situation for a small company:

	Balance as of the end of last year	Credit sales increasing the accounts receivable balance during the year	Cash collections decreasing the accounts receivable balance during the year
Accounts receivable	$12,000	$90,000	$85,000

What will be this company's accounts receivable balance at the end of the year? The answer may be derived as $12,000 + 90,000 - 85,000$, yielding $17,000. If this company makes all its sales on credit, what dollar revenue amount would the company report on its income statement? The answer is $90,000. From a cash perspective, however, how much cash did the company receive this year, generated by its sales activities? That answer is $85,000. Therefore, by how much does net income differ from cash inflows from sales? The answer is that this company recognized $5,000 more in revenues than actually received in cash. (That is, $90,000 - 85,000 = $5,000$.) Please note that this $5,000 figure is precisely equal to the amount by which the accounts receivable grew ($17,000 - 12,000 = $5,000$). Therefore, since the statement of cash flows starts with a net income figure that includes more (sometimes less) revenue than cash received from sales, the company's statement of cash flows must include a line item to show the amount by which its accounts receivable balance changed during the year. That amount is exactly the amount by which income statement revenues differ from sales-related cash collections.

Generalizing, if a firm's accounts receivable balance increases during a year, that means it's sold more than it's collected from customers, and the amount of the accounts receivable increase that year should be deducted from the net income figure on the statement of cash flows. By contrast, if its accounts receivable balance *decreases*, that means it's collected more than it's sold. The revenues on the income statement then wouldn't be large enough to reflect cash collections, and, in the conversion to a cash-based performance measure, the amount of the accounts receivable net decrease should be *added back* to net income on the statement of cash flows. (For example, see the Car Seats, Inc. adjustment for receivables in the amount of $11,190.) Please note that a decrease in the accounts receivable balance would *not* indicate that customers paid for more than they bought. Rather, it merely reflects payment for some of the prior year's credit sales, along with collections on a good part of the current year's sales.

Finally, the CFFO section of the statement of cash flows ends with a figure labeled "net cash provided by operating activities," or words to that effect. This is a useful figure. For a mature, healthy company, it should be positive and growing from year to year, as it depicts the firm's ability to generate positive net cash inflows

> **Insider's Note**
>
> *A company's CFFO should be large, positive, and getting bigger each year.*

from its core business activities. Clearly, if this number is negative and/or diminishing, the company's core business is not healthy or is weakening.

Cash Flows from Investing Activities

If you think about it for a moment, what can a company do with the cash generated by its core operations? In essence, it can do many of the same things you or I might do with the money left over from our paychecks, after living expenses, assuming we don't want to hold it in cash. We might buy a car, refrigerator, or washing machine—our own version of long-lived operating assets. We might invest in the stock market. Or we might pay down our mortgages or credit card debt. Similarly, corporations use their available cash to invest in long-lived assets and securities, and to repay their financiers. The CFFI section of the statement of cash flows depicts the company's activities in the first of these two categories.

The CFFI section reports the cash that a company deploys for investments in such items as land, buildings, and equipment, and in other companies. For an example of the former, see the $17,410 investment by Car Seats, Inc. in "additional property" in its statement of cash flows (Figure 4.3). The CFFI section also shows the proceeds received from sales of investments previously acquired, such as the $1,320 generated this year by Car Seats, Inc. on its "disposal of assets."

Generally speaking, a net negative total for the CFFI section is not a bad thing. On the contrary, it suggests that the company is making more long-term investments than it is liquidating. Such a situation is a sign of the company's optimism for the future. It may reflect a commitment to modernize its infrastructure, or to expand into new domains. On the other hand, a yearly, recurring, net positive total for CFFI is probably not good news. It may indicate that the company is downsizing, leaving markets, liquidating investments, or selling its crown jewels to generate cash to repay creditors or fund daily operations.

> ### Insider's Note
>
> *If a company's CFFI is positive (negative), the company is selling (buying) more investments than it is buying (selling). In general, and over time, CFFI should be a negative figure.*

CFFF: Cash Flows from Financing Activities

The CFFF section reports cash *used* in financing activities—debt service to creditors, dividend payments to shareholders, and repurchases of the firm's own stock from the public. This section also depicts cash *generated* by financing activities through the issuance of new stock to investors, or the raising of funds through new bonds, loans, or commercial paper.

Readers must interpret the CFFF section of the statement of cash flows in concert with the other two sections, as

> ### Insider's Note
>
> *The details of the CFFF section of a statement of cash flows depict the extent to which a company has raised funds from, or paid funds to, its shareholders and creditors. A net negative or positive CFFF must be interpreted in conjunction with the other parts of the cash flow statement.*

many interaction effects can be expected. Recurring, strong net income, for example, will often be accompanied by sizable dividend payments to investors in the CFFF section. If a company shows weak cash flows from operations, in tandem with ongoing investments under CFFI, it can be expected to report a net positive CFFF figure as it raises funds to cover these through new borrowings or sales of stock.

On the other hand, after several years of weak or negative CFFO, along with net positive figures for CFFI, a firm may suffer an overall weakening of its financial prospects and condition. Readers might find signs of this in the CFFF, where they'd see a discontinuation of dividends and an inability to obtain additional cash through new borrowings. Clearly, that would not be a good story. But it would be an important one, and it would be visible in the statement of cash flows.

The Inside Scoop

The annual report presents a trilogy—three separate financial statements. One of these is the balance sheet, which depicts a company's assets, liabilities, and owners' equity. The balance sheet tells the story, as of a precise moment in time, of what a company owns and what it owes. The difference between these figures is, in essence, the equity held by owners in the company.

The income statement reports a company's sales and expenses for a year, or some other, specified period of time. The difference between these figures constitutes the firm's net income, or loss.

The statement of cash flows portrays the company's ability to generate cash, and the ways in which it used that cash during the course of a year.

Each of these statements tells a story. Each is important. Each is different.

Practical Application

On the Car Seats, Inc. balance sheet, verify that $A = L + OE$. On the income statement, note the format that leads through multiple earnings-oriented subtotals to arrive at a single bottom line, labeled "net income." Take a bit more time with the statement of cash flows. Note first that it starts with the "net income" figure from the income statement, and ends with the cash balance that appears on the balance sheet. In a very real way, the statement of cash flows acts as a bridge between these other two financial statements.

Next, identify the three parts of the cash flow statement—CFFO, CFFI, and CFFF. Within the CFFO section, note (1) the adjustments to add back noncash expenses, such as depreciation, which had previously been deducted in the calculation of net income on the income statement, and (2) the adjustments that capture changes in various balance sheet current accounts such as accounts receivable. Refresh your memory as to the logic (discussed in the preceding pages) behind those adjustments. In the CFFI and CFFF sections, take a moment to interpret the events described. If you have time, try this also with the annual report you were invited to obtain in Chapter 2.

In Anticipation of the Next Secret

The procedures for capturing, codifying, and communicating corporate financial data are quite simple. Let's take a peek at the process.

Secret #5

It's as Simple as 1-2-3

It's all about ins and outs;
ups and downs!

The questions behind Secret #5:

- Can the accounting process be explained in simple terms?
- What merit is there in understanding the accounting process?
- Are there any inviolate financial reporting relationships that provide a framework and foundation to help us understand an annual report's financial statements?
- What are the connections among an annual report's three financial statements?
- The statement of cash flows is unique. How and why?

Fundamentally, if you can add, subtract, keep one equation in balance, and learn some basic vocabulary, you can quickly master an annual report's underlying accounting processes.

The Source of All Truth (Well Some Truth, Anyway)

In the course of our lives, we've all encountered rules designed to bring certainty and simplicity to a complex world. Unfortunately, not all of these work. Sitting now at my keyboard, I find that I'm still scratching my head over a few that I learned in my earliest classes. In third grade spelling, for example, my teacher taught me to place "i" before "e." That seemed an excellent rule. It worked for "friend" and "French fries"—crucial terms for an eight-year-old. Then, however, my teacher added, "except after 'c.' " Okay, I thought, a little exception. No big deal. It worked for "ceiling" and "receive." But my teacher wasn't done. "Or when it sounds like 'a,' " she said, as in "neighbor." Or in special cases, such as "weird." At that point, I got frustrated. What kind of rule was this, I thought, that has so many exceptions, including exceptions to the exceptions?

Fortunately, the rules of financial reporting aren't quite like that. The following relationships codify the foundations for the three key financial statements in annual reports that we have already discussed:

In Regard to the:	*The Reliable Rule is:*
Balance Sheet →	Assets = Liabilities + Owners' Equity
Income Statement →	Net Income = Revenues − Expenses
Statement of Cash Flows →	Ending Cash = Beginning Cash + Cash from Operating Activities + Cash from Investing Activities + Cash from Financing Activities

These are the cornerstones of an annual report's financial statements. They provide an unwavering basis for understanding additional details pertaining to those financial statements.

Assets = Liabilities + Owners' Equity

In an earlier chapter, and again just now, we introduced the fundamental balance sheet relationship: $A = L + OE$. Let's build on this relationship. The entire financial reporting framework at work in the corporate world can be extrapolated from the relationships embedded in this one equation. Therefore, let's begin by exposing some of these more detailed relation-

Insider's Note

All of the financial statements presented in a corporate annual report spring from the $A = L + OE$ relationship.

ships. Each of the three elements of this equation can be divided into two subcategories as depicted below:

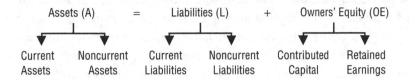

Assets

Each of these subcategories is straightforward, and yields a bit more insight for readers of an annual report. *Current assets*, for example, are those assets which, through the normal operations of the company, will be converted to cash within one year. They include:

- Cash, of course.
- Accounts receivable (A/R): These are sums due from customers who bought goods or services on credit, generally requiring payment within 30 days.
- Inventory (Inv): These are goods purchased or manufactured by a company, and intended to be sold to customers. Wal-Mart, for example, carries an inventory of jeans in its stores. It intends to sell these and get paid for them within a year, if not sooner.
- Prepaid assets (Ppd/A): These are items for which a company has paid in advance, and from which it expects to derive benefits over the ensuing year. When a company buys insurance, for example, it generally pays a premium at the beginning of the policy, and receives the benefit of the resulting protection over the next 12 months. That prepaid insurance policy would be classified as a current asset as of the date its premium was paid.[1]

Noncurrent assets, by contrast, consist of all balance sheet assets that do not qualify for the "current asset" category. These longer-term assets include buildings, land, vehicles, and investments.

Liabilities

What are *current liabilities*? As I'm sure you surmised, these are obligations owed by a company, due to be paid within the next 12 months. The logic here is similar to that applied among current and noncurrent assets. By separating current from noncurrent liabilities, a company distinguishes between those obligations that assert a claim on cash in the near term—within 12 months—and those that don't. Current liabilities include:

- Accounts payable (A/P): Amounts owed to suppliers
- The current portion of long-term debt
- Wages payable (W/P)
- Interest payable (I/P)
- Taxes payable (T/P)
- Near-term (e.g., 90-day) bank loans

As you might expect, *noncurrent liabilities* are obligations with due dates beyond the next 12 months. Examples include the noncurrent portions of mortgages, bonds, taxes owed but long deferred, and retirement benefits owed employees.

Owners' Equity

Contributed capital represents the funds paid by owners and investors to the company to acquire shares of its stock when those shares were first offered to the public. Note the "first offered" part of this definition. When you call your broker and ask her to buy 500 shares of IBM, she can do this because, somewhere in the world, another investor is looking to *sell* 500 shares of IBM. The resulting transaction will probably take place on the New York Stock Exchange, which, like similar exchanges around the world, is a market for buying and selling stocks that are already in the hands of the public. Consequently, when you pay for your 500 shares of IBM, the money won't go to IBM. It will go to the seller of the shares.

A company only receives money from the sale of its shares when *it* sells them to investors in an *initial public offering*—an IPO. Thus, within the owner's equity section of a balance sheet, "contributed capital" represents the proceeds of a company's own stock sales, particularly IPOs. To be complete, we should mention that this sum will be reduced by the costs a company incurs if it buys some of its shares back from the public. The shares acquired in such a repurchase program—*treasury stock*—will therefore be counted as an offset to contributed capital, representing previously issued but no longer outstanding shares of the company's stock.

The last of our OE sub-categories, *retained earnings*, is an interesting item. It's equivalent to a company's historical, cumulative net income, less historical, cumulative dividends paid to shareholders. But this, of course, begs the question: to whom do a company's earnings belong? The answer: they belong to the company's owners, not its managers. The company, after all, is a legal entity conducting business on behalf of its owners. The company's net income, therefore, is the return due to those owners (i.e., you and me if we are shareholders) on their equity interest in the company. Of course, companies seldom pay owners their total proportionate share of a given year's net income. And owners don't demand that they do. In most mature companies, however, owners do expect *some* periodic cash return on their investment. Consequently, many companies pay dividends representing a percentage of a given year's reported net income. Annually, these dividends may amount to 5%, 10%, or even as much as 60% of net income.

But this introduces an interesting wrinkle. Remember: Net income is not a cash figure. It's an accrual-based figure. Dividends, however, are generally paid in cash. Thus, as retained earnings are calculated as cumulative net income earned, less cumulative dividends paid, it's not a pure cash figure either. Indeed, there's no corporate vault holding the cash equivalent of a company's retained earnings.

But this prompts yet another question: Why do shareholders allow a company to retain earnings at all? If they own the firm, why don't they insist that it pay the full amount of its net income as dividends? The answer is straightforward: owners trust the company's managers to use undistributed earnings within the business to generate even greater returns in the future. If a company succeeds at that, the owners will be happy, and this arrangement will continue. By contrast, if the company disappoints owners with its level of ongoing income, shareholders may demand increased dividend payout rates. Or they may sell the company's stock and invest elsewhere.

In summary, retained earnings can be divided into two parts and its net income part can also be displayed as consisting of two additional parts—revenues and expenses.

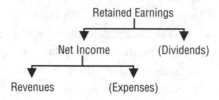

Accounting 101—*in 10.1 Minutes*

IBM must process thousands of business transactions every day. Corporations like IBM need efficient, robust, systematic processes to account for their businesses in an orderly, accurate way. In truth, the process aspect of accounting is nothing more than a system to capture, codify, control, and communicate business data. This system may focus on a single business event, such as the purchase of a building, or on a series of regularly recurring events, such as the monthly payment of employee wages. In either case, in capturing and codifying a business transaction or event, the system must make three determinations: Which components in the financial reporting diagram are affected? By how much? And in what direction? Throughout the accounting process, the system must maintain the integrity of the basic equation:

> **Insider's Note**
>
> *The essence of Accounting 101 involves identifying which component part of the expanded financial reporting equation is impacted by a business event and then either increasing or decreasing that component by the proper monetary amount, all the while keeping the equality of $A = L + OE$.*

$A = L + OE$. Figure 5.1 helps show the component parts of this equation, in conjunction with some of the new accounts we've just introduced.

Figure 5.1 points toward the interconnectedness of the three primary financial statements in an annual report. While all of the accounts are linked, note that those in italics will be used to construct the income statement. Those shaded will appear on the balance sheet. The bolded "cash" account warrants and receives its own dedicated financial statement, detailing its sources and uses. Stay tuned for more about that.

Meanwhile, let's use Figure 5.1 to help us master Accounting 101. Suppose a company just bought a new truck for $25,000 in cash. Which

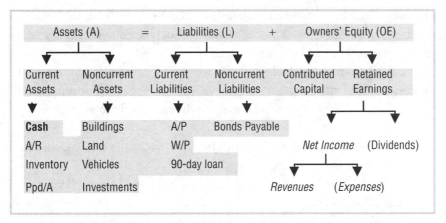

Figure 5.1 The Components of A = L + OE

parts of the diagram will be impacted by this event? Clearly, the "cash" and "vehicles" accounts. Next, what was the magnitude of the impact? $25,000 in each account. Last, in what direction were they impacted? "Cash" declined by $25,000, while "vehicles" increased by the same amount. Both are assets—one current; the other, noncurrent. The net financial effect of this event leaves the equality of the basic equation, A = L + OE, true.

Let's take another example. Suppose a company takes out a 90-day bank loan totaling $50,000. What parts of the diagram *now* will be affected and how? Simple. "Cash," a current asset, increases by $50,000, while "90-day loan," a current liability, increases by the same amount. Both sides of the equation rise by $50,000, and the full A = L + OE relationship remains in balance.

Now, suppose you've just completed a week's work, and your employer owes you $2,000 in wages. Payday, however, won't roll around until next week. What part of the diagram has been impacted as of *today* and how? From the company's perspective, *wages payable* (W/P) have increased by $2,000. Likewise, *expenses*—or, more specifically, *payroll expenses*—also increased by $2,000. Is the basic equation still in balance? Look carefully . . . you'll need to interpret the parentheses around "expenses" as a reduction in the item immediately above it. That item, of course, is *net income*. "Net income," in turn, feeds into *retained earnings*. Thus, the increase in wages payable, a liability, has been counterbalanced by a decrease in "retained earnings," a component of owner's equity. Thus, the equality expressed by the fundamental equation remains true.

And that, in a nutshell, is how it works. All accounting systems and processes, from the simplest manual ledgers to the most sophisticated, high-volume computer networks, execute the same functions:

- They establish any number of line item accounts under each category of the basic equation.
- They identify the line item accounts impacted by a particular business event.
- They quantify the monetary amounts of these impacts.
- Finally, they increase or decrease the targeted line item accounts, as appropriate, such that the equality of the basic financial reporting equation remains true.

(Notice that we did not use words that you may have encountered before like debit, credit, journal entries, trial balance, and posting. For understanding corporate annual reports and their financial statements, such terms are irrelevant.)

Assessing the Financial Statement Effects of Business Transactions

Even though you may never have aspirations to be an accountant or a bookkeeper, the ability to think through the financial reporting effects of business transactions is an important skill. This is true because of one simple fact—corporate managers are *not* ambivalent about the story presented in their year-end financial statements. They know what story they want to tell. In order to nudge, push, or even steer financial statements in the desired direction, managers structure their firm's business events in ways that lend themselves to the preferred financial statement effect. Of course, not every

Insider's Note

Corporate managers are not ambivalent about how a business event gets reported. Thus, they may structure a business event so as to prompt the most desirable financial statement portrayal.

business event is amenable to proactive steering. Wages are wages, and customer collections are customer collections.

Let's explore this idea with a more flexible transaction, however. Let's say a company needs a new fleet of delivery vehicles. To fill this need, corporate managers may buy trucks with cash on hand (Option A). Or they may take out a loan, and use its proceeds to buy the required trucks (Option B). Or they may rent trucks for short terms, on an as-needed basis (Option C). Or they may execute any combination of these options. Any of these might fill the business need. They will entail different costs. Managers will consider those. However, they will also consider the ways in which each option affects the company's financial statements. For example, the first year's balance sheet and income statement effects for each option are represented in Figure 5.2.

Clearly, these financial statement effects are quite different from one another. And those differences may have a powerful impact on the way in which management prefers to acquire its new delivery capacity. Let's say management doesn't want more debt on its balance sheet. In that case, Option B would not be viable. By contrast, if management

	Balance Sheet	Income Statement
Option A	-Current asset (cash) *decreases* by purchase price. -Noncurrent asset (vehicles) *increases* by purchase price.	-Depreciation expense *increases* by proportion of vehicles' lives represented by one year.
Option B	-Noncurrent asset (vehicles) *increases* by purchase price. -Current liability *increases* by amount of coming year's principal repayment due on loan. -Noncurrent liability *increases* by remainder of loan principal.	-Depreciation expense *increases* by proportion of vehicles' lives represented by one year. - Interest expense *increases* by the amount of interest charged on the loan for that year.
Option C	-Current asset (cash) *decreases* only when and to the extent that vehicles are rented.	-Rent expense *increases* only when and to the extent that vehicles are rented.

Figure 5.2 Three Ways to Acquire a Truck: The Financial Statement Effects

doesn't want long-term assets on the balance sheet, then Option C would be attractive. The goals, tactics, and possibilities would branch out from there, and could become very complex. The underlying point, however, is quite simple: Managers have goals and preferences for the stories told in their companies' financial statements. These preferences influence the ways in which business transactions are structured. That is, managers can—and often do—engineer their companies' financial stories through their decisions regarding the structure of business transactions.

This is not sinister. It is, however, a reality. And it casts the annual report financial stories we read in a proactively authored, partially engineered light. The preferences reflected in these financial stories will be specific to the managers who generate them, and to the situations in which they work. Consequently, it's important to read the narrative material preceding the financial statements in an annual report, in order to learn about the company's management team and its perspective on such issues as performance, risk, strategy, new versus established markets, the company's stock price, debt, and competitive position. Such information will begin to give us a feel for the company's financial preferences and tendencies. In the end, we must decide if we're comfortable with what we learn about the company and its managers, because we must acknowledge that the financial story they tell us—and about which they hope we'll be excited—will be to some degree emblematic of their preferences and perspectives.

A Closer Look at the Statement of Cash Flows

If you're comfortable with the financial line items, relationships, and connections we've discussed in Figure 5.1 let's use these to bring the statement of cash flows into sharper focus. Dust off that high school algebra; we're going to use it.

First, let's expand the fundamental $A = L + OE$ relationship by substituting into it the items depicted in Figure 5.1 equation #3 expresses that full-blown diagram.

1. Assets = Liabilities + Owners' Equity

2. Current Assets + Noncurrent Assets = Current Liabilities + Noncurrent Liabilities + Contributed Capital + Retained Earnings

3. Cash + A/R + Inv. + Ppd/A + Vehicles + Buildings + Land + Investments = A/P + W/P + 90-day loans + Bonds Payable + Contributed Capital + Net Income – Dividends

Now let's consider the two equations below. The first of these (#4) simply takes equation #3 and isolates *cash* on the left hand side of the equals sign. To do that, we subtract from both sides of the equation the items we need to delete from the left in order to isolate "cash."

The second equation below (#5) is exactly the same as #4, except that the Greek letter delta (Δ) has been inserted to express the concept of *change*. This is customary notation. Whenever you encounter the symbol Δ, followed by the name of an account, it merely signals the change in that account. ΔCash, for example, refers to the change in cash; ΔA/R, to the change in accounts receivable. (Note net income has been moved to the front of the right-hand side of the equation and does not carry the Δ symbol.)

4. Cash = Net Income – A/R – Inv. – Ppd/A – Vehicles – Buildings – Land – Investments + A/P + W/P + 90-day loans + Bonds Payable + Contributed Capital – Dividends

5. ΔCash = Net Income – ΔA/R – ΔInv. – ΔPpd/A – ΔVehicles – ΔBuildings – ΔLand – ΔInvestments + ΔA/P + ΔW/P + ΔI/P + Δ90-day loans + ΔBonds Payable + ΔContributed Capital – Dividends

Insider's Note

The statement of cash flows depicts the sources and uses of cash for a company by reporting the amount of change that occurred in all the other balance sheet items for that period of time.

The delta (Δ) notation here is important. And its purpose is quite straightforward. Because the statement of cash flows is a report pertaining to a period of time, as opposed to a moment in time, it summarizes events that have *changed* the cash asset balance during that period. Specifically, the statement of cash flows explains the net change in cash that occurred during a period of time by depicting the changes in all balance sheet accounts *except* cash. In essence, this is like the task many of us were presented with in our early school years—defining a new vocabulary word without using that word in the definition. In this context, dividends and net income are also inserted into the equation in lieu of ΔRetained Earnings, since they represent the components of one year's change in retained earnings.

Equation #5 provides the mathematical logic behind our discussion of the statement of cash flows in Chapter 4. It explains, for example, why a net *increase* in accounts receivable during a year is *deducted* from net income in the CFFO section of the cash flows statement. If a company's total accounts receivable increased during a year (positive Δ), then its net income must rest in part upon sales for which it has not yet been paid. Consequently, in calculating cash actually generated by operations, that growth in accounts receivable must be subtracted from the net income figure that begins the statement of cash flows. This appears in equation #5 as $-\Delta$A/R.

Similarly, an increase in wages payable (again, positive Δ) is added to accrual-based net income on the statement of cash flows in calculating cash generated by operations. If wages payable by a company increased during the year, that means there are incremental wage expense amounts built into the net income number for which workers have not yet been paid. Therefore, in converting accrual-based net income to a cash-based figure, the increase in wages payable must be used to add back that part of wage expense not yet paid by the company.

As one final step, let's take equation #5 and display it in a vertical format (see Figure 5.3). In so doing, let's position ΔCash at the bottom of the display, since a typical statement of cash flows will derive—and

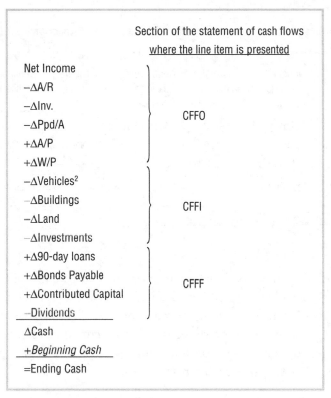

Figure 5.3 A General Statement of Cash Flows Template

conclude with—that yearly change. (Note that this vertical display parallels the actual statement of cash flows for Car Seats, Inc. presented in Chapter 4.)

The Inside Scoop

All financial statement information in a corporate annual report springs from one basic relationship: $A = L + OE$. This simple formula can be expanded as in Figure 5.4.

The accounting process is, essentially, the practice of describing business events in ways that increase or decrease two or more parts of this diagram, while maintaining the equality of the starting equation. Moreover, a

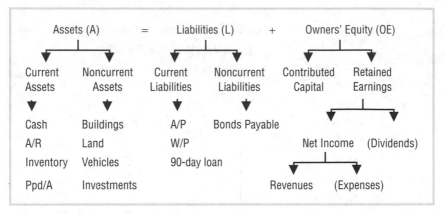

Figure 5.4 Revisting the Components of A = L + OE

statement of cash flows depicts the major changes in its cash balance during a year without presenting all the specific ins and outs found in its checkbook registers. By isolating cash on one side of the expanded version of the accounting equation, we see that the statement of cash flows uses the changes in all balance sheet line items—except cash—to explain the year's change in cash (see equation #5 above).

Practical Applications

In Figure 5.5, you'll find some typical, independent business events and their financial statement effects as of the time they occur. Please review these events, and make sure you understand their impact. This will help you master the Accounting 101 process as well as the evaluation of financial statement effects from specific events. (Note: M = million, K = thousand.)

From this exercise, we can see how this analysis could be used to project the financial statement effects of *proposed* business transactions. Once a transaction is analyzed in a manner similar to this, if the projected financial statement effect is not to management's liking (e.g., decreased CFFO from buying a car with cash) managers could consider alternative ways to structure the deal (e.g., finance the car with a loan). The financial statement effects of most every business transaction can be easily under-

Event	Balance Sheet				Income Statement	Statement of Cash Flows		
	Total Current Assets	Total Assets	Total Current Liability	Total Liability	Net Income	CFFO	CFFI	CFFF
1. Took out a 60-day, $1M loan	+1M	+1M	+1M	+1M	—	—	—	+1M
2. Incurred and paid $8K in interest	−8K	−8K	—	—	−8K	−8K	—	—
3. Bought car with $9K cash	−9K	—*	—	—	—	—	−9K	—
4. Paid $1K in wages	−1K	−1K	—	—	−1K	−1K	—	—
5. Bought $3K of goods on credit	+3K	+3K	+3K	+3K	—	−3K	—	—
6. Owe $60K of income taxes	—	—	+60K	+60K	−60K	—**	—	—
7. Paid $10K dividend	−10K	−10K	—	—	—	—	—	−10K
8. Record $1K electric bill to be paid next month	—	—	+1K	+1K	−1K	—**	—	—

* The net effect on total assets is zero because a current asset (cash) decreases by the same amount a noncurrent asset (vehicles) goes up.

** The net effect on CFFO is zero because net income goes down due to the expense effect on net income but the CFFO adjustment for an increase in a current liability offsets that decrease.

Figure 5.5 The Financial Statement Effects of Eight Business Events

stood using the Accounting 101 mindset and approach presented in this chapter.

In Anticipation of the Next Secret

Financial reporting is like a hospital gown . . . it reveals what's mostly behind.

Secret #6

It's Old News

Is it relevant, reliable, neither, or both?

The questions behind Secret #6:

- Why is the historical cost of an item such a key focus in financial statements?
- What information is lost when historical costs are embraced?
- Once presented in financial statements, are historical costs left untouched forever?
- Are all assets reported on an identical basis? If not, what are the differences in their treatment?

It is time to explore the undergirding conventions that ultimately shape the contents of corporate financial statements and consequently, their interpretation. As we embark on this path in the remainder of this book, please be mindful of an overarching truth—financial reporting is as much (maybe even more) art and nuance as it is science and precision.

Teeing Up the Tension between Relevance and Reliability[1]

If you could go on an all-expenses-paid vacation to Hawaii or the Greek islands, which would you choose? If you loved to sing *and* dance, but could excel at only one, which would you prefer? If you could receive highly relevant or highly reliable corporate financial information, but not both, which would you value more?

We seldom relish such "either/or" decisions. In fact, we often try to dodge them. "Why can't I learn to sing *and* dance?" you might ask. Theoretically, you could. (Personally, of course, I can't. But that's another story.) Similarly, in the realm of annual reports, we'd like information that's both reliable *and* relevant. But those two qualities rarely coexist in a single financial measure. Today, annual reports presume to favor reliability.

Historical Cost: Reliable, but Is It Relevant?

Any item represented on a balance sheet—any asset, liability, or component of owners' equity—can be shown to possess a number of attributes. A warehouse, for example, has a clearly defined age and storage capacity. It's equipped with specific measures for security and climate control. Likewise, from the perspective of the company that owns it, one attribute of the warehouse is its historic purchase price. Another is its current market value. Of these two—historical cost and current value—which can be measured more reliably?

For purposes of this discussion, let's define a reliably measurable monetary amount as one on which many—if not all—observers would agree. On this basis, it's clear that the historic purchase price of the warehouse is a highly reliable figure. Any observer could establish it by a review of actual transaction records. These would leave little room for speculation or debate, regardless of whether the company paid for the warehouse by cash, check, stock, the origination or assumption of a loan, or some combination of these.

In assessing the financial health and prospects of the company that owns the warehouse, however, is its historic purchase price a *relevant* figure? Many financial readers would say no—particularly if it was purchased years ago. These people would prefer to know the facility's current market value. But this introduces challenges of its own. If you asked three observers to establish the current market value of the warehouse, each might ask the opinion of his or her own favorite real estate appraiser. All might compare the warehouse to different facilities, recently sold elsewhere in town. All might imagine different uses for the site, if transferred to a new owner. These differing sources, assumptions, and analyses would yield different estimates of the property's current value.

Thus, the more reliable figure, historical cost, is not the most relevant. The more relevant figure, current market value, is not the most reliable. This gives rise to one of the key tensions in financial reporting: Should annual reports present reliable measurements with questionable contemporary relevance? Or should they present the most relevant measures, despite their uncertain reliability?

Stew, Anyone?

Over the years, we've all enjoyed at least one batch of really good homemade stew. "Stew" seems to be a catchall term for various combinations of leftovers, prepared at different times and with different ingredients and seasonings, all left to simmer on the stove for some extended, indefinite time. This variety is precisely what gives stew its appeal. At times, however, it also gives rise to the question: "What's in this?"

While variety may be quite welcome in stew, it's less so in the depiction of balance sheet amounts—particularly for assets. On a typical corporate balance sheet, the figures reported for assets often represent a variety of monetary measurements. "But wait," you may ask, "didn't we just say all assets are reported at historical cost?" In fact, we did. But historical cost is just the starting point for the presentation of assets[2] in corporate balance sheets. To that historical-cost basis, companies make a number of adjustments over time—different adjustments for different assets—which dilute the reliability of that reported measurement. Let's explore five such scenarios.

Land and Goodwill: Stuck in the Asset Museum

Most companies own land, on which they build plants, warehouses, distribution centers, office buildings, parking lots, laboratories, and other facilities. At a young company, or a long-standing one that's relocated, this land may have been purchased quite recently. In a stable real estate market, its current market value may be close to the price at which it was acquired.

By contrast, at an older company, occupying a site purchased years ago, the price paid for land may bear no resemblance at all to its current market value. Think of the land underneath Macy's in Manhattan, or Sears in Chicago. These parcels of real estate were purchased for a fraction of the prices they would fetch in today's market. Yet on the balance sheets of these companies, land is reported at historical costs that may be several decades old. From the date that it's purchased and recorded on a firm's balance sheet, land remains on the books at its original purchase price. Adjustments are made to reflect *improvements*, such as landscaping, or *impairments*, such as designation as a toxic site. Under normal circumstances, however, the financial record of the land remains unchanged—regardless of changes in the market, which can be substantial. It's as if land costs are displayed in an asset museum, behind a sign reading: "Don't touch."

The same is generally true for the balance sheet asset termed *goodwill*. A corporation reports goodwill on its balance sheet when it purchases another company at a price greater than the appraised value of the acquired company's net assets—that is, its total assets less total liabilities. The acquirer may pay such an amount if it believes the target company possesses attributes—or offers synergies—that make it more valuable than the mere collection of net assets conveyed. Such attributes might include talented employees, a history of innovative product development, a reputation for service excellence, or an outstanding distribution network.

Some corporate balance sheets include very substantial figures for goodwill, resulting from just one or two major acquisitions. When Hewlett-Packard acquired Compaq for $24 billion, for example, approximately 60% of that purchase price was classified as goodwill. When AT&T acquired Bell South for $67 billion, more than 80% of that total was deemed goodwill. Alternatively, a balance sheet may show a large figure for goodwill, traceable to no single acquisition, but rather to a long string of more modest corporate acquisitions. United Technologies and Microsoft, for example, have a history of such acquisitions.

As with land, once a company records goodwill on its balance sheet, it leaves this line item alone, unless: (1) it buys more companies, generating more goodwill, or (2) the goodwill asset is impaired. Goodwill might be impaired by a number of factors. The acquired company might suffer an exodus of talent. Products anticipated from its innovation pipeline may fail to materialize. Its reputation may be tarnished through a subsequent lawsuit. Any number of possible events could depress the upside that the acquirer expected to derive from its acquisition of another company. AOL Time Warner provides a vivid example of goodwill impairment. When American Online acquired Time Warner, it classified a substantial amount of its $147 billion purchase price as goodwill. Among other things, management expected to derive valuable synergies through the combination of American Online's operations and resources with Time Warner's. Unfortunately, not everything went as planned. Shortly after the merger, the consolidated balance sheet took a *$54 billion* write-down of its goodwill asset.

Thus, companies record land and goodwill on their books as of the date they purchase them, and then leave them untouched for years, assuming no impairment in value below their original cost. If there is a perceived, significant impairment of their worth and future utility to the company, then a write-down is required. The process of quantifying this decrement is so full of judgments and estimates that the reliable historical cost amount initially reported for those assets is abandoned. I'm sure that corporate write-downs for goodwill or land impairments are the result of a rigorous estimation methodology. And I'm also sure that process includes a number of carefully researched, highly defensible assumptions. But by their very nature, those assumptions could have been different and also defensible. Without a doubt, those alternative assumptions would yield a different write-down amount than what was actually recorded.

Insider's Note

Land and goodwill assets are reported at their historical cost and left at that figure for years and years unless there has been an event diminishing their value, at which time, they would be reduced.

Let's be clear. It's not fraudulant, sneaky, or misleading to take a write-down on the historical cost of an asset when its usefulness and value

Land and goodwill are recorded at cost. Neither asset is depreciated. Goodwill represents the excess of acquisition cost over the fair value of the net assets purchased in a corporate acquisition. The company continually evaluates whether circumstances indicate the balance sheet amount for land, goodwill, and other long-lived assets may be impaired. These evaluations are based on the assets' discounted projected future cash flows and require significant management judgment. If impaired, an asset's balance sheet amount is reduced and income statement earnings are reduced.

Figure 6.1 Land and Goodwill Prototype Disclosure

have dropped below the level of its original purchase price. In fact, this is a prudent and conservative thing to do. Indeed, financial reporting should generally err toward prudence and conservatism. But there is a lack of symmetry here. Companies don't make postpurchase disclosures or adjustments related to their land or goodwill accounts when these assets appreciate in value; only when they diminish. Moreover, once a company does report such a reduction on its balance sheet, the resultant amount is no longer a reliable, historical cost. The reduction made for impairment is, in essence, an educated guess. Exemplifying the foregoing discussion, an annual report's *Significant Accounting Policies* footnote will often present such information as is shown in Figure 6.1.[3]

Buildings, Equipment, and Vehicles: Driving to Zero

By contrast with land and goodwill, companies bring *depreciable assets* onto their balance sheets at historical costs as of the date of purchase, and then systematically reduce these figures over a preferred period of time, using a methodical but largely arbitrary system, without regard to real market changes in value. These depreciable assets—which include buildings, vehicles, machinery, computers, and the like—are assumed to be "used up" as a company employs them in its business. Now, we all know that as you occupy a building or drive a truck, there is not a literal, physical using up of that asset. Walls don't evaporate. Trucks don't shrink. There is,

Buildings, equipment, and vehicles are reported at cost, less depreciation recorded to date. Depreciation is computed using the straight-line method over estimated useful lives of 12 to 40 years for buildings, 4 to 10 years for equipment, and 3 to 5 years for vehicles. These assets are reviewed annually for possible impairment to their balance sheet amount.

Figure 6.2 Buildings, Equipment, and Vehicles Prototype Disclosure

however, a valid assumption made that the usefulness of the asset diminishes over time. In essence, such assets have a finite utility. As a result, they are, in financial reporting terms, depreciated over an estimated life. To this end, a company's financial statement footnotes will disclose information like what is shown in Figure 6.2.

A popular approach to depreciation, and the one noted in the footnote prototype in Figure 6.2, is to assume that an asset's economic utility will be "used up" in equal annual amounts over its financial life. That is, its recorded cost will diminish evenly over time. As an example, assume that a $12 million headquarters building is presumed to have a lifespan of 30 years. Using the so-called straight-line method of depreciation, the company that owns this asset would book a $400,000 reduction in the asset's recorded balance sheet cost each year ($12 million ÷ 30 years) to reflect the "using up" of its utility. The company would also record a depreciation expense of $400,000 on its income statement in each of these 30 years. A similar approach is used for equipment, vehicles, and other assets from which a company expects to derive benefits over a finite number of years.

Companies must present numerical data in their annual reports, depicting the amount of depreciation taken on their assets to date, enabling readers to make a rough determination of their assets' overall age. Let's explore two examples, either of which might appear in an annual report's financial statement footnotes. One example pertains to a company we will call Old Company, Inc. while the other pertains to New Company, Inc. (see Figure 6.3). Both companies use the *straight-line method of depreciation*.

Assume Old Company and New Company paid $8,110 for their buildings, equipment, and vehicles. The change in this figure from last

	Old Company, Inc.		New Company, Inc.	
	This Year	Last Year	This Year	Last Year
Buildings	$ 6,333	$ 5,444	$ 6,333	$ 5,444
Equipment	1,222	1,111	1,222	1,111
Vehicles	555	400	555	400
	8,110	6,955	8,110	6,955
Accumulated depreciation	(6,800)	(6,100)	(2,300)	(1,800)
	$ 1,310	$ 855	$ 5,810	$ 5,155

Figure 6.3 Old Company versus New Company

year to this year—from $6,955 to $8,110—indicates the net effect of buildings, equipment, and vehicles purchased, less the historical cost of those sold this year. Under *accumulated depreciation*, both companies report the total depreciation they've taken to date on their comparable year-end portfolio of buildings, equipment, and vehicles. Note that Old Company shows greater accumulated depreciation than New Company. This suggests that Old Company assets are, on average, at a later stage of their estimated usefulness than New Company's.

Perhaps more than any other asset on a company's balance sheet, buildings are reported in a manner that conflicts with the average person's view of such assets. You and I view our homes as appreciating—not depreciating—assets, despite the fact that we use them on a daily basis. We expect their values to rise. In fact, we receive unwanted mail solicitations from lenders, inviting us to take advantage of that increase by taking out home equity loans.

Companies, however, do not portray their office buildings, warehouses, and factories as appreciating assets in their annual reports. Rather, they depreciate these structures in their financial statements, even if the market for such assets is appreciating. In fact, a company may run a factory, occupy a building, and even operate a delivery truck long after these assets are fully

Insider's Note

Assets such as buildings, equipment, and vehicles are initially reported at their historical cost but every year that monetary amount is reduced by recording a depreciation expense to reflect their use.

depreciated in its annual report. In such an instance, those assets would appear on the firm's balance sheet, if they're fully depreciated, at zero. Yet the company still uses them, and might well be able to sell them for more than their original historical cost.

Inventory and Accounts Receivable: IBM, LCM, and WHAM!

A third asset, inventory, represents the goods that a company holds pending sale to customers. These goods are initially recorded at the historical cost that the company incurs to purchase or manufacture them. At the end of each year, however, the company must subject any goods remaining in inventory to a test, in which it adjusts its balance sheet to reflect these goods at the *lower of cost or market (LCM)*. In the course of this test, the company determines the current market price at which it could replace each of the items in its inventory. If that price is lower than the historical cost incurred for them, the company reduces the asset amount recorded on its balance sheet accordingly. Figure 6.4 shows what a typical annual report inventory footnote might disclose in this regard.

So, if a retailer carries a vast inventory of a recently retired and disgraced professional athlete's dolls, and their popularity with customers has come and gone, the company's LCM test may signal the need to write them down. If so, it must reduce the balance-sheet inventory asset figure pertaining to those dolls and report a corresponding amount as an inventory market adjustment expense on its income statement.

Similarly, if IBM, or any of its competitors, held a number of computers in inventory with Pentium X technology. When Pentium X + 1s come out, the older models will lose a great deal of their marketability. Under the LCM test, IBM would probably need to reduce the inventory asset amount it reports for them and—Wham!—the company will take a reduction to its

> Inventories, net of reductions for any obsolete items, are stated at the lower of cost or market.

Figure 6.4 Inventory Prototype Disclosure

income statement earnings figure for getting caught with outdated product inventory.

Thus, inventory, generally one of the largest asset categories on a retailer's or manufacturer's balance sheet, is initially recorded at a reliable, historical cost figure. This figure may subsequently be reduced—but never increased—due to changes in the price these goods command in the market. Naturally, firms try to avoid holding inventory that's exposed to such market impacts. Toward that end, they strive to carry minimal amounts of inventory, or to buy or produce goods only when they have reliable customer demand for particular items. This issue is especially important in industries that produce fashion goods, or goods that rely on rapidly changing technologies, and in industries that must endure long product development cycles, during which alternatives may arise, undermining the need for the goods under development.

Like inventory, *accounts receivable* are also initially reported at historical cost and may subsequently be reduced. As you'll recall, accounts receivable represent the monetary amounts that customers promise to pay a company for the goods or services sold to them on credit. Frequently, a company grants customers 30 days to pay for such goods. If customers fail to pay in that time, the company may remind them of their obligation. If they still don't pay, and their accounts remain even longer on the books as unfulfilled promises to be paid, the selling company may have to adjust the accounts receivable asset figure downward, reflecting managers' growing pessimism that they'll be paid. This is cautious and conservative—and often realistic.

Insider's Note

A company's inventory and accounts receivable assets are reported at historical cost but adjusted yearly to reflect any estimated loss of marketability (for the inventory) or collectability (for the receivables).

As receivables "age," customers' ability and/or willingness to pay them can change, casting their promises to pay into doubt. When such doubts arise, and certainly as they mount, the company to which the money is promised must reduce its accounts receivable asset in order to reflect the amount believed actually to be collectible. The company must simultaneously create a corresponding expense account on its income statement. (Note that accounts receivable, like inventories, are never adjusted up— only down.) With this in mind, annual reports often contain a financial statement footnote paralleling what appears in Figure 6.5.

The Company offers credit terms to customers that meet our credit criteria. Accounts receivable are initially recorded at the sales price customers are billed. This amount is reduced by an estimate of the amount of probable uncollectible accounts receivable based on such factors as the age of specific customer accounts receivable, historical trends, customer disputes, and economic conditions.

Figure 6.5 Accounts Receivable Prototype Disclosure

Partially Owned Affiliates: "As If" Asset Changes

As another example of the stewlike amalgamation of historical–cost based asset amounts on balance sheets, let's consider the asset representing a sizable but not controlling investment in another company's stock. By way of example, if Ford Motor Company buys 25% of the outstanding stock of Car Seats Inc., it will initially record that investment at the price it pays in the open market—that is, at historical cost. In subsequent years, however, it will increase this asset figure on its balance sheet by the amount of its proportionate share of Car Seats' annual income. It will similarly decrease the figure if Car Seats, Inc. generates a loss.

This is known as the *equity method* of accounting for investments. Companies must use this method when they acquire between 20% and 50% of the shares of another firm. The logic behind these percentages is straightforward: at these levels of ownership, the investing company is presumed to exert significant influence, but not control, over the decisions of the company in which it has taken such an ownership position.

In the financial reporting for partially owned affiliates, a company may *increase* as well as decrease the recorded cost of its assets. The amount by which it makes this adjustment, however, is simply an arithmetic figure. It's a percentage of the investee company's net income. There is an intriguing logic to this departure

> ### Insider's Note
>
> *When companies buy 20–50% of the stock of another company, that investment is initially reported at its historical cost. In each subsequent year, that investment is increased (decreased) by the investor's proportionate share of the investee's net income (dividends).*

Investments in other companies where the company has a 20% to 50% voting interest, and where the company exercises significant influence over the investee, are accounted for using the equity method. The company's ownership share of earnings or losses in those investees is included in our income statement operating results and the balance sheet investment account is increased or decreased, accordingly.

Figure 6.6 "Significant Influence" Ownership Investment Prototype Disclosure

from historical cost: Because, at a 20% to 50% ownership level, the investing company is deemed to hold significant influence over the company in which it has invested, it's presumed that this influence must contribute to the latter company's financial performance. Therefore, in our example, 25% of Car Seats' net income is ascribable to Ford's involvement, and Ford's investment-related accounts should reflect that. In this regard, annual reports often carry financial statement footnotes that communicate something like what appears in Figure 6.6.

Following this policy, when Car Seats, Inc. generates positive net income, Ford would increase the balance sheet account of its investment in Car Seats, Inc., while posting an equivalent increase to an income statement account titled "earnings from affiliates," or words to that effect. Please note: This earnings amount represents no transfer of cash. It is not tied to any share-price appreciation. It is simply an arithmetic calculation—a pro rata share of another company's accrual-based net income figure.

Passive Investments in Stocks: Some Real Market Values

Finally, we encounter one asset category in which a company's historical costs are adjusted on the balance sheet each year to show its current market values. These assets are the firm's passive investments in the stock of other companies. For financial reporting purposes, a "passive" investment is defined as a holding of less than 20% of the investee's publicly held shares. A holding of this size is assumed to be insufficient to give the investor company significant influence over the company in which it has acquired a stake. Con-

Passive investments in other companies' equity securities
are reported by the company at fair value. Fair value is based
on quoted market prices.

Figure 6.7 "Passive" Ownership Investment Prototype Disclosure

sequently, the equity method of accounting does not apply. Rather, to reflect the changing worth of its investment at year end, the investor company "marks it to market." That is, the investor company determines the current market value of the shares it owns. It then adjusts its balance sheet investment asset account accordingly. With regard to the balance sheet's reported amount for such investments, a corporate annual report's financial statement footnotes will frequently declare something similar to what is shown in Figure 6.7.

In line with this policy, if a passive investment appreciates, the company holding it shows an increase in the appropriate asset account, reflecting the increase in its value since the company's last balance sheet date. A corresponding gain is also recorded on its income statement.[4] Likewise, if the share value of the passive investment declines, the company books a decrease in the asset on its balance sheet and records a corresponding loss on its income statement. This holding gain or loss represents one of the few instances in which an annual report actually reports the monetary value associated with something *not done*. That is, a holding gain or loss is the measured amount associated with management's decision *not* to sell an investment. Generally, recorded gains and losses must be consummated by a marketplace sales transaction. In this instance, however, an actual sale of the shares need not take place for a gain or loss to be reported.

So, passive investments are carried on the balance sheet at current market values when other assets are not. What is it about this asset—or its market value— that leads to this policy? The answer is quite simple: If three of us are asked to determine the current market value of

Insider's Note

Passive investments in another company's stock (i.e., less than 20%), are reported by the investor company at the market value of the shares held.

1,000 shares of Microsoft stock, we'll all report the same figure. We can all turn to *The Wall Street Journal*, or an Internet quote service or similar source, and obtain an objective, market-determined value. Thus, by contrast with other assets, the current value of a passive investment can be determined in both a relevant *and* reliable manner. That ability drives the financial reporting pertaining to this asset to the use of market values.[5]

Should We Quit Making Stew?

In financial statements, is it better to provide reliable, somewhat irrelevant measurements? Or do readers prefer more relevant, less reliably measured amounts? Personally, I wish the financial reporting practices pendulum would swing a bit toward the latter position. In my view, contemporary balance sheets are not as reliable as their historical cost basis would lead us to believe. This is a result of the many different, judgmentally determined ways in which historical costs are adjusted. I've heard many arguments against reporting market values—mainly because they're too subject to management manipulation. But similar objections are also applicable to many of the adjusted historical cost amounts currently reported.

Moreover, some would also argue that we should use just one means of asset valuation—or, at least, *fewer* methods than we currently employ. By way of analogy, note that maps do not report the distance from New York to Chicago in miles, Chicago to Dallas in furlongs, and Dallas to New York in football-field equivalents. If they did, travelers would be hard-pressed to determine the total length of such a journey, or which of its legs would be longest. In the United States, the traveling public has agreed to use one measure—miles—to make all such distances comparable and additive.[6]

Similarly, I believe there is *one* means of valuing long-lived assets that would be most relevant for corporate balance sheets. This is what appraisers call an asset's *value in use*—that is, its appraised value "as is and where is."[7] The reasons for this are: In assessing a company's financial health and prospects, the current market values of its assets are more relevant than historical costs. Furthermore, professional appraisers can determine these values. Indeed, this has been done for some balance sheet assets, such as buildings, in other countries in times past. Perhaps corporations will do this one day, making long-lived asset values more relevant, comparable, and additive. For now, it's stew.

The Inside Scoop

In measuring the monetary amount to report for corporate assets, their historical cost is viewed as a reliable figure. It is objectively and uniformly determinable. It is not, however, a particularly relevant figure, in terms of being current and indicative of value. Nonetheless, the U.S. financial reporting model has a long tradition rooted in the use of historical costs. That is also true for many, if not most, other countries around the world.

Even though historical cost begins as a reliable measure the day an asset is purchased, that measurement basis becomes less reliable over time through a variety of different adjustments for different assets:

- The market value of land and buildings, for example, generally appreciates over time. But land is left on the balance sheet at its original purchase price, while buildings are actually depreciated over time on corporate balance sheets.
- Inventories and accounts receivable are initially recorded at their historical costs, but then subjectively reduced (never increased) to reflect management's judgments regarding any projected financial decrement to those assets.
- Investments in other companies—of such a size to give the investor significant influence over the company whose stock it holds—are reported and adjusted on the balance sheet on an "as if" basis. That is, the investment asset and the income statement earnings of the investor company are increased by its proportionate share of the earnings of the investee company, as if the investor had generated those earnings itself. To qualify for such treatment, an investment must represent 20% to 50% of the publicly held shares of the investee.
- On the other hand, passive investments in other companies are maintained on the balance sheet of the investor company in a manner that departs from historical cost, reflecting changes (up or down) in market values at every successive balance sheet date. Only this asset category and its mode of financial reporting can be viewed as objectively providing both reliable and relevant figures. Passive investments represent less than 20% of the publicly held shares of the investee.

Ask yourself if you prefer contemporary or historical data. Do you believe you'd have a better sense of my financial standing, for example, if I told you what I paid for my house 15 years ago, or if I shared a current appraisal of my home? If you answered the latter, you have an explicit preference for current market value information in addition to, or in lieu of, historical cost information. For now, however, companies for the most part are required to report various forms of historical cost data in their financial statements. And all significant departures from historical cost must be disclosed in the financial statement footnotes. It's important to recognize that, and to understand the ways in which these adjusted data are derived and do or do not reflect current market values.

Practical Application

Figure 6.8 is the asset section of a hypothetical, but typical, corporate balance sheet. We now know that the dollar amounts reported for the assets listed comprise a financial stew. That is, each asset is initially recorded by the company at its historical cost. In subsequent years, however, many of their reported monetary amounts depart from this foundation. In the listing below, take a moment to identify the assets that may be associated with departures from historical cost. Which ones depart? What is the essence of each departure? Where would a company typically present and discuss the details associated with that departure?

Let's answer the last question first. Firms generally summarize their accounting policies in the first or second footnote to the financial statements in their annual reports. In that footnote, they disclose the basis on which they measure their major asset categories. Therein lies the recipe for their financial stew.

Moving on to an identification of the assets that potentially—and quite frequently—depart from their roots in historical costs, the line items you should have flagged are: (1) receivables, (2) inventories, (3) property, plant, and equipment, (4) goodwill, (5) equity in net assets of nonconsolidated affiliates, and (6) marketable equity securities. Please note that cash does not appear on this list. Also, we did not flag the asset labeled "other." Balance sheets often contain such a line item. When its monetary amount is relatively small, companies generally do not provide details as to what appears in this catchall asset basket. Thus, we have no way of knowing

Assets	This year	Last year
Current assets		
Cash and equivalents	$ 27,700	$ 23,800
Receivables (net)	273,900	279,800
Inventories	260,500	250,600
Other current assets	6,200	2,800
Total current assets	568,300	557,000
Property, plant and equipment (net)	210,500	212,700
Goodwill	32,000	43,400
Equity in net assets of nonconsolidated affiliates	56,000	60,100
Marketable equity securities	79,300	68,100
Total assets	$ 946,100	$ 941,300

Figure 6.8 The Weird Hats Corporation Consolidated Balance Sheet (Assets Only) as of December 31

what its measured financial attributes are, although our default assumption is historical cost.

The likely departures from historical cost for each of the six items flagged are:

- Receivables: This asset is reported at historical cost, less the monetary amount of management's estimate of total customer promises to pay which are not likely to be fulfilled. This new, reduced figure may be described as the estimated "net realizable value" for accounts receivable.
- Inventories: This asset is reported at a "lower of cost or market" figure, in which a market value below cost indicates that the asset items in this category have been deemed obsolete, damaged, or otherwise saleable only at a price below the company's original cost to make or buy them.
- Property, plant, and equipment: This asset is reported at a monetary amount equivalent to the items' historical cost less accumulated depreciation. It is important to note that accumulated depreciation is a function, among other things, of the estimated

useful life established for those items which are depreciated. Land, by contrast, is not depreciated. It is reported at its historical cost indefinitely. All items in this bundle, including land, are subjected to an annual impairment review to ensure that their value to the company—in the roles they were intended to serve—has not diminished below the monetary figures at which they're carried on the balance sheet. If an asset has experienced such impairment, its reported amount is reduced accordingly.

- Goodwill: The financial reporting for this asset is similar to that for land. It is initially recorded at historical cost, and then left alone unless it's judged to be impaired by subsequent business, competitive, and/or economic conditions that cause its worth to the company to decline below this level.

- Equity in net assets of nonconsolidated affiliates: Corporations account for this asset by the "equity method." That is, they record the initial investment (representing 20% to 50% of the publicly traded shares of the investee) at historical cost. They then increase (decrease) this figure each year by an amount equivalent to the investor company's proportionate share of the investee company's net income (loss). The carrying amount of this asset may also be decreased by the investor company's proportionate share of any dividends paid by the investee.

- Marketable equity securities: This asset pertains to passive investments in other companies, in which the level of investment does not reach the 20% threshold that triggers the equity method of accounting. This is, in essence, the only asset on a corporate balance sheet that is adjusted each year, up or down, to its market value. That value figure is frequently derived from year-end prices quoted on the appropriate stock exchange.

Note two key insights that may be derived from this discussion: (1) even within a single balance sheet, assets are measured in many different ways, and (2) to the extent that reported asset amounts depart from historical costs, those departures entail a good deal of judgment, calling into question the oft-cited reliability of historical costs as the preferred balance sheet measure. Authorities have long cited the reliability of historical costs as the principal reason for embracing that means of asset measurement in financial statements, despite the greater relevance of market values in assessing the financial condition of a company. Unfortunately, to the extent that historical costs are adjusted as described above, readers of financial statements end up with asset measures that are less reliable than they're presumed to be, and perhaps less relevant than they could be.

In Anticipation of the Next Secret

Boxers or briefs? It's a choice every day.

Secret #7

It's Full of Choices

What's your pleasure?

The questions behind Secret #7:

- Do generally accepted accounting principles permit different methods for reporting a financial statement item?
- If so, what are some of the more significant choices permitted?
- How can readers of an annual report know which choices were made?
- Do these choices really matter? Don't they all result in basically the same financial picture?

Going out tonight, would you prefer to wear black tie, shabby chic, Brooks Brothers, or business casual? It's up to you. It's a matter of taste. But your choice may have consequences. In making it, you may want to consider what you plan to do this evening and the impression you hope to make.

Likewise, and for example, when companies report inventories and facilities assets on their balance sheets—or cost of goods sold and depreciation expense on their income statements—they face choices between higher and lower dollar amounts. These choices are distinct from, and incremental to, the lower of cost or market and impairment adjustments discussed with regard to inventories and facilities in the prior chapter.

Inventory: Physical Flows versus Cost Flows

Envision the inventory on the shelves of a Wal-Mart store. There must be thousands of different items, and sizable quantities of each. Now, think of all the Wal-Mart stores around the world, which also carry the same array of items. The total dollar figure for inventory on Wal-Mart's corporate balance sheet is a huge number. In fact, inventory represents a sizable asset for most retail and manufacturing companies. As discussed previously, this asset is reported on balance sheets at its historical cost, subject to subsequent *lower of cost or market* (LCM) adjustments. There is, however, an additional financial reporting dimension to the balance sheet inventory asset.

One may imagine that a company tracks every item it buys or makes in order to know which one it just sold. Companies do maintain such records for quality assurance and safety. For financial statement purposes, however, it does not matter to a retailer like Wal-Mart whether the jeans I just bought from its Denver store were purchased by the company from a supplier yesterday or last week. Even if it paid slightly different prices on those dates, the retailer still doesn't care. And yet, at year end, companies must assign a monetary figure to their inventory on hand. They must also quantify the historical cost of all the inventory sold during the year, in order to report an expense figure for cost of goods sold on their income statements. To do this, companies may use any of at least four different financial reporting methods for inventory: Specific Identification, FIFO, LIFO, and Average. Let's explore each of these, focusing on their differential impact on balance sheets and income statements. Toward that end, a simple example may help.

> ## Insider's Note
>
> *The financial measurement of inventories sold and still on hand at year end can be done using any one, or a combination, of four different methods: specific identification, LIFO, FIFO, and average.*

As I write this, the sun is rising over the hills of western North Carolina, where my wife and I are staying at a lovely bed and breakfast with two other couples. I can smell the aroma of bacon, eggs, coffee, and sweet rolls, wafting up the stairs to our room. Sue, our host, rose before dawn to make her famous omelets. For a gastronome, Sue's omelets are an indefinable and

	Purchased two weeks ago for:	Purchased last week for:	Purchased yesterday for:
1 carton of eggs	$3.00		
1 carton of eggs		$3.30	
1 carton of eggs			$4.00

—2½ dozen eggs were used in the breakfast—

Figure 7.1 Breakfast Example: Purchases

transcendent experience. From an accountant's perspective, however, they involve a simple conversion of inventory—eggs—into goods sold.

Taking the accountant's point of view, let's assume that at dawn, Sue had three full cartons of eggs in her refrigerator, purchased on different days at different stores for different prices. While preparing breakfast, Sue *could* keep track of which eggs went into each omelet. She could then join us at the table and point out that I got the cheapest omelet, while Harry, another guest, received a costlier one. As you might expect, this is not Sue's way. But what if she had a son-in-law who wanted to bring financial precision to her B&B? He might watch her at the stove with his green eyeshade and clipboard, and if Sue didn't chase him out of the kitchen fast enough, he might have noted some information about breakfast as shown in Figure 7.1.

But this still begs the question: under GAAP, what was the total cost of eggs consumed in Sue's breakfast? And that begs another: What do you want it to be?

Specific Identification = Name It and Claim It

First, please remember that the preparation of this breakfast involved a physical flow of components. Sue pulled specific eggs from their cartons while leaving others behind. If Sue's son-in-law had noted which eggs were drawn from which cartons, he could have identified the specific costs of those eggs. For example, if Sue had used the entire carton purchased two weeks ago, half the carton from last week, and the entire carton bought yesterday, her son-in-law could have calculated the cost of those eggs used as $3 + (\frac{1}{2} \times \$3.30) + \$4 = \$8.65$. He might then have recorded $8.65 as that day's cost-of-eggs-used expense on her B&B income statement. Likewise, accounting for the half carton of eggs still in Sue's refrigerator, he would have recorded ½ × $3.30, or $1.65, as that day's ending inventory balance for eggs on her balance sheet.

Obviously, neither Sue nor her son-in-law actually does this. Sue and her husband, Sam, buy hundreds of cartons of eggs each year at various prices. They don't track the cost of each egg. After all, an egg is an egg, and as each one isn't tagged with a price at the grocery store, it quickly becomes impossible to tabulate its specific cost in any breakfast, or to determine which eggs, purchased at which price, remain in the refrigerator at midnight, December 31, when Sue and Sam prepare their yearly B&B financial statements. If Sue and Sam were in the business of crafting fine jewelry or custom homes, they would likely use the specific identification method in accounting for their inventory. But when a company makes thousands of inventory transactions each year, involving similar, relatively low-cost items, the specific identification method quickly becomes too burdensome to employ. Companies use simpler methods to determine their year-end balance sheet inventory and income-statement cost of goods sold expense amounts.

> **Insider's Note**
>
> *The specific identification method for inventory items is most applicable to unique, high-value items that are easily distinguishable and tracked.*

FIFO = LISH

One such simpler method is first-in, first-out, abbreviated as FIFO. In order to report inventory and cost of goods sold during a year under the FIFO method, the B&B in our example would need to track just a few data points: the quantity and prices paid for the eggs (1) on hand at the beginning of the year, (2) purchased during the year, and (3) on hand at the end of the year. It would not be necessary to identify and track specific eggs used each morning. At year end, the B&B would simply assign costs to the eggs used according to a chronological FIFO cost flow. In our breakfast example, the pertinent information would be shown in Figure 7.2.

Thus, under FIFO, the cost-of-eggs-used expense is $8.30. On the balance sheet, the ending inventory of a half carton of eggs is assigned a $2 cost from the latest purchase (½ carton × $4.00). Under FIFO, the expense figure of $8.30 and the inventory asset figure of $2.00 would be appropriate

	Quantity	$
Beginning of year supply of eggs	-0-	-0-
Eggs purchased two weeks ago	1 carton	$3.00 ....
Eggs purchased last week	1 carton	3.30 ......
Eggs purchased yesterday	1 carton	4.00 × ½
Total cost of eggs available for use	3 cartons	10.30
Less: Total FIFO cost of eggs used	(2½ cartons)	(8.30) ....
Ending inventory of eggs	½ carton	$2.00

Figure 7.2 Breakfast Example: FIFO

regardless of which eggs were actually used or on hand in our example. Thus, under FIFO, the eggs purchased earliest are *assumed* to be the ones used first, and the eggs purchased most recently are *assumed* to be the ones still on hand at the end of the period (last in, still here—LISH).

LIFO = FISH

LIFO stands for last in, first out. Like FIFO, this accounting method is based on a chronological flow of historical costs assigned to inventory, independent of the actual physical flow of those goods. By contrast with FIFO, however, LIFO reverses the direction of the flow. Thus, under LIFO, the cost of the 2½ cartons of eggs used in our breakfast example would be calculated as follows: one carton purchased yesterday ($4) + one carton purchased last week ($3.30) + one-half carton purchased two weeks ago (½ × $3, or $1.50), for a total of $8.80. The cost of a half carton of eggs on hand at the end of breakfast—that is, the egg inventory remaining on the B&B's balance sheet—would be deemed to be ½ × $3, or $1.50.

In referring to this method as LIFO, a company explicitly focuses on its use in deriving the income statement's cost of goods sold expense amount by assigning the latest costs incurred to the inventory items sold. The complement of this term is FISH—first in, still here—which focuses on the costs assigned to the inventory asset on the balance sheet.

In our breakfast example, we've applied both the LIFO and FIFO methods as if our B&B's purchases of eggs had been chronologically stacked during

Insider's Note

LIFO and FIFO are opposite inventory cost flow assumptions. FIFO (LIFO) assigns the oldest (most recent) inventory costs to the items sold in deriving the income statement cost of goods sold expense amount.

the year, with the latest purchase on top and the oldest one at the bottom. In determining the cost of eggs used in making breakfast, FIFO worked upward from the bottom of the pile, while LIFO worked downward from the top (see Figure 7.3 below for a visual aid in this regard). At the end of this process, under both methods, whatever remained in the pile would appear on the balance sheet as inventory. The cost of the cartons removed would appear on the income statement as cost of goods sold.

Average = KISS

Under a fourth approach, companies keep it severely simpler. They derive ending inventory and cost of goods sold figures by calculating the average cost—that is, the average price they paid—for an item throughout the period in question. In our B&B example, that figure would be $(\$3.00 + \$3.30 + \$4) \div 3 = \$3.43$ per carton of eggs. Thus, after using 2½ cartons in making breakfast, the B&B would report cost-of-eggs-used on its income statement as $(2\frac{1}{2} \times \$3.43 = \$8.58)$. It would report ending inventory on its balance sheet as $(\frac{1}{2} \times \$3.43 = \$1.72)$.

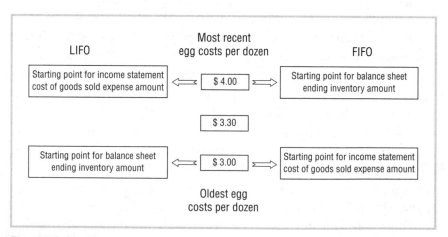

Figure 7.3 Breakfast Example: LIFO versus FIFO

Comparing Inventory Methods

In reporting financial results at their B&B, Sue and Sam could choose any of these four accounting methods. They have that choice, even though the cost-of-eggs-used expense on their income statement, and the inventory asset on their balance sheet, would differ among these methods as shown in Figure 7.4.

Now, the monetary amounts derived under these methods are clearly different, but they don't seem to differ by much. Even at the extremes, both the expense and asset lines under FIFO versus LIFO vary by only $0.50. The cost-of-eggs expense under LIFO is only 6% greater than that calculated under FIFO. Ending inventory under LIFO is 25% less than that under FIFO. Let's reexamine these percentages, however, in the context of a well-known company. Recently, on its annual income statement, Wal-Mart reported $220 billion in cost of goods sold. On its balance sheet, the company reported inventory of $30 billion. Applying the percentages above to these figures, a 6% difference in cost of goods sold would equate to $13 billion. A 25% change in inventory would amount to $7.5 billion. That's real money!

In accounting for inventory flows, Wal-Mart and other large, public companies face the same choices as Sue's B&B. These firms must inform readers of their annual reports, however, as to which inventory methods they employ. According to recent declarations in annual reports, Sherwin-Williams Company uses LIFO; Rolls Royce uses FIFO; Micron Technology uses the average-cost method; and NVR, Inc. (owner of Ryan Homes) uses specific identification.

	Allowable Inventory Method			
	Specific ID	FIFO	LIFO	Average
Cost-of-eggs-used expense on the B&B income statement	$8.65	$8.30	$8.80	$8.58
Ending inventory asset on the B&B balance sheet	1.65	2.00	1.50	1.72
Total cost of eggs available for use	$10.30	$10.30	$10.30	$10.30

Figure 7.4 Breakfast Inventory Example: Comparative Summary

Disclosing Inventory Methods

If a company uses LIFO for some or all of its inventories, it also must report the valuation at which its inventory would have appeared on the balance sheet if it had used FIFO. This is intended to help readers make an "apples to apples" comparison between companies using FIFO and LIFO. This is only required of companies that use LIFO. None of the other methods need be converted on a what-if basis. Nonetheless, here is a prototype of what such a financial statement footnote might disclose (see Figure 7.5).

Insider's Note

The use of LIFO carries with it two requirements: (1) the financial statement footnotes must disclose what inventory would have been had FIFO been used, and (2) the company must use LIFO on its tax return.

In this example, the company would have reported $48 million *more* in inventories on its balance sheet if it had used FIFO rather than LIFO. Please note two important points:

1. This company's expense for cost of goods sold has generally risen over time. Remember: A LIFO-based balance sheet assigns the *oldest* costs to inventory (FISH), while a FIFO-based report assigns the *most recent* costs to this asset (LISH). As the prototype footnote declares, balance sheet inventories would have been reported at a greater value under FIFO than under LIFO and we can infer that this company's costs to buy and/or make inventory have risen over time.
2. Let's revisit the $A = L + OE$ relationship. If the company's inventories were increased by $48 million under FIFO vis-à-vis LIFO, this would boost the Asset (A) side of the equation. But that

Inventories are stated at the lower of cost or market. Cost is determined by the last-in, first-out (LIFO) method. Current cost, determined on the FIFO method, exceeded LIFO cost by $48.0 million and $40.5 million at the end of this year and last year, respectively.

Figure 7.5 LIFO Prototype Disclosure

raises a question: what else would be affected to keep the equation in balance? Clearly, the firm does not incur greater Liabilities (L) as a result of this accounting method. It does not suffer a reduction in another asset. In fact, the offsetting increase appears in Owners' Equity (OE). The reason for this is straightforward: excluding tax effects, if the ending inventory asset amount increases by $48 million under FIFO vis-à-vis LIFO, then the corresponding expense for cost of goods sold must decrease by the same amount. The company's earnings would therefore be $48 million greater under FIFO than under LIFO (again, excluding taxes). These increased earnings would flow through to Owners' Equity.

The latter point is particularly noteworthy. For this company, the choice to use LIFO rather than FIFO has *reduced* reported pretax profits by $48 million. Why would a company do that? Here again, the reasoning is straightforward: When supply and/or manufacturing costs are rising, many companies use LIFO on their tax returns. This reduces their taxable income, and so cuts the taxes they must pay. If they use LIFO for taxes, however, these firms must also use LIFO in their annual reports. In this example, assuming a corporate tax rate of 35%, the company has saved roughly $16.8 million in taxes ($48 million × 35%) during its years on LIFO. For some companies, accumulated LIFO-based tax savings run 10 or 20 times that amount. Since shareholders generally prefer that companies generate more cash, sooner, with greater certainty, this cash saving—generated simply by an accounting method—can be highly appealing even when earnings are dampened by the use of the LIFO method.

Facilities and Other Long-Lived Assets: "Using Them Up"

Returning to my stay at the bed and breakfast in North Carolina: I'm pleased to report that the setting was lovely. From an artist's perspective, Sue and Sam have a beautiful house on a golf course with spectacular mountain views. The entire upstairs consists of guest quarters. The B&B is open year-round. Now, from an accountant's point of view, let's assume that the second floor comprises half of the square footage in the structure, and that the house cost $500,000. Then $250,000 of the house can be viewed as an explicit B&B asset—facilities. Such an asset, with a multiyear usefulness (life), would be depreciated for financial-statement purposes.

As noted earlier, depreciation entails a systematic, periodic expense to the yearly income statement, writing down a portion of a long-lived asset's historical cost. This portrays the gradual "using up" of the asset's benefits to the business. Certainly, Sue and Sam are not physically "using up" the second story of their house. Under GAAP, however, that doesn't eliminate the need to report depreciation expense on their income statement. Naturally, depreciation will affect their balance sheet as well. As Sue and Sam recognize yearly depreciation expense amounts, they will also reduce the monetary amount of their facility asset, leaving less and less of its historical cost on their B&B balance sheet each year.

Insider's Note

Depreciation is the financial equivalent of "using up" a building, vehicle, or piece of equipment.

Sue and Sam may choose from among at least three methods for depreciating their $250,000 facilities asset. Each will generate a different depreciation expense on their B&B income statement and a different asset amount reported on their B&B balance sheet. Let's explore each in turn.

Straight Line: Equal over Time

In depreciating long-lived assets, such as buildings or equipment, one of the most frequently used and easily implemented methods is based on the assumption that the asset's usefulness declines *steadily* over time. This generates an equal amount for depreciation every year throughout the economic life of the asset. Applying this straight-line method, if Sue and Sam's B&B facility was judged to have an economic life of 25 years, they would divide their asset's historical cost by that figure. This would yield an annual depreciation expense—and corresponding reduction to the facilities asset account on the balance sheet—of $10,000 a year ($250,000 historical cost ÷ 25 years). Sue

Insider's Note

Both the straight-line and double-declining-balance methods of depreciation assume time is the key factor giving rise to a depreciable asset's decreased utility.

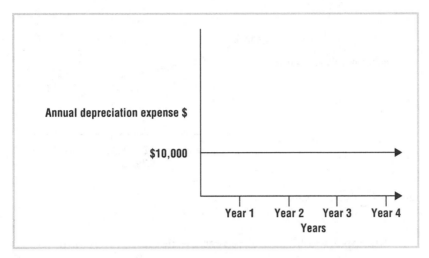

Figure 7.6 Straight-Line Depreciation Portrayed

and Sam would report that expense each year for 25 years. In graphical form, this approach may be depicted as shown in Figure 7.6.

Accelerated: More Early, Less Later

In some instances, as with vehicles, a business may judge that the economic benefits of an asset are "used up" at a greater rate in the early years of its life, and at a lower rate later. Here again, the business does not require physical evidence for this phenomenon. It need not see a vehicle's body deteriorate or its carrying capacity decline over time. Nonetheless, GAAP permits a depreciation method that reflects greater financial reduction to an asset's historical cost in its early years, and less later. In fact, it permits an entire family of such methods. Collectively, these are known as accelerated depreciation.

One popular form of accelerated depreciation is the double-declining-balance method. Businesses may implement this technique as follows:

1. Estimate the useful life of the asset, in years. For Sue and Sam's B&B facility, for example, this would be 25 years.
2. Using that figure, calculate the percentage write-down of the asset's original historical cost that would be incurred each year under straight-line depreciation. A 25-year economic life, for

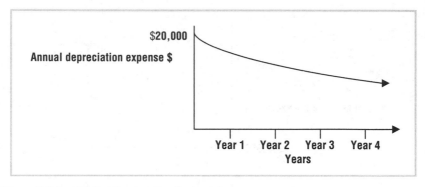

Figure 7.7 Accelerated Depreciation Portrayed

example, would generate a yearly write-down of ⅟₂₅ of the asset's original cost, or 4%.
3. Double the straight-line depreciation percentage. In our example, this would yield $4\% \times 2 = 8\%$.
4. Each year, calculate depreciation expense by applying that doubled rate to the asset's remaining, undepreciated historical cost.

At Sue and Sam's B&B, this technique would generate the following expense figures for depreciation during the first four years of their asset's life:

Year 1: $0.08 \times \$250{,}000 = \$20{,}000$
Year 2: $0.08 \times (\$250{,}000 - \$20{,}000) = \$18{,}400$
Year 3: $0.08 \times (\$250{,}000 - \$20{,}000 - \$18{,}400) = \$16{,}928$
Year 4: $0.08 \times (\$250{,}000 - \$20{,}000 - \$18{,}400 - \$16{,}928) = \$15{,}574$

Graphically, over time, this pattern may be viewed as shown in Figure 7.7.

Units of Production: Use It and Lose It

While both the straight-line and accelerated methods view time as the crucial factor in calculating depreciation, there is a third technique that denominates the usefulness of an asset in terms of productive capacity. By way of example, a company might view a vehicle's economic life not as five years, but as 120,000 miles. It might estimate a jet engine's life to be 20,000 flight hours; a robotic welder's to be 50,000 welds; or a CT scanner's to be 15,000 images.

The key attribute of any asset's capacity to provide service can be adopted as a basis for expressing its useful life. Thus, if a company buys a truck for $48,000, and estimates that the useful life of this vehicle is 120,000 miles, then it will generate $0.40 in depreciation expense—that is, $48,000 ÷ 120,000—as it drives that truck

Insider's Note

The units-of-production method of depreciation assumes the physical use of a depreciable asset is the key factor giving rise to its decreased utility

each mile. If it drives the truck 10,000 miles in its first year, it will report $4,000 in depreciation expense (10,000 × $0.40), and take a corresponding write-down to the historical cost of the truck asset on its balance sheet. If it drives the truck 24,000 miles in its second year, depreciation expense for that period will be $9,600 (24,000 × $0.40). Thus, under the units-of-production method, depreciation expense may rise or fall from year to year, depending on the use of the asset.

Returning to the B&B example, Sue and Sam might express the useful life of their guest rooms in terms of "guest-nights," in which one paying couple, staying one night in one room, represents one guest-night. If they expect their four guest rooms, in the aggregate, to yield 25,000 guest-nights during their economic life, then each guest-night will trigger a depreciation expense of $10 ($250,000 historical cost of facilities ÷ 25,000 guest-nights). If the B&B generates 850 guest-nights in its first year, then depreciation expense will be 850 × $10, or $8,500. If guest-nights total 1,100.

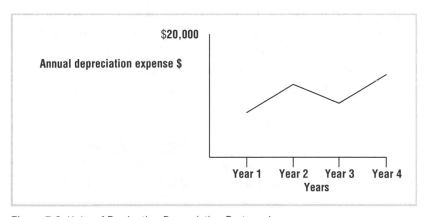

Figure 7.8 Units of Production Depreciation Portrayed

in year two, 900 in year three, and 1,200 in year four, then annual depreciation expense will be:

Year 1: $10 × $850 = $8,500
Year 2: $10 × 1,100 = $11,000
Year 3: $10 × 900 = $9,000
Year 4: $10 × 1,200 = $12,000

Graphically, this pattern may be viewed as shown in Figure 7.8.

Made-to-Order Profits?

As we've seen, a company must depreciate its long-lived assets such as buildings, vehicles, equipment, and machinery in order to financially reflect the "using up" of those assets as it employs them in business. A company may, however, choose from among at least three allowable methods to calculate depreciation expense. These methods will generate very different depreciation expense amounts for the same asset, used in the same way, during the same year. Just in the first year of our B&B example, these amounts ranged widely, as summarized in Figure 7.9.

Clearly, over the life of the B&B's facility, the maximum dollar amount that can be depreciated will be its original historical cost of $250,000, regardless of the method used to determine the yearly steps toward this total. The same is true for all depreciable assets at all companies: the maximum total expense for depreciation, over the life of an asset, is that asset's historical cost. If you ran a business that owned depreciable assets, however, and you wished to impress shareholders with your operating profits, you might have a preference as to which method to use. If you ran Sue and Sam's B&B, for example, how much would you want to deduct from earnings for purposes of depreciation: $8,500, $10,000, or $20,000? Excluding tax con-

	Depreciation Methods		
	Straight line	Double-declining	Units of production
Depreciation expense amount	$10,000	$20,000	$8,500

Figure 7.9 Depreciation Example: Comparative Summary

sequences, and all other factors being neutral, most managers would choose $8,500 . . . at least in year one.[1]

Large, publicly held companies vary in their selection of depreciation methods. The Coca-Cola Company, for example, uses straight-line depreciation. Nike uses the double-declining-balance method on its equipment and machinery, whereas the Louisiana-Pacific Corporation uses the units-of-production method on the same type of assets. These choices are within the companies' discretion, and their financial effects are significant. Texas Instruments (TI), for example, recently announced a change from accelerated to straight-line depreciation. In just its first quarter of using the new method, TI incurred almost $30 million less in depreciation than it would have under its previously used method. This represented a 10% decrease in depreciation expense for the quarter—simply by executing a change in financial reporting policies. That's not too shabby. A TI plant manager would have to work pretty hard to save an equivalent amount in manufacturing expenses.

12 + Combinations

The choices we've discussed so far—four methods of accounting for inventory, and three approaches to depreciation—generate 12 combinations of accounting methods, just for a subset of a company's total assets. These combinations, in turn, will yield 12 different income figures and balance sheet totals for the same company, conducting the same business, over the course of the same year. Please note that all 12 of these financial results would be allowable under GAAP. But this raises a challenge in comparing the financial results of any two companies. Unless those companies have made precisely the same choices of financial reporting methods, such a comparison will have an "apples to oranges" quality. That is, their relative results will be a function not only of performance, but also of financial reporting policy choices.

Moreover, the complexity doesn't end there. There are at least three more depreciation methods available to companies, other than those already described. In the oil and gas industry, under GAAP, there are two ways of accounting for costs and assets related to the exploration and development of those natural resource reserves. In long-term construction projects, such as the building of skyscrapers, bridges, and power plants, there are also two methods for reporting costs and profits on such contracts.[2] And with each of these options, the number of combinations of financial reporting methods—all acceptable under GAAP—rises multiplicatively. With such options available, it is not surprising that different companies actually do choose different combinations of methods.

But wait, there's more. A company may also use LIFO for one part of its inventory and FIFO for another. It may use straight-line depreciation for one category of depreciable assets and units-of-production for another. Thus, the number of potential combinations of financial reporting methods is greater still. This range may be further increased by variations in the LCM or impairment adjustment of historical costs, discussed in the prior chapter. It will be increased yet again by possibilities to be addressed in chapters to come. For the moment, however, please recognize one overarching point: financial statements are neither as precise nor as comparable as one might presume.

Insider's Note

A single company may choose from numerous approved financial reporting methods for certain, specific asset(s). Exercising those options, in different combinations, would give rise to scores of different balance sheets and income statements for that company.

This raises an important question: how can readers of annual reports make sense of data that can vary so fundamentally? The answer resides in the financial statement footnotes, where the reporting company must address three points on this topic:

1. It must identify the financial reporting methods it has selected.
2. It must declare any changes in these selections and, if possible, report the cumulative financial impact of these. That is, it must discuss how its financial statements would have looked if the new methods had always been in use.
3. It must provide a rationale for each change.[3]

For any single asset or expense account, however, a company need not disclose information pertaining to a range of possible reported amounts. Perhaps the footnotes should present that information. Without it, we have only an imperfect basis for assessing a company's financial position and performance, or for comparing it with others.

The Inside Scoop

As we've seen, a company faces numerous choices in crafting its financial statements. Regarding inventory, it may select among at least four accounting methods, including specific identification, LIFO, FIFO, and average. Regarding depreciation of certain long-lived assets, it may select among at least three methods—straight line, accelerated, and units of production. This generates 12 combinations of financial reporting methods solely with regard to these two classes of assets.

A company may choose its financial reporting methods. This choice is not unlimited or unregulated, however. It is not intended to facilitate a manipulation of earnings. Once a company chooses its financial reporting methods, it must apply these consistently, unless it has a strong reason to change. It must also disclose its choices. If it changes its financial reporting methods, it must disclose the reason for that change in the footnotes to its financial statements. If possible, it must also isolate and report the cumulative financial effects of the change. Readers of annual reports, for their part, must strive to understand the implications of various financial reporting methods, and how they compare and contrast.

Practical Application

To explore the financial reporting methods discussed in this chapter, let's revisit the balance sheet of Car Seats, Inc., last seen in Chapter 4. As you peruse the assets in this financial statement, your eye may now linger on the lines for inventory and property, plant, and equipment (PP&E). You may recall that these lines should be further illuminated by footnotes discussing their subcomponents, as well as the accounting methods used to calculate inventory cost flows and PP&E depreciation. Please find these footnotes below (all amounts are in thousands). Note that the bottom-line dollar amounts in the Figure 7.10 and 7.11 footnotes are identical to those which appear on the Car Seats, Inc. balance sheet.

Reviewing the Figure 7.10 disclosure, let's explore a few questions. First, does Car Seats, Inc. maintain all its inventories on the same basis? No. The company accounts for roughly three-fourths of its inventories under LIFO, and the remainder under FIFO. Companies seldom tell us the

Inventories are reported at the lower of cost or market. Cost is calculated on the last-in, first-out (LIFO) basis for approximately 75% of inventories. Cost is calculated for all other inventories on a first-in, first-out (FIFO) basis.

	This year	Last year
Raw materials	$ 58,200	$ 57,700
Work in process	64,900	66,400
Finished goods	146,800	131,700
FIFO inventories	269,900	255,800
Excess of FIFO over LIFO	(21,400)	(19,300)
Total inventories	$248,500	$236,500

Figure 7.10 Car Seats, Inc. Inventory Disclosure

reason for using two different inventory accounting methods. Companies don't have to report that information.

Over time, have inventory costs increased or decreased at Car Seats, Inc.? They've increased. We can see that, because we're told that a pure FIFO-based inventory calculation for this year would have been $21,400 greater than that reported with LIFO included in the calculation.

Cumulatively, over all the years Car Seats, Inc. has applied the LIFO method, by how much would pretax earnings have differed if it had used only FIFO in accounting for inventories? Earnings would have been $21,400 greater. The logic behind this is as follows:

- Purely under FIFO, at the end of this year, inventories would have been $21,400 *greater.*
- Consequently, the cumulative expense for cost of goods sold would have been $21,400 *less.*
- Therefore, cumulative pretax earnings would have been $21,400 *greater.*

Why might Car Seats, Inc. have chosen to adopt LIFO, especially when this method results in lower reported profits in its annual report? Car

Seats, Inc. may seek to use LIFO for tax purposes, as this method's reduction of reported earnings will reduce the company's tax obligation, conserving near-term cash flow. In order to use LIFO on its tax return, however, Car Seats, Inc. must also use this method in its annual report.

To date, how much has Car Seats, Inc. saved on taxes by using LIFO rather than FIFO? Applying an estimated 35% tax rate to the $21,400 reduction in pretax earnings generated by LIFO, we can infer that the company has saved approximately $7,490 in taxes.

Now, let's turn to the firm's PP&E disclosure in Figure 7.11.

Examining this statement, we can see that Car Seats, Inc. has elected to use the straight-line method for depreciation. What other options did the company have? It could have chosen either an accelerated or a units-of-production method. Can we tell what Car Seats, Inc.'s accumulated depreciation would have been if it had chosen one of these alternatives? Unfortunately, we can't.

What is the approximate age of Car Seats, Inc.'s portfolio of depreciable assets? We can estimate that, on average, the firm's assets are roughly 56% of the way through their useful lives. This approximation rests on two known

Property, plant, and equipment are recorded at cost. Depreciation is computed using the straight-line method over the estimated useful lives of the assets.

	Estimated useful lives	This year	Last year
Buildings and fixtures	3–40 years	$206,000	$202,500
Machinery and equipment	3–30 years	144,300	146,200
Information systems	3–10 years	30,100	33,800
Land improvements	3–30 years	28,760	26,220
Vehicles	3–10 years	10,120	9,530
Land		18,340	16,990
		437,620	435,240
Less accumulated depreciation		233,260	226,740
Property, plant, and equipment (net)		$204,360	$208,500

Figure 7.11 Car Seats, Inc. Property, Plant, and Equipment Disclosure

facts: (1) the straight-line method applies a constant, yearly expense for depreciation to a given set of assets, and (2) land is not depreciated. With this in mind, we can deduct the cost of the company's land from the original, historical cost of its PP&E. We can then divide this figure into Car Seats' accumulated depreciation (that part of the firm's fixed assets which is deemed to have been "used up"). The result will represent the proportion of these assets which has been used up, or—under straight-line depreciation—the weighted average age of these assets, as a percentage of their estimated useful lives. Mathematically, this may be expressed as follows:

$$\underbrace{\$233{,}260}_{\substack{\text{Accumulated}\\\text{depreciation}}} \div (\underbrace{\$437{,}620}_{\text{Total PP\&E}} - \underbrace{\$18{,}340}_{\text{Land}}) = 56\%$$

Please note that this calculation can only be used to infer age under straight-line depreciation.

In Anticipation of the Next Secret

Look at the nearest stranger. Guess his or her weight. What are the odds that you are correct? Would you answer differently if you had to tell the person your guess?

Secret #8

It's Imprecise

Give it your best guess!

The questions behind Secret #8:

- Do the financial statements in annual reports include any estimates, or are all figures accurate and precise?
- If there are estimates, where do they reside? What are some examples?
- Are the effects of these estimates significant?
- How can financial statement footnotes help us ascertain the type and extent of any management estimates?

Around the house, I am a do-it-yourself handyman. Sadly, I must confess, there are a number of projects started long ago, still unfinished. I never fail to misestimate the time and money needed for my projects. Perhaps you do the same. None of us has perfect foresight, not even seasoned managers of large, public companies.

Welcome to a World of Financial Estimates

The financial statements in annual reports are built upon numerous management estimates. Indeed, the process of making these estimates is a natural and necessary part of telling a company's financial story. Like those we make in our own lives, a company's estimates may vary from actual outcomes. Further, each estimate made is but one that could have

Insider's Note

Estimates play a huge role in crafting the contents of the financial statements presented in a corporate annual report.

been made. Like the historical cost adjustments and financial reporting choices discussed in the prior chapter, estimates weaken the supposed objectivity and certainty of the figures that appear in financial statements. In light of the number and significance of these estimates, we must view corporate financial statements as products of preference as well as calculation.

To explore the role of estimates in financial statements, let's examine three examples: (1) useful lives and residual values for depreciable assets, (2) uncollectible accounts receivable, and (3) certain factors affecting a company's obligation for retirees' health care benefits. In each of these cases, estimates can have a sizable effect on the associated line items in a company's balance sheet and income statement.

Lives and RVs

Many companies maintain large investments in facilities, equipment, and vehicles, which must be depreciated for financial-reporting purposes. As discussed in the prior chapter, managers may select the method by which their company depreciates such assets. Choices include straight-line and accelerated depreciation over time, as well as a method based on the assets' use in service or production. In addition, managers must make estimates in determining depreciation: managers estimate the useful life of each depreciable asset, as well as its residual value at the end of that life.

In estimating the lifespan of a depreciable asset, corporate managers must consider the manner in which that asset will be used and maintained. Generally, managers assume their company will perform normal repairs and maintenance to keep assets in good operating condition. Based on that premise, they estimate a depreciable asset's lifespan to be the length of time that it can reasonably be expected to last before it physically wears out. When an asset's life is influenced more by the passage of time than by use, as in the case of a building, managers estimate it in years. When the reverse is true, when lifespan is more influenced by an asset's use than by the passage of time, managers express it in terms of service or output, such as units produced by a manufacturing device or miles driven in a car.

For many depreciable assets, however, technological life has greater relevance than physical life. Technological life refers to the time frame during which a depreciable asset is expected to generate economic benefits before it becomes obsolete. In this regard, two types of obsolescence are pertinent: product obsolescence and process obsolescence. Product obsolescence pertains to the market lives of the goods produced by the depreciable asset. For example, car manufacturers normally depreciate the machines used to stamp auto body panels over a period of four or five years—not because the machines wear out in that time, but because changes in auto models render them obsolete. In process obsolescence, by contrast, the depreciable asset itself becomes obsolete as a result of technological improvements in subsequent generations of such assets. When estimating the useful lives of computers, for example, companies anticipate that process obsolescence will occur—due to such innovations as higher-speed processors[1]—long before the equipment physically wears out.

> **Insider's Note**
>
> *Many factors go into estimating the useful lives of depreciable assets, including time, use, product obsolescence, and process obsolescence.*

Regardless of these complexities, a company must estimate the useful life of a depreciable asset at the time it is acquired. The impact of this estimate can be substantial. If a company makes a $10 million investment in equipment and depreciates it on a straight-line basis, even the difference between an 8-year and a 10-year useful life wll be sizable—and will affect both the income statement and the balance sheet—as illustrated in Figure 8.1.

Figure 8.1 depicts an asset with no residual value (discussed below). As you would expect, total depreciation expense adds up to the asset's historical cost—in this example, $10 million—regardless of its estimated useful life. But, for any given year, different estimated lives have significant differential effects on a company's income statement and balance sheet.

In preparing to depreciate an asset such as a building or a vehicle, managers must also estimate its *residual value* (RV). By definition, RV is that portion of a depreciable asset's historical cost that will be left on the balance sheet at the end of its useful life, because the company has projected that it will be worth at least that much. In practice, however, this can

Income Statement Effects

Years	Annual depreciation expense when the life is:		More (less) annual depreciation expense with 8 years as base case
	8 years	10 years	
1 thru 8	$1,250,000	$1,000,000	**$250,000/year**
9 and 10	—	$1,000,000	**($1,000,000)/year**

Balance Sheet Effects

At end of year:	Equipment asset amount when the life is:		More (less) asset amount with 8 years as base case:
	8 years	10 years	
1	$8,750,000	$9,000,000	**($250,000)**
2	7,500,000	8,000,000	**(500,000)**
3	6,250,000	7,000,000	**(750,000)**
4	5,000,000	6,000,000	**(1,000,000)**
5	3,750,000	5,000,000	**(1,250,000)**
6	2,500,000	4,000,000	**(1,500,000)**
7	1,250,000	3,000,000	**(1,750,000)**
8	-0-	2,000,000	**(2,000,000)**
9	-0-	1,000,000	**(1,000,000)**
10	-0-	-0-	**-0-**

Figure 8.1 Financial Statement Impact of Different Depreciation Lives for a $10 Million Depreciable Asset

be a questionable concept, as many depreciable assets actually *appreciate* in value. Nevertheless, under GAAP, companies are allowed to estimate an asset's RV, and cease depreciating that asset once its reported balance sheet amount reaches this figure.

In the Figure 8.1 example, in which a firm made a $10 million investment in equipment, the estimated RV of that asset was zero. This can be seen, as the firm fully depreciated its historical cost. If management had estimated that the equipment would have an RV of $1 million, only $9 million of its historical cost would have been depreciable over its useful life. Annual depreciation expense then would have been $1,125,000 for an eight-year estimated life, or $900,000 over a 10-year span. Thus, the depreciation expense that appears in a company's income statement—and the asset amount on its balance sheet—is affected by multiple factors, including depreciation methods chosen, estimated lives, and estimated RV.

Call the Good Fellas

As noted in an earlier chapter, many companies make sales on a credit basis. Not to me, of course. When I shop, I need to bring cash or a credit card. But when one company sells to another, it often extends credit. That is, it delivers goods in return for a promise of future payment. In the process, the selling company records revenue and an account receivable on the sale, and expects payment within an agreed time—often 30 days.

On the surface, this appears straightforward. Most companies, however, find it impossible to collect all of their accounts receivable. There are many reasons for this. Customers fall on hard times or go out of business; they dispute the quality or quantity of goods received; they object to payment terms. No company makes a credit sale *expecting* a credit customer to default. But among hundreds or thousands of customers and sales, involving thousands or even millions of dollars, it can expect that some number of these will prove uncollectible.

With this in mind, companies are required to estimate the monetary amount of accounts receivable that they won't be able to collect. They must record this as an expense, matched against revenues on the income statement for the related period. They must do this prior to actually finding out which specific customers will not honor their agreement to pay. The logic behind this is as follows: Uncollectible accounts are deemed an expense of making credit sales, and must therefore be anticipated and linked to the revenues they helped generate.[2] In recognizing this expense, management records a corresponding reduction in accounts receivable on the balance sheet. This is logical. After all, the company has already projected that, in the aggregate, these payment promises will generate less cash than it hoped at the time of the original sale.

A company may use any process it deems reasonable to estimate its

> ### Insider's Note
>
> *Not all of a company's customers will pay for the goods and services they purchased. Selling companies must estimate and record the monetary amount of those uncollectible accounts receivable as of each year end.*

uncollectible accounts receivable. Of course, it should base this estimate on historical experience, informed by current economic conditions and customer profiles. Beyond that, however, it may record its best educated guess. And rest assured, this estimate *is* a guess. It blends the science of data-based analysis with the art of managerial judgment. Ultimately, only time will tell which customers will default on their trade credit—and by how much.

The monetary amounts can be sizable. Boeing's balance sheet, for example, recently reported gross accounts receivable of $5,336 million, offset by $90 million in estimated uncollectible accounts. That is, Boeing estimated that 1.7% of its receivables would be uncollectible. In making this estimate, the company likely considered a broad range of factors, including prior collections experience; the financial condition of its customers, the airlines; the probability that disputes might arise with those customers; and the nature of such potential disputes. All of this left a good deal of room for judgment and estimation. Different evaluations of any of these factors could have resulted in a substantially different estimate. That, in turn, would have had a sizable impact on Boeing's reported financial results. A mere 0.5% increase in the percentage of accounts receivable that were estimated to be uncollectible, from 1.7% to 2.2% (the percentage from the year before), would have reduced the firm's net accounts receivable by $27 million ($5,336 million × 0.005), and increased its estimated uncollectible accounts expense by the same amount.

With a more pessimistic perspective, Boeing could possibly have justified a higher percentage. Perhaps the firm could also have made a case for an uncollectible accounts percentage 0.5% *lower* than that reported. It was, to a large extent, managers' choice and judgment. They had the challenge to derive an estimate they could defend and substantiate—a task with no precise, right answer.

It's Not Only Rock and Roll

My wife and I saw the Rolling Stones in concert a few years ago. What a great show! Locally, some called it the "Rickety Bones Concert," because the average age of the fans was likely over 50. The Stones, of course, have been around the block once or twice themselves. But so what? Mick Jagger, truly one of rock's elder statesmen, put on a mesmerizing performance.

With his energy and showmanship, he looked set to deliver "Satisfaction" well into his seventies.

Now, let's pretend that Mick Jagger and other great but aging performers are employees of Really Old Concert Knights, Inc.—ROCK, Inc.—a public company that stages performances by artists "who've been around for long, long years." Let's further imagine that ROCK, Inc. offers a postretirement health-care plan that will cover much of its employees' medical needs from the date of their retirement until death. In the company's annual report, it will need to report the existence of this plan. On its balance sheet, it will need to report a liability, representing its obligation to employees under the plan. On its income statement, it will need to report a yearly expense, representing the annual growth in that obligation, as employees earn benefits under the plan through their work for ROCK, Inc.

> ## Insider's Note
>
> *Postemployment health care benefits promised to employees represent a huge corporate obligation. Measuring the monetary amount of this obligation requires a number of estimates.*

Determining the company's liability under this plan, however, presents a challenge. Management will need to make a host of estimates to derive the figure, including considerations such as the following:

- How many of ROCK, Inc.'s current employees will ultimately retire from the company? Or, conversely, how many will quit or die before they retire?
- Among those who retire from ROCK, Inc., when will they do so?
- How long will they live after they retire?
- What sorts of medical care will they need during their retirement years?
- How much will medical care cost during those years?
- What rate of return will ROCK, Inc. earn on funds set aside for its postretirement health-care plan?

It's difficult to answer these questions as they might pertain to any one employee, never mind hundreds or thousands of other ROCK, Inc. employees. And yet, companies that offer postretirement health-care plans must answer them, not only for current employees, but also for those already retired and still covered by the plan. The process of responding to such questions is fraught with estimates and, not infrequently, sheer guesses. Can you anticipate medical costs 15 years from now? I can't. Nonetheless, companies must make these estimates in order to quantify their liabilities and expenses under such benefit plans. And the numbers are not trivial. For large, long-standing, people-intensive companies, these obligations can approach $100 billion. Even net of funds set aside for the obligation, the totals can still be in the billions.

Let's say you needed to estimate the six items listed above, in order to determine the postretirement health-care obligation at your company. It's possible, even likely, that any two people assigned this task would arrive at varying estimates. And yet, these liabilities, as reported by publicly traded companies, are heavily subject to such estimates. As input factors may vary

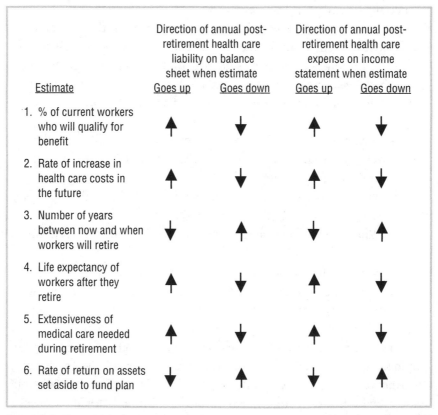

Figure 8.2 Financial Statement Impact of Different Post-retirement Health Care Estimates

within a single company, they will certainly vary *among* companies, making the financial statements of companies less comparable. It's therefore important to read a firm's disclosures in this regard. In reviewing a company's annual report, take care to identify its benefit-plan estimates, and to understand the general effects of these estimates on its financial statements, as per Figure 8.2.

Other Areas of Embedded Estimates

We've discussed only a few of the financial statement items in which estimates play a significant role. Many other parts of financial statements also rest, to varying degrees, on estimates, assumptions, and managerial judgments. These include, but are not limited to:

- The likely amount of an obligation to be generated in defense of a lawsuit, or in fulfilling a government order for environmental remediation
- The obligation arising from a defined-benefits pension plan
- Compensation expense pertaining to stock options granted to employees today, but not exercisable for several years
- The obligation to fulfill warranties granted in conjunction with the sale of products
- Estimated quantities of natural resource assets
- And let's not forget the estimates we highlighted in Chapter 6, pertaining to:
  - A lower of cost or market adjustment to inventory, and
  - Material impairment of a company's recorded long-lived assets, such as land, facilities, and goodwill

The specific financial reporting details for these additional estimates are beyond the scope of this book. Please recognize, however, that all of these financial statement items require significant estimations.

Confessions about Estimates

Making estimates is a normal and necessary part of crafting a company's financial story in its annual report. Readers of corporate annual reports, however, must recognize where estimates are at work, so they can view the relevant figures as approximate and subject to management discretion. Due to the quantity and significant impact of such figures, companies are required to alert readers to the fact that estimates are a part of their financial statements. Such alerts appear in the MD&A section of an annual report and in its financial statement footnotes. A company must also highlight its key estimates and assumptions, provide a rationale for each, note any changes in them from the prior year, discuss the sensitivity of balance sheet and income statement amounts to such changes, and provide information on the accuracy of its past estimates.

Among the items on this list, sensitivity disclosures have particular significance. And foremost among the sensitivity analyses that appear in financial statement footnotes are those which pertain to postemployment benefits. By way of example, General Motors' reported a net postretirement health-care liability of $34 billion from a few years ago. In connection with this reported amount, GM made several disclosures. In its financial statement footnotes, it disclosed the rate of increase it had estimated for future health-care costs, the rate of return it expected to earn on funds set aside for the benefit plan, and the effects of a 1% increase or decrease in the estimated trend for future health care costs. GM noted that the $34 billion net liability would have been $9 billion higher, and the program's expense figure for the year would have been roughly $630 million greater than reported, if the company had estimated that future health-care costs would increase at a rate 1% greater than that projected. Conversely, GM reported that, its net liability would have been $8 billion less, and the related expense would have been roughly $520 million lower than reported, if they had estimated that future health care costs would increase at a rate 1% lower than anticipated. Those are substantial differences!

The Inside Scoop

We all make estimates in order to function in our daily lives. We estimate the travel time to a friend's house for a party that starts at 8 P.M. We estimate the likelihood of rain when we leave the house with—or without—an umbrella. We estimate the cost of a vacation when we start saving for it. Sometimes, our estimates become more accurate as we make more of them, and compare them with actual results. Sometimes, they don't.

Companies, too, make estimates. In fact, estimates constitute a normal, necessary, and significant part of a company's financial story. Companies estimate the life spans and residual values of depreciable assets, such as buildings, vehicles, equipment, and machinery. They estimate the portion of accounts receivable that will prove uncollectible. In evaluating their liabilities under postretirement health-care plans, companies make a wide range of estimates.

These estimates may have a direct and sizable effect on the amounts presented in companies' balance sheets and income statements. Despite their aura of precision, corporate financial statements include many estimates. Readers of annual reports must strive to recognize these, and to understand their effects. Toward that end, companies must disclose and discuss their key estimates.

Practical Application

To reinforce our understanding of estimates in financial statements, let's focus on a company that acquires a facilities asset for $100 million and depreciates it on a straight-line basis. Let's imagine the company is considering various estimates for this asset's life span and residual value. Figure 8.3 shows a range of figures for annual depreciation expense, generated by different combinations of these two asset attributes requiring estimates. Please verify the calculation of one or two of these amounts to cement your understanding of life span and residual value as factors influencing the determination of depreciation expense.

As can readily be seen in Figure 8.3, the depreciation expense figures vary widely. Over a 30-year life, assuming a 15% residual value, the company in this example would depreciate its $100 million asset by $2.83 million per year. By contrast, over a 20-year life, assuming a 1% RV, annual depreciation expense would increase to $4.95 million per year—almost twice as much. Theoretically, the company might choose among any of the combinations of estimates in the table above, and many others. Please note, however, that while holding other assumptions steady, annual depre-

		Useful Life (in years)				
		20	22	25	27	30
Residual Value (% of asset's historical cost)	1%	$4,950	$4,500	$3,960	$3,667	$3,300
	5%	4,750	4,318	3,800	3,519	3,167
	10%	4,500	4,091	3,600	3,333	3,000
	15%	4,250	3,864	3,400	3,148	2,833

Figure 8.3 Annual Straight-line Depreciation Expense Amount (in Millions) for a $100 Million Asset When . . .

ciation expense declines as depreciable life lengthens, and as estimated residual value increases. Consequently, in reading a firm's annual report, it's important to note any changes—and particularly, any increases—in either of these estimates. If the firm *has* increased the estimated useful lives or residual values of its depreciable assets, we can anticipate that this will reduce depreciation expense and so increase earnings. If that earnings increase is significant—and if, without it, corporate earnings would have fallen short of shareholder expectations or the prior year's results—we must ask ourselves if the company is managing earnings. Such a concern would prompt further research to learn what professional financial analysts are saying about the company.

By contrast with estimates pertaining to depreciable assets, those concerning uncollectible accounts receivable must be made every year. Generally, if a company's estimated uncollectible accounts—as a percentage of gross accounts receivable—remains stable over time, we can infer that the firm has been consistent in its extension of credit, its collections, and the credit profile of its customers. If that percentage trends down, we might infer that the company has tightened credit, improved its collections efforts, and/or focused its sales on a healthier customer base. If the company's uncollectible accounts percentage trends upward, we might well view that as a warning sign of declining financial health in the company's market, weakened collections efforts, and/or an increased willingness by the company to chase sales, regardless of the credit risk posed by its customers. We would not want to see such an upward trend, unless the sales and profits generated by relaxed credit terms and a riskier customer base outweighed the losses caused by increased uncollectible accounts receivable.

By way of example, a popular home products manufacturer recently reported $270 million in net accounts receivable and $14 million of estimated uncollectible accounts, yielding gross accounts receivable of $284 million ($270 million + $14 million). Interestingly, the company's estimated uncollectible accounts—as a percentage of gross accounts receivable—have trended downward in recent years. At $14 million, they represented approximately 5% of gross receivables. Three years earlier, estimated uncollectible accounts comprised roughly 8% of the company's gross receivables. What might explain such a significant decline in this percentage over three short years? Perhaps the company strengthened its collections practices, reducing the estimate needed for uncollectible accounts. Perhaps the company has been more stringent in its credit requirements among potential customers. So long as tighter credit did not disproportionately dampen sales, this is a good move. This raises the question: What *has* been the sales trend? Unfortunately, over the three years in question, the company's sales have declined by 7%. In this context, a reduction in estimated uncollectible accounts from 8% to 5% of gross receivables does not appear to represent entirely good news.

This suggests yet another question. At $284 million in gross accounts receivable, how much more would the company have expensed if its estimated uncollectible accounts had remained 8% of gross receivables, rather than declining to 5%? The answer is $8.5 million ($284 million × (8% − 5%)). At some companies, this might look like an opportunity. If I were a manager at a company whose annual profits were about to miss projections by $8 or $9 million, would I adjust my uncollectible accounts estimate to make up the shortfall? I hope not. In fact, I'm confident that most managers at reputable companies wouldn't. But the temptation exists. In reading financial reports, it's a good idea to be mindful of such possibilities.

With regard to retiree health-care plans, the following excerpts from a recent PepsiCo annual report—from its MD&A section and financial statement footnotes—are typical.

In the disclosures shown in Figure 8.4, PepsiCo alerts readers of its annual report to several key estimates and assumptions. The company provides a brief indication of how those estimates are derived (i.e., historical experience, managerial judgment). It also specifies its estimates regarding the rate of increase in health-care costs (i.e., 10% this year, declining gradually to 5% per annum). The company also tells us how the current year's balance sheet liability and income statement expense amounts would change if health-care costs were projected to rise at rates 1% greater or less than the declared estimates.

The point of such information is not to encourage readers to judge certain estimates as better or worse, right or wrong. Rather, these disclosures help readers to view the company's financial condition and performance as residing within a range—as opposed to hitting precise, specific targets. In the year in question, for example, the postretirement health-care liability on PepsiCo's balance sheet was $1,004 million. With a 1% increase in the estimated trend for future rises in health care costs, that figure would have risen

Significant assumptions used to measure our annual retiree medical expense include [among others]:

- certain employee-related factors such as turnover, retirement age and mortality;
- and health-care cost trend rates.

Our assumptions reflect historical experience and management's best judgment regarding future expectations. An average increase of 10% in the cost of covered retiree medical benefits is assumed this year. This average increase is then projected to decline gradually to 5% [four years from now and thereafter]. These assumed health-care cost trend rates have an impact on the retiree medical plan and expense and liability. A 1% change in the assumed rate would have the following effects:

	1% increase	1% decrease
This year's expense	$3 million	($2 million)
This year's liability	$38 million	($33 million)

Figure 8.4 Excerpts from a PepsiCo Annual Report Related to Retiree Health Plans

to $1,042 million. With a 1% decrease, it would have declined to $971 million. Thus, the disclosures map out a range of values for this liability.

Such disclosures can also be useful when readers of annual reports seek to establish a common basis for assessing the financial condition and performance of multiple companies. Imagine, for example, that a PepsiCo competitor used an estimate of 8% for the growth rate of health-care costs, while PepsiCo used 10%. Under this scenario, we could draw upon the +1% sensitivity analysis data from the competitor and the −1% data from PepsiCo, and adjust the firms' respective income statements and balance sheets to a more common basis for comparison.

In Anticipation of the Next Secret

Is there anything under that kilt? Something seems to be missing.

Secret #9

It's Incomplete

Something is missing

The questions behind Secret #9:

- Are there any assets or liabilities that *don't* appear on corporate balance sheets?
- If so, why are they omitted?
- If they're excluded, they must not be very important . . . right?
- Do financial statement footnotes compensate for these omissions? If so, how?

In 1990, amid such momentous events as German reunification and the freeing of Nelson Mandela, an incongruous song hit the pop music charts. Believe it or not, "Itsy Bitsy Teeny Weeny Yellow Polka Dot Bikini" briefly hit number 1. Can you believe it? I'd have thought that song would be better suited to the innocence of the 1950s than to the era of grunge rock and Kurt Cobain. And yet, there it was, at the top of the charts. Apparently, our interest in the bikini never wanes. Why is that?

I learned the answer from a friend from Brazil—a nation justly proud of its swimsuits and beaches. As this gentleman explained, "We're attracted by what the bikini shows us, and curious about what it doesn't." Being a finance professional, he added, "Accounting is like that, too." And I must admit, he was right. Annual reports do reveal a great deal about a company's financial condition and performance. There are important elements, however, that they don't show us.[1]

Invisible Intangible Assets

Do you have an auto mechanic, insurance agent, dentist, or electrician to whom you are loyal? If so, why is that? Are you drawn by their friendly attitude? Their proven expertise? Their track record of standing behind their work? Or do they have an employee whom you like and trust? Whatever it is, there's often an intangible factor behind our decision to engage one vendor rather than another. The vendors know this, of course, and work hard to nurture the intangible attributes that attract us.

Intangible assets are among the key factors that help large corporations acquire customers, build markets, and compete against rivals. Examples include the research-and-development skills of software engineers at SAIC, brand image and reputation at the Walt Disney Company, the power of Amazon.com's proprietary information systems, and the unabashed customer loyalty at Apple, Inc. All of these companies have invested substantial resources in such internally created advantages, and reap considerable returns from them. And yet, these distinctive, beneficial advantages don't appear as reportable assets on their balance sheets. Quite frankly, contemporary balance sheets do not present much, if any, information on internally created intangible assets. Neither do financial statement footnotes.

> **Insider's Note**
>
> *Many important, internally created intangible assets are not monetarily measured and reported in a company's financial statements.*

It's not hard to identify a company's intangible assets. Ask corporate executives about the keys to their company's success, and they'll invariably mention two or three of them. What is hard is establishing agreement as to the most appropriate *measure* for these assets. The prevalent financial reporting practice is that data in—or associated with—financial statements must generally meet two criteria: (1) they must be objectively determinable by a marketplace transaction, and (2) they must be financial. If these criteria can't be met, potentially informative data are often not reported. Let's consider both of these criteria.

It's long been assumed that internally created intangible assets are not objectively measurable in financial terms. Many still believe this to be the case. But measurement techniques *have* been developed for intangible assets, and used outside annual reports. M-CAM, Inc., for example, has developed a valuation process for intellectual property, which has been used by the Securities and Exchange Commission, the Internal Revenue Service, banks, insurers, and the NASDAQ stock exchange. Moreover, *Business Week* magazine runs a regular feature on the value of corporate brands, as determined by Interbrand Corporation. Interbrand has quantified values for these brands, even though many of them were created by the firms that own them rather than purchased them from other entities in marketplace transactions. The argument that internally created intangible assets cannot be objectively measured is simply no longer valid.

Annual reports have also tended to avoid reporting a wide range of nonfinancial metrics, treating such data as off limits. In many ways, this is unfortunate. Readers of annual reports could gain a broader view of a company's performance and capabilities if they had access to its product returns data, as well as win rate on competitive bids, research-and-development yields, and other nonfinancial, performance-oriented data. After all, the companies themselves use such measures in managing their operations. And many of these metrics are amenable to verification by independent auditors. They'd be useful additions to the stories presented in annual reports.

Insider's Note

Annual reporting practices shy away from presenting audited, nonfinancial performance metrics that would be helpful in gauging the worth of various intangible assets.

And yet, the very exclusion of internally created intangible assets from balance sheets represents an implicit financial valuation: zero. Granted, zero is a cautious, conservative estimate. But it's not a valid or informative one. Nor is it more reliable or useful than a specific monetary figure or other numerical description might be. If required, managers could identify the most critical internally created intangible assets at their companies. External experts could value these, and companies could report them in a special section of their balance sheets. Footnotes could describe the valuation methods employed, and auditors could attest to their results. For those intangible assets not amenable to valuation, annual reports could provide nonfinancial measures, indicative of their contribution to corporate performance. Currently, however, such information is not required in annual reports.

Certain Liabilities Don't Make It onto the Balance Sheet

Rent to De-own

If you personally lease a car or an apartment, you probably factor monthly rent into your financial planning. In fact, most of us would consider these commitments to be among the highest priorities in our budget, and would pay them before even *thinking* about spending money on recreational items, such as concert tickets or a movie.

Companies, too, view their rent payments as high priorities. It may be surprising to learn, however, that they may not have to record these multiyear obligations on their balance sheets. An airline, for example, may lease an entire fleet of planes without showing them or the lease obligations on its balance sheet. That is possible if the airline structures its leases in accordance with certain financial-reporting rules, those contracts will qualify as operating—rather than capital—leases. In that case, the lease data will only surface in the annual report's financial statement footnotes. An airline can fly with no planes on its balance sheet? Yes. A construction company can build bridges and dams with no earth-moving equipment on its balance sheet? Yes. What are the financial-reporting criteria that make this possible?

> **Insider's Note**
>
> *It is not unusual for multimillion dollar leased assets, and related liabilities, to not appear on corporate balance sheets.*

To qualify as an operating lease—and so, to be excluded from the lessee's balance sheet—a rental agreement must pass a negative test. That is, it must possess *none* of the following attributes:

1. An option to purchase the leased asset at a bargain price at the end of the lease term
2. Conveyance of title to the asset at the end of the lease term

3. A present value of the aggregate minimum rental payments under the lease greater than or equal to 90% of what it would have cost to buy the asset outright at the time the lease was signed
4. A lease term greater than or equal to 75% of the leased asset's useful life

If a lease meets *any* of these criteria, it is a capital lease. For financial reporting purposes, the leased asset must then be treated as if it were not merely rented, but rather purchased by the lessee with borrowed funds. Upon leasing an asset under a capital lease agreement, a company must record on its balance sheet, at the signing of the lease, both the leased asset and an equivalent liability for the lease obligation.

If, on the other hand, a lease meets *none* of the four criteria above, then it qualifies as an operating lease. In that case, the lessee does not report either the leased asset or liability on its balance sheet. Rather, it treats the lease simply as a rental, periodically reducing cash on its balance sheet and increasing rent expense on its income statement.

These four "bright line" tests enable managers to avoid adding assets and liabilities to their company's balance sheet, simply by structuring leases to avoid all four of the criteria above. This is important, as most companies do *not* want to report any more liabilities than they must. That preference, in conjunction with clear financial-reporting criteria, often prompts managers to structure leases deliberately to avoid the four capital lease criteria. That is, they negotiate leases with no bargain purchase option, no ultimate conveyance of title, a term less than 75% of the leased asset's useful life, and lease payments with a discounted present value less than 90% of the asset's purchase price. In this way, they gain the use of assets without recording them—or the associated lease obligations—on their corporate balance sheet. This is popularly known as "off-balance-sheet financing."[2]

> ### Insider's Note
>
> *"Bright line" financial reporting rules for leases make it easy for companies to utilize "off-balance-sheet financing" arrangements.*

Now, simply because an operating lease doesn't appear on the balance sheet, that doesn't mean readers of a company's annual report are denied all information pertaining to what may be a long-term, substantive financial arrangement. In its financial statement footnotes, a company must acknowledge its operating leases and provide a summary schedule of payments under them. The goal of this disclosure is to inform readers of the nature, timing, and extent of the company's operating lease obligations, despite their exclusion from the balance sheet. Figure 9.1 is a prototype lease footnote, modeled on numerous real-world examples. It reports more than $9.7 million in operating lease obligations—a contractual sum that does not appear on the lessee company's balance sheet, but that dwarfs the $3.8 million (present value) in capital lease obligations that do.

By keeping leased assets and liabilities off their balance sheets, companies generally seek to enhance the financial stories perceived in a traditional analysis of their financial statements. By way of example, consider

The company leases warehouse space, office facilities, space for retail stores and production equipment under non-cancelable operating and capital leases. The following is a schedule of future minimum lease payments as of December 31 this year:

In thousands	Operating	Capital
Due at end of next year	$3,444	$2,000
Due at end of the second year	3,100	600
Due at end of third year	1,220	450
Due at end of fourth year	740	280
Due at end of fifth year	222	114
Thereafter	1,000	700
Total future minimum lease payments	$9,726	$4,114
Less amount representing interest Present		(312)
value of future minimum lease payments		3,802
Less current maturities of obligations		
under capital leases		(2,012)
Long-term lease obligations		$1,790

Rent expense for this year was $3,122. Last year, it was $2,098 and for the year prior to that it was $1,110 (in thousands).

Figure 9.1 Prototype Annual Report Lease Disclosure

the balance sheets of two firms—Op Company and Cap Company—which are identical in all ways but one. Both firms lease a warehouse. While Op Company uses this facility under an operating lease, Cap Company's rental agreement includes a bargain purchase option. This obligates Cap Company to report the agreement as a capital lease, and to carry both the warehouse and associated lease liability on its balance sheet (see Figure 9.2).

If we analyze these statements under the fundamental equation, $A = L + OE$, we might reach two erroneous conclusions. First, because its reported assets are numerically greater, we might infer that Cap Company is larger than Op Company. That would be an incorrect, or at least useless, comparison. Second, if we wish to know the extent to which each firm has used debt to finance its assets, we might divide total liabilities by total assets and express the result as a percentage. This would yield a quotient of 38% for Op Company ($15,000 ÷ $39,000), and 48% for Cap Company ($23,000 ÷ $47,000). This might lead us to conclude that Cap Company is more reliant upon and weighted with debt than Op Company. But that, too, would be incorrect.

Remember, the resources and operations of these firms are identical, with the exception of a single clause in a single rental contract. In reality,

	Op Company, Inc.	Cap Company, Inc.
Assets:		
Current assets	$15,000	$15,000
Office building	20,000	20,000
Warehouse under capital lease	—	8,000
Other noncurrent assets	4,000	4,000
Total assets	$39,000	$47,000
Liabilities:		
Current liabilities	$10,000	$10,000
Capital lease liability	—	8,000
Other noncurrent liabilities	5,000	5,000
Total liabilities	15,000	23,000
Owners' Equity	24,000	24,000
Total liabilities and owners' equity	$39,000	$47,000

Figure 9.2 Operating versus Capital Lease Balance Sheets

Op Company is neither smaller nor less reliant on debt than Cap Company, despite the appearance of their balance sheets. As readers of their annual reports, we must read the financial statement footnotes to uncover Op Company's warehouse operating lease data to make a more valid comparison between the companies.

Digging for Retirement Obligations

Defined-benefit pension plans represent one of the largest obligations at many companies. By contract, these plans guarantee specific cash payments to former employees during their retirement years. Postretirement healthcare plans constitute a related obligation, also potentially quite large, as they provide former employees with certain levels of medical care during their retirement. Companies strive regularly to set aside funds to cover projected future payouts under both these plans. Nonetheless, until slightly more than a decade ago, annual reports and balance sheets provided scant information about either these obligations or the funds set aside for them.

Only recently have companies been required to report the over- or underfunded status of these plans in their balance sheets. Even now, on their balance sheets, companies show neither their gross liabilities (that is, their total obligations) under these plans, nor the assets they've set aside to fund these obligations. That information is only in the financial statement footnotes, along with an overall description of the plans and some of their key assumptions. Readers of an annual report must therefore dig through the footnote pertaining to pensions and other postretirement benefit plans in order to ascertain a company's gross obligations under these programs.

Insider's Note

Certain postretirement contracts between employers and employees result in huge corporate financial obligations. Neither that gross liability nor the assets set aside to fund those obligations are reported on corporate balance sheets.

By way of example, let's assume that a company's annual report includes a pension footnote, informing us that it had a year-end obligation of $4.9 billion under its defined-benefit pension plan. Let's assume further that the company has set aside $3.4 billion to cover that obligation. Clearly, the plan is underfunded by $1.5 billion. Underfunding is not uncommon among these plans. For our purposes, the key point is that only the $1.5 billion shortfall is reported on the balance sheet. Neither the full obligation of $4.9 billion nor the $3.4 billion in earmarked funds would appear there. These figures would be found only in the financial statement footnotes.[3] For that matter, prior to 2006, even the $1.5 billion shortfall would have been excluded from the balance sheet.

For many companies with defined-benefit pension plans that are underfunded, the social, economic, and balance-sheet burdens of this obligation weigh heavily. Employees worry that the security of their retirement years is in jeopardy. Obligated to fund their plans, companies feel mounting pressure on their cash flows. Meanwhile, the liability grows on their balance sheets. Faced with these pressures, many companies are now shifting to defined-*contribution* pension plans. Such plans simply require companies to make periodic, contractual payments into employees' retirement accounts, with no guarantee of specific payouts during retirement years. This eliminates the need to report projected balance sheet liabilities for workers' retirement years. It also obviates the issue noted above, in which total liabilities and plan assets fail to appear on the balance sheet. Under defined-contribution plans, companies also escape the financial burden of supporting an ever-growing retiree population at stated, contractual levels. This burden can be substantial, as retirees now outnumber the active work force at many large U.S. corporations. For all of these reasons, companies are likely to embrace defined-contribution plans—and to forego or terminate defined-benefit plans—at an accelerating pace in the years to come.

Contingent Liabilities Are Seldom Seen

Lawsuits are a common feature of the business landscape and can generate substantial future obligations, particularly as they relate to product liability, environmental remediation, employment discrimination, and unfair competitive practices. Nonetheless, under current financial reporting rules, defendant companies are not required to report a liability for such lawsuits on their balance sheet unless, as of the date of the financial statements (1) it is *probable* that the obligation will come to pass,

Insider's Note

Potential obligations contingent on the occurrence of specific trigger events need not be reported as balance sheet liabilities unless the trigger event is probable and the resultant monetary amount is estimable.

and (2) its financial consequences are *estimable*. If a potential obligation meets only one of these criteria, a company may simply discuss the situation in its financial statement footnotes, and this will be deemed sufficient.

In this context, the probability judgment boils down to a yes/no assessment. That is, legal liability is projected to be "probable" or "not probable." But let's think about that for a moment. Could a company numerically estimate the likelihood of losing a lawsuit, and incorporate the result into a probability-weighted liability on its balance sheet? Yes, I believe it could.

With regard to the second criterion, above: in their financial statement footnotes, companies often conclude that a potential contingent liability is "not estimable." This eliminates the need to attach a value to what may become a significant future cash outflow. And yet, in the preceding chapter, we saw that companies can and do make a host of estimates concerning accounts receivable, depreciable assets, and postretirement health-care benefits. In my judgment, they should be required to make their best estimates regarding contingent liabilities as well, and then include these figures on their balance sheets, or at least in their financial statement footnotes.

Companies argue—with some merit—that including in their financial statements the potential impact of events that "might happen," as opposed to reporting the actual impact of those which "have happened," will weaken the reliability of financial reporting. This, of course, keeps contingent liabilities off their balance sheets. This is the state of affairs today. It is likely to remain so for the foreseeable future. Consequently, with regard to litigation-related contingent liabilities, we'll continue to see financial statement footnotes that include passages much like the following excerpts from an annual report issued by Altria, the parent company of Philip Morris.

Insider's Note

Millions of dollars in corporate contingent liabilities are never discussed in monetary terms in the financial statement footnotes, let alone ever presented on the balance sheet.

The paragraphs of Figure 9.3 were extracted from a recent Altria annual report, after reading through about 10 pages concerning tobacco-related litigation contingencies. In those pages, Altria describes major cases decided for and against the company, as well as the status of numerous pending suits, both in the United States and overseas. In this disclosure, the

[Altria] and its subsidiaries record provisions in the
consolidated financial statements for pending litigation
when they determine that an unfavorable outcome is
probable and the amount of the loss can be reasonably
estimated. Except as discussed elsewhere in this [note]: (i)
management has not concluded that it is probable that a loss has
been incurred in any of the pending tobacco-related litigation; (ii) management is unable to make a meaningful estimate of the amount or range
of loss that could result from an unfavorable outcome of pending tobacco-
related litigation; and (iii) accordingly, management has not provided any
amounts in the consolidated financial statements for unfavorable outcomes, if any.

The present legislative and litigation environment is substantially
uncertain, and it is possible that the business and volume of [Altria's]
subsidiaries, as well as Altria Groups, Inc.'s consolidated results of operations, cash flows or financial position could be materially affected by an
unfavorable outcome or settlement of certain pending litigation or by the
enactment of federal or state tobacco legislation.

Figure 9.3 Excerpt from an Altria Contingent Liability Disclosure

company does state that it has reported some income statement expense
and balance sheet liability amounts (i.e., "record provisions") for those situations where management believes losses are probable and estimable. It is
my assumption that those accrued amounts are for the cases that have been
lost, and in which all appeals have been exhausted. It is not clear from all the
footnote verbiage that that is the case, but the narrative seems to suggest it.

More important, however, is the clear statement in the footnote excerpt that no expense or liability has been recorded for many of the pending lawsuits because management does not believe the losses are probable
or estimable. Given all the prior history with such lawsuits and the growing
public sentiment against large tobacco companies, I must admit, that is an
interesting position to take. Readers can take comfort in the fact that auditors

have signed off on the company's financial statements and associated foot-notes, and that this disclosure would have been part of the package that they reviewed and deemed appropriate. And, to be fair, Altria has adhered to GAAP and we are told that if certain cases are lost, the financial effects could be material. We're not told, however, how material. We might well ask ourselves: if the company lost these cases, would it simply endure a couple of years of net losses, or would it slide into bankruptcy? Other firms have suffered the latter fate, with no warning in their annual reports.

The Inside Scoop

Annual reports, and financial statements in particular, have a tabular, nu-merical look that conveys a sense of precision, specificity, accuracy, and—as a result—completeness. In this chapter, however, we've seen that they are not comprehensive.

Financial statements exclude several important pieces of informa-tion. Internally created intangible assets, for example, generally do not appear on a company's balance sheet. Even such highly valuable, mission-critical assets as Coca-Cola's brand or Microsoft's resident intellectual capital cannot be found in their respective firms' financial statements. To learn more about such intangibles, which often play crucial roles in the success and future of a company, interested parties must pursue other sources of information, such as financial analysts' reports and the busi-ness press.

Several important liabilities—or potential liabilities—are also pre-sented in an incomplete manner, or not at all, in corporate financial state-ments. Operating leases, for example, constitute a means of off-balance-sheet financing. The gross liability and plan assets for defined-benefit pension plans and postretirement health-care benefits do not appear on balance sheets either. The potential obligations related to contingent liabilities are also frequently omitted from these statements. Companies present infor-mation about these liabilities, rather, in their financial statement footnotes. Even there, however, disclosures on these subjects often leave much to be desired. Let's be clear. All of these omissions are a function of current GAAP—not a function of devious corporate managers or remiss external auditors. GAAP would need to change for these items to be included in the financial statements.

Practical Application

Brands: Often Not There

To see just how much brands can be worth—and how little of this may appear on their owner's balance sheet—let's consider a recent PepsiCo annual report MD&A excerpt (see Figure 9.4).

In its financial statement footnotes in that same annual report, PepsiCo reported $2.5 billion, before amortization (in essence, depreciation), for the brands reported on its balance sheet. At about the same time, however, the Interbrand annual ranking of "Best Global Brands," published in *Business Week*, valued PepsiCo's brands at $12.9 billion.[4]

What do we learn from this? First, from the annual report, we learn that PepsiCo distinguishes between the brands it creates internally and those which it acquires through marketplace transactions. When it spends money on the former, it expenses these funds as incurred. As a result, the development of internally created brands does not lead to a posting of assets on the balance sheet. When PepsiCo acquires brands developed by others outside the company, however, this does affect its balance sheet. Its financial statement footnotes show a $2.5 billion historical cost associated with the purchase of certain brands. PepsiCo has amortized its investment in some of these brands, yielding a balance sheet figure for purchased brands of about $1.8 billion—roughly 28% less than their original cost. And yet, none of these figures even approaches the value estimated for PepsiCo's brands by an objective third party. If Interbrand's $12.9 billion valuation is correct, PepsiCo holds an unrecorded asset worth $11.1 billion (that is, $12.9 billion–$1.8 billion). This unreported figure is equal to more than

> We sell products under a number of brand names, many of which were developed by us. The brand development costs are expensed as incurred. We also purchase brands . . . in acquisitions. Upon acquisition, the purchase price is first allocated to identifiable assets and liabilities, including brands, based on estimated fair value, with any remaining purchase price recorded as goodwill.

Figure 9.4 Excerpt from a PepsiCo Annual Report MD&A Discussion of Brands

one-third of the monetary amount of all the assets PepsiCo *does* report on its balance sheet! Such a situation is in accordance with GAAP and not unusual for companies with long-standing, recognizable brands.

Operating Leases: Off-balance Sheet

Assume you saw the financial statement footnote depicted in Figure 9.5 in a corporate annual report. What monetary amounts would you expect to find on the company's balance sheet—as assets and liabilities—related to these leases?

The answer: none at all. From a financial reporting perspective, *capital* leases are viewed as a means of acquiring assets with borrowed funds. They are therefore posted to a company's balance sheet. But this excerpt concerns *operating*—not capital—leases. And from a financial reporting perspective, an operating lease is viewed as a mere period-to-period rental. Consequently, the company in this example would not include in its balance sheet any part of its $350 million in operating leases. It would not show the leased goods as assets. It would not show its operating lease obligations as liabilities. It would merely record periodic rent payments as

We have operating leases for production plants, administrative offices, distribution centers, vehicles, and information systems. The operating leases expire at various dates thereafter. The future minimum rentals for all noncancellable operating leases are:

(Amounts in thousands)	Future minimum rentals
Due at end of next year	$ 35,200
Due at end of the second year	34,700
Due at end of third year	33,500
Due at end of fourth year	31,200
Due at end of fifth year	25,900
Due at end of sixth year and beyond	189,500
Total	$ 350,000

Figure 9.5 Sample Lease Footnote Disclosure

expenses on its income statement. For this reason, the use of assets under operating lease arrangements is frequently referred to as off-balance-sheet financing.

Defined-Benefit Pension Plans: Net Not Gross

Most publicly traded companies include in the footnotes of their annual reports a set of disclosures on employee benefit plans. If a company maintains a defined-benefits pension plan, it will display in these footnotes three key line items pertaining to it. By way of example, consider Figure 9.6.

On the basis of such disclosed data, can we determine whether this company's plan is over- or underfunded? We can indeed. It's underfunded by $190 million. That is, while the company has incurred pension obligations of $478 million to its current and retired employees, it has set aside only $288 million to fulfill these. Assuming the company doesn't terminate its plan, it will have to make up the resulting $190 million shortfall at some time in the future.

This raises a further question: Where do these substantial figures appear on the company's balance sheet? Actually, of these three dollar amounts, only the $190 million—the funding shortfall—appears on the balance sheet. And its inclusion has only recently been required. The company's $478 million in benefit obligations and $288 in plan assets are not on the balance sheet.

Contingent Liabilities

Many corporations include a line item in the liabilities section of their balance sheets titled "Commitments and contingencies," or words to that

(Amounts in millions)	Defined-benefit pension plans
Benefit obligation, end of year	$478
Plan assets at fair value, end of year	$288
Funded status of plans, end of year	($190)

Figure 9.6 Partial Pension Plan Footnote Disclosure

effect. More often than not, this line shows no monetary amount. Its purpose is to notify readers that the company has some commitments and contingencies which did not warrant a monetary posting on the balance sheet. The line is also intended to direct readers to the financial statement footnotes for further information.

But this raises a question: If a company has contingent liabilities, why aren't they reported—monetarily—on the balance sheet? The answer: The company did not deem them to be both *probable* and *estimable*. For a contingent liability to appear on the balance sheet, it must fulfill both of those criteria.

In its financial statement footnote on contingencies, a company will usually describe, in general terms, the different categories of lawsuits pending against it. It will discuss the nature and status of various suits. These narratives often include language along the following lines: "We cannot estimate the possible loss or range of loss which may arise from these lawsuits." This explains why the balance sheet includes no monetary amount for contingent liabilities. Confronted by such language, we might infer that a loss is "probable," as the company offers no statement to the contrary. If that is the case, however, it raises yet another question: If contingent liabilities are probable, how could they be totally nonestimable, either individually or collectively? In light of the many estimates that companies make all the time for other balance sheet items, weighting contingencies in the light of probabilities and experience, seems doable. Yet, we're often told: contingencies are nonestimable. GAAP sanctions such a conclusion. Auditors verify it. We must accept it.

In Anticipation of the Next Secret

Hopefully someone will say the emperor has no clothes on when he doesn't.

Secret #10

It's Blessed (Most of the Time)

Of controls and certifications

The questions behind Secret #10:

- What assurance do we have that corporate financial stories are not fiction?
- What do external auditors do?
- Who are the other audit-related groups involved in corporate financial reporting and what do they do?
- What is an audit failure?

Think about all the third-party assurances we have in our daily lives. As I walk through my home, I see the Underwriters Laboratories insignia on electrical products, the Green Seal check mark on environmentally friendly products, and the AAA logo on brochures for hotels and auto repair shops. Such symbols (see Figure 10.1) signify that knowledgeable experts have, on our behalf, verified that a product or service has met certain performance standards.

In addition and in the United States, we appreciate that the meat we eat has been processed according to USDA requirements; the airplanes we buckle into have been FAA approved; and our places of work are subject to OSHA safety standards. Our lives are populated with third-party reviews and assurances, many of which we take for granted.

Note: Symbols reproduced with permission.

The UL mark is owned by Underwriters Laboratories, Inc.

Figure 10.1 Popular Symbols Conveying Assurances

It is probably not an overstatement to declare that the reviews and assurances that external auditors bring to the financial marketplace are also taken for granted. They are taken for granted until they fail us. All it took was the collapse of Enron to put auditors on the front page of every newspaper in the country. As a result, they became the focus of a speech by the leader of the free world (George W. Bush) and the target of a massive legislative reform (the Sarbanes-Oxley Act). The external auditor's assurance attached to Enron's financial statements and relied on by the financial marketplace was found to be without merit and billions of dollars of retirement account, college fund, and rainy-day savings were destroyed almost overnight.

Auditing = Assessing = Attesting

The financial markets need and rely on independent, third-party, well qualified, tough-minded external auditors to render professional audits. Those audits are aimed at assessing and attesting to three things: First, do a company's financial statements conform to GAAP? Second, does the company have an effective system of internal financial controls? Third, taken as a whole, do the financial statements present fairly the company's financial condition and performance? The external audit function plays a vital role in communicating to the financial marketplace

Insider's Note

Financial statements without an external auditor's blessing are more likely to contain inaccuracies and misleading information than financial statements that have been reviewed and blessed by an external auditor.

whether or not a company's financial story may be believed. Without the proper functioning of the external audit, the autobiographical financial performance stories that companies publish would run the risk of being totally self-serving, perhaps to the point of misleading or even false.

Audit Opinions

As a result of a typical external audit, auditors render three key opinions that are communicated to the public along with the audited company's financial statements. The first pertains to the fairness of the financial statements. Second, recall from an earlier chapter that an annual report must contain a letter from the company's CEO and CFO regarding the reliability of their company's internal financial controls. External auditors must review that letter and report to you and me whether or not they agree with the CEO and CFO's evaluation. The third opinion rendered by the external auditor pertains to their direct assessment of the adequacy of the company's internal financial control systems. Figures 10.2 and 10.3 are prototypes of good news audit opinions pertaining to each of these three foci.

Insider's Note

A typical annual report contains three evaluative opinions rendered by the company's external auditor. Be sure to read these.

The key words in these audit reports are: "present fairly" and "maintained in all material respects effective internal control." These words convey the auditors' opinion that in all significant ways, everything is OK. These are the words the company wants to hear. These are the words financial analysts want to hear. These are the words you should look for when reviewing a company's annual report. In essence, the auditors are saying that the company's autobiographical performance story is a viable story. Words to the contrary from the external auditor seldom appear in an annual report. When they do, assume the financial story presented in that annual report is, in part, not as reliable as we would prefer.

The Art of Auditing

To quickly get a feel for the nature of the external audit task, consider this question. If you had to attest to the accuracy of my personal tax return for

We have audited the accompanying balance sheets of W Company as of December 31, 20x3, and 20x2, and the related statements of operations, stockholders' equity, and cash flows for each of the three years in the period ended December 31, 20x3. These financial statements are the responsibility of the Company's management. Our responsibility is to express an opinion on these financial statements based on our audits.

We conducted our audits in accordance with the standards of the Public Company Accounting Oversight Board (United States). Those standards require that we plan and perform the audit to obtain reasonable assurance about whether the financial statements are free of material misstatement. An audit includes examining, on a test basis, evidence supporting the amounts and disclosures in the financial statements. An audit also includes assessing the accounting principles used and significant estimates made by management, as well as evaluating the overall financial statement presentation. We believe that our audits provide a reasonable basis for our opinion.

In our opinion, the financial statements referred to above *present fairly,* in all material respects, the financial position of the Company as of [at] December 31, 20x3 and 20x2, and the results of its operations and its cash flows for each of the three years in the period ended December 31, 20x3, in conformity with U.S. generally accepted accounting principles.

Source: Public Company Accounting Oversight Board Web site (May 2007, Emphasis added).

Figure 10.2 Example of an External Auditor's Unqualified Opinion on a Client's Financial Statements

this year, how would you do that? Chances are you would ask to see evidence (i.e., supporting documents) justifying all of the line item amounts listed on it. For example, to validate the amount reported for charitable donations, you would ask for copies of cancelled checks or receipts from the charitable organizations. On the other hand, to verify that the line items with zeros were valid, you would probably ask me questions related

We have audited management's assessment . . . that W Company maintained effective internal control over financial reporting as of December 31, 20x3, based on criteria established in Internal Control—Integrated framework issued by the Committee of Sponsoring Organizations of the Treadway Commission. W Company's management is responsible for maintaining effective internal control over financial reporting and for its assessment of the effectiveness of internal control over financial reporting. Our responsibility is to express an opinion on management's assessment and an opinion on the effectiveness of the company's internal control over financial reporting based on our audit.

We conducted our audit in accordance with the standards of the Public Company Accounting Oversight Board (United States). Those standards require that we plan and perform the audit to obtain reasonable assurance about whether effective internal control over financial reporting was maintained in all material respects. Our audit included obtaining an understanding of internal control over financial reporting, evaluating management's assessment, testing and evaluating the design and operating effectiveness of internal control, and performing such other procedures as we considered necessary in the circumstances. We believe that our audit provides a reasonable basis for our opinion.

A company's internal control over financial reporting is a process designed to provide reasonable assurance regarding the reliability of financial reporting and the preparation of financial statements for external purposes in accordance with generally accepted accounting principles. A company's internal control over financial reporting includes those policies and procedures that (1) pertain to the maintenance of records that, in reasonable detail, accurately and fairly reflect the transactions and dispositions of the assets of the

(continued)

Figure 10.3 Example of an External Auditor's Unqualified Opinion on: (1) Management's Assessment of the Effectiveness of Internal Control over Financial Reporting, and (2) on the Effectiveness of Internal Control over Financial Reporting

Figure 10.3 (*continued*)

company; (2) provide reasonable assurance that transactions are recorded as necessary to permit preparation of financial statements in accordance with generally accepted accounting principles, and that receipts and expenditures of the company are being made only in accordance with authorizations of management and directors of the company; and (3) provide reasonable assurance regarding prevention or timely detection of unauthorized acquisition, use, or disposition of the company's assets that could have a material effect on the financial statements.

Because of its inherent limitations, internal control over financial reporting may not prevent or detect misstatements. Also, projections of any evaluation of effectiveness to future periods are subject to the risk that controls may become inadequate because of changes in conditions, or that the degree of compliance with the policies or procedures may deteriorate.

In our opinion, management's assessment that W Company maintained effective internal control over financial reporting as of December 31, 20x3, *is fairly stated,* in all material respects, based on criteria established in Internal Control—Integrated Framework issued by the Committee of Sponsoring Organizations of the Treadway Commission. *Also in our opinion,* W Company *maintained, in all material respects, effective internal control* over financial reporting as of December 31, 20x3, based on criteria established in Internal Control—Integrated Framework issued by the Committee of Sponsoring Organizations of the Treadway Commission.

We have also audited, in accordance with the standards of the Public Company Accounting Oversight Board (United States), the balance sheets as of December 31, 20x3, and 20x2, and the related statements of operations, stockholders' equity, and cash flows for each of the three years in the period ended December 31, 20x3 of W Company and our report . . . expressed an unqualified opinion.

Source: Public Company Accounting Oversight Board Web site (May 2007, emphasis added.)

to those line items and see if my answers sounded reasonable to you. For example, if you saw that I did not report any interest income, you would probably ask if I had any interest-bearing bank accounts. You would expect me to say no. If you were a bit skeptical about my "no" answer though, you might send letters to the local banks asking if they had any accounts in my name. Again, you would expect the bank's answers to be "no." Such is the probing process of obtaining corroborating evidence to support the tax return information I filed.

The audit of a company's financial statements and internal controls over their financial transactions begs the same question: how would you go about attesting to the appropriateness of those financial statements and the reliable functioning of those systems? Like your audit of my tax return, the task involves obtaining corroborating evidence from reliable sources to support the financial statement items reported (and not reported) and to verify that sound financial controls are in place and working.

Visualize the millions of financial transactions that Microsoft must process every year. Unlike the financial transactions that I engage in during the course of the year that are represented in my tax return and that you could comprehensively review, there is no way an auditor can review every one of Microsoft's financial transactions. Thus, the external audit process is one of selective testing and review, all done in a carefully planned, scientific way. Statistical sampling techniques are used and mathematical confidence levels are calculated as auditors aim to render their ultimate audit conclusion. That is why the audit opinions presented above repeatedly mention *reasonable assurance* as opposed to complete, or total, or precise assurance that things are as they should be. Audits are not endeavors to verify 100% of all financial statement details. They are rigorous endeavors geared to gain well grounded, statistically supportable, reasonable assurances regarding the information contained in the financial statements and the financial control systems designed to accurately process, capture, and codify a company's financial transactions.

> ### Insider's Note
>
> *External audit activities focus on gathering evidence to provide reasonable assurance regarding the appropriateness of the contents of a company's financial statements.*

The external audit process requires healthy skepticism. For a moment, assume you are a corporate executive and you are fully aware that implementing GAAP involves judgments, estimates, and choices—all of which affect reported financial results. Would you prefer to report in your financial statements: (1) more revenues or less? (2) more expenses or less? (3) more liabilities or less? Your answers, in order, would probably be "more, less, and less." Moreover, if your year-end bonus calculation was a function of GAAP-based financial results, the most self-serving estimates, judgments, and choices might be quite tempting to make. Now, an external auditor should: (1) anticipate such possibilities, and (2) devise audit tests to assess whether or not a client has erroneously or maliciously violated GAAP in striving to report more revenues, less expenses, and less liabilities. Auditors must bring a healthy skepticism to bear on all their clients in order to evaluate the appropriateness of the company's financial story portrayed in their annual report.

Here are some of the specific ways auditors obtain evidence to verify the information contained in a company's financial statements. Audits generally include various and repeated combinations of the following:

- Written or oral inquiry to third parties and/or client management
- Observation of company personnel at work
- Inspection and counting of assets
- Third-party confirmations
- Examination of company supporting documents
- Re-performance of company procedures or calculations
- Mathematical reasonableness tests

Consider, for a moment, just the inventory asset account an audit client might possess. It is common for the external auditor to physically count all, or a sample of, that company's year-end inventory in order to verify its existence. Similarly, the auditor would send letters to a client's customers, asking them to confirm the year-end monetary amounts they owe the client for the goods they have received but not paid for yet. To ascertain whether the LIFO inventory method has been properly applied, an auditor would review the client's calculations, recalculating some of those figures. As an overall check on the reasonableness of a company's cost of goods sold expense on the income statement, an auditor would calculate the gross margin percentage (i.e., (sales – cost of goods sold) ÷ sales) to see if it is in line with prior years' percentages. Indeed, the art of auditing is finding the most reliable and the most objective sources of evidence to support the financial figures reported by the company.

Auditors and Audit Firms

It is possible that somewhere, sometime, someone will write a version of Willie Nelson's famous song, "Mamas Don't Let Your Babies Grow Up To Be Cowboys" and title it, "Mamas Don't Let Your Babies Grow Up To Be Auditors." I hope not . . . it is a noble and needed profession. In spite of the infamous Enron audit failure, there are thousands of auditors around the world doing a magnificent job of providing sound, positive assessments of corporate financial statements, where warranted. To render such assessments, an auditor must be a licensed certified public accountant (CPA) in the United States and the equivalent elsewhere in the world (e.g., a Chartered Accountant in the United Kingdom and a *Wirtschaftsprüfer* in Germany). Generally, CPAs can practice their profession just as doctors and lawyers do—alone as a sole practitioner or in small, medium-sized, or even large groups. As you might expect, the largest audit firms are the ones that audit the major, publicly held companies like Toyota, IBM, and Unilever.

Auditors have a body of standards that they must follow in conducting their audits. In the United States, auditing standards are promulgated by the Public Companies Accounting Oversight Board (PCAOB) which establishes:

- appropriate codes of conduct for auditors
- minimum quality control standards for audit firms
- required audit processes and procedures for obtaining and evaluating audit evidence, and
- appropriate means for dealing with audits that uncover client financial reporting deficiencies

Any of the more than 1,500 audit firms registered with the PCAOB, and their member auditors, who violate the PCAOB's auditing standards are subject to sanctions levied at the discretion of

Insider's Note

External auditors have professional and legal guidelines they must follow aimed at insuring the quality of their audits.

the Securities and Exchange Commission (SEC), the PCAOB, and any U.S. court.

Today, the world's largest audit firms are collectively referred to as the "Big 4." Not too long ago, there was a "Big 8." But, just as the corporate mergers of Boeing with McDonnell-Douglas, Northrup with Grumman, AOL with Time Warner, and Exxon with Mobil have reduced the number of players in their respective industries, so too have a number of recent audit firm consolidations served to reduce the number of large, global players in the auditing industry. Even though there are over 1,500 audit firms registered with the PCAOB, the truth is that the "Big 4" account for a disproportionate share of the audits of the companies traded on the U.S. stock exchanges. The ancestral roots of the "Big 4" audit firms go back to the mid-nineteenth century. The firm names today frequently still carry the names of their nineteenth-century founders, men who had a calling to be the eyes and ears of absentee corporate owners. If there is a bit of the genealogist in you, you might find Figure 10.4 of interest.

In spite of any noble historical lineage shown in Figure 10.4 (before you wonder aloud, no, I am not related to Charles Waldo Haskins, who was one of the founding partners of Haskins & Sells), the "Big 4" firms have a critical and mostly thankless role to play in our current financial environment. Like it or not, they are the most visible, most vulnerable, and most important standard-bearers for the auditing profession. The men and women of the Big 4 must strive to be ever-better advocates for you and I, the absentee owners of the companies they audit. They must nurture and believe in the societal stewardship role they play. Yes, they are businessmen and -women in their own right, seeking to run their firms profitably and successfully, but they are first and foremost called to audit on our behalf. That is true for the "Big 4" and for all audit firms that audit publicly held companies.

Additional Audit Actors

So far, the discussion of auditors has focused on external, independent auditors. These are the non-company employees who arrive during the course of the year to check on things. Publicly held companies are required to open their doors to them. There are, however, two other important

Firm roots go back at least to:	Firm			
1849	Whinney, Smith & Whinney			
		1979 Ernst & Whinney		
1903	**Ernst & Ernst**			
			1989 ***Ernst & Young***	
1894	**Arthur Young & Co.**			
1917	Klynveld, Main, Goerdler			
		1987 ***KPMG***		
1870	**Peat, Marwick, Mitchell**			
1854	**Coopers & Lybrand**			
		1998 ***PricewaterhouseCoopers***		
1849	**Price Waterhouse & Co.**			
1854	Deloitte, Plender, Griffin			
		1978 Deloitte, Haskins & Sells		
1886	**Haskins & Sells**		1989 ***Deloitte & Touche***	
1900	**Touche Ross & Co.**			
1913	**Arthur Andersen & Co.**	➤ —2002 mostly defunct—		

Note: Firms in bold roman font, were referred to as the Big 8 for many years. The firms in bold and italics are the current Big 4.

Figure 10.4 Genealogy of the "Big 4" Audit Firms

audit-related parties that operate within the walls of the companies whose stocks and bonds we buy and sell.

The IA Group

Frequently, movies and television shows that center on the activities and intrigue within a police department depict either good cops who are wrongly accused of misdeeds or bad cops who seem to be getting away with misdeeds. There is, however, the inevitable moment in the show when IA—the Internal Affairs group—gets involved. In a police department setting, IA is the in-house group of investigators who are above reproach, report directly to the police commissioner, have direct access to a powerful outside authority, and who are given free rein to investigate the activities and personnel of the police department. As we watch the IA team arrive on the scene, we are always led to believe that they will root out the truth, leaving no stone unturned, and that their mere presence induces worry, anxiety, and a bit of fear among those likely to be touched by their investigation.

With much less drama but with no less purpose, companies have their own IA groups—internal auditors. These professionals perform many of the same tasks that the external auditors do, they just do it on a continuous basis and as employees of the company. In multinational, and in multi-divisional domestic companies, internal auditors frequently travel to numerous, far-flung company sites to perform their tests. What are they testing? They are striving to verify that: (1) financial data processing systems are functioning well, (2) policies and procedures of the company are adhered to, and (3) appropriate safeguards are in place and working to protect the assets of the company. With their intimate knowledge of the company, internal auditors make a significant contribution to the reliability of the financial data that flows into a company's annual report. As a colleague once asserted, internal auditors are the "moral hard wiring" of an organization.

> ## Insider's Note
>
> *A company's internal audit group makes a valuable, daily contribution to the financial reporting process that leads to the publication of a corporate annual report.*

The AC Group

In some quarters, AC refers to Atlantic City, New Jersey, the city that by its own admission is "always turned on." In financial quarters, AC is shorthand for the audit committee of a company's board of directors. By the admission of many who have historically observed and relied on audit committees to be an active and vital part of a company's corporate governance, ACs have not always been earnestly tuned in to their task. Whether that is true or not

> ## Insider's Note
>
> *Corporate audit committees are a vital part of a company's board of directors governance structure. They hire, compensate, and oversee the external auditor.*

is debatable and it is also irrelevant in this post-Enron era. It is irrelevant because it is now very clear that audit committees must:

- consist of independent board members (i.e., no company executives)
- have at least one member who is a financial expert, with all other members being at least financially savvy
- hire, compensate, and oversee the external auditor
- be the company group to whom the external auditor reports
- preapprove any and all auditing services conducted by the external auditors and any other pertinent, audit-related parties
- establish and implement procedures for receiving, inviting, addressing, and keeping confidential any complaints pertaining to auditing and accounting issues

Audit committees are in a position of authority and power to expect, demand, and probe until they get clear answers to their questions. The rest of the board of directors depends, to a great extent, on the AC to fulfill the overall board's fiduciary financial responsibility. An AC must continuously assess its company's financial results in the context of the tone set by the top executives, the nature of the company's business and industry, and the pressures/temptations created by the company's executive compensation plans and the stock market's expectations regarding the company's earnings performance. As is true of external auditors, healthy skepticism should be an AC hallmark.

Auditors ≠ Saints

What do the following organizations have in common?

WorldCom	Adelphia Communications
Tyco International	Xerox Corporation
HealthSouth Corp.	Waste Management Inc.
MicroStrategy Inc.	Miniscribe Corp.
Gemstar-TV Guide Int'l.	Qwest Communications
Sunbeam Products, Inc.	Baptist Foundation of Arizona
Royal Ahold	Rite Aid Corp.

Along with Enron, they have had, or are alleged to have had, a modern day, significant audit failure. An audit fails when the external auditor fails to find, or fails to require a change in, a corporate financial reporting disclosure or practice that was subsequently deemed inappropriate, misleading, and/or fraudulent by an authoritative body such as the SEC or a court of law. These were organizations that failed, on at least one occasion, to adhere to what was expected of them and their internal auditors, external auditors, and/or audit committees failed to uncover the financial misrepresentations. These disasters, and others similar to them, generate substantial monetary losses and tarnished reputations that are difficult to rebuild.

What do Cynthia Cooper and Sherron Watkins have in common? Were they two sprinters on the U.S. track and field gold medal relay team? Did they have the number 1 country and western hit this past summer? Nope. They were two of the three "Persons of the Year 2002" as named by *Time* magazine. In particular, Cynthia Cooper blew the whistle on the accounting shenanigans at WorldCom and Sherron Watkins blew the whistle at Enron. For their bold adherence to the notion of what was right, they were recognized as exemplars of how to stand tall against extensive personal and financial pressures to remain silent. At one level, we can celebrate them and what they did. On another level, it is deeply disappointing that we needed them. We so want to assume that the financial story conveyed by companies is fair, honest, and accurate. We so want to believe that the audit parties have acted in our best interest and have diligently executed their tests and exercised tough-minded judgments. In most companies, most of the time, such views are justified. Ah, but we are naïve to hold such views without bringing to bear a bit of our own knowledge, our own healthy skepticism, and our own diligence in using multiple sources of information in evaluating a company's financial situation.

Who Pays the Auditors?

As has been mentioned several times throughout this book, financial reporting, and even the role of auditors, is a dynamic, evolving component of the financial marketplace. GAAP changes, audit guidelines change, and shareholder expectations increase. Who knows what the audit function of 2020 will look like? There is, however, an interesting aspect of the audit arena that, in my opinion, should change and would be easy to change in a very short time.

There is an inherent contradiction in the basic nature of the auditor/client/public relationship. For some, me included, this inherent contradiction is thought to be at the root of some audit failures. What is the contradiction? Well, for the moment, consider the following—then draw your own conclusion.[1]

It is axiomatic that auditors are to conduct audits as the investing public's informed, inquisitive, independent agent. Historically though, public companies have solicited, selected, and paid the external auditor who performs their mandated audit. For a very long time the financial community relied on the personal integrity of individual auditors as the last line of defense against a client's exploitation of the financial reporting rules, and against outright fraudulent behavior. The heartbreaking audit failures we too frequently have read about suggest that those client pressures grew past the tipping point, at least for some auditors. The cost of those failures by a handful of individual auditors to the financial community, to the auditing profession, and to their audit firms is staggering.

At least as far back as the early seventeenth century, an enduring and well-known payment principle was established—*who pays the piper, calls the tune* (see "The Legend of The Pied Paper of Hamelin"). In this, the twenty-first century, the principle still holds. I believe investor confidence in a company's reported financial results—as well as the integrity of the external audit itself—would be greatly enhanced by changing *who calls the tune* and to do that requires changing *who pays the piper*.

Shareholders need to call the tune—after all, the audit is conducted for their benefit. Given the dispersion and transience of stockholder interests, some might say this is impossible, but not so. Since stockholder interests coalesce in the stock exchanges, it seems reasonable that the stock exchanges should hire and compensate the auditors who audit their listees' financial statements.[2] Such an arrangement would

Insider's Note

Rather than the company audited hiring and paying the external auditor, why not have the SEC or the stock exchanges do that on behalf of investors?

better align the interests of shareholders and auditors. In one simple move, real external audit independence, objectivity, and stewardship of a public trust would take center stage. No such new arrangement is in the works—maybe some day.

The Inside Scoop

Auditing and auditors are important. They are the eyes and ears of those of us who entrust companies with our retirement funds, our college education accounts, and our savings. Internal and external auditors, together with the audit committee of a company's board of directors, all serve to provide assurances that the financial reports we receive are fair and complete depictions of how our money was put to use and what that money produced in the way of returns (or the lack thereof).

Auditors and audit committees have not always lived up to their responsibilities. For sure, business press headlines have announced many such failings. But, with the passage of the Sarbanes-Oxley Act in 2002, the creation of the Public Company Accounting Oversight Board in 2003, and the improved independence and auditing standards pertaining to external auditors (and to audit committees, for that matter), the future looks positive for better corporate governance, better audits, and for better financial reporting.

Practical Application

The Philosophy of Auditing is one of the classic books in the auditing arena. It may be hard to imagine that there is an actual philosophy of auditing, never mind one conveyed in nearly 250 pages of finely crafted prose and logic, but there is. Among other things, the book's authors posit that "auditing is concerned with *social responsibility* and *ethical conduct* as well as with the *collection and evaluation of evidence*" (emphasis added).[3] In cementing some of the key points made in this chapter, let's focus on the three italicized parts of this quote. What is an external auditor's social responsibility? Why is ethical conduct a critical dimension of the external audit function? Why is there an external audit focus on both the collection and evaluation of evidence?

Social Responsibility

Bluntly, external auditors are ultimately not accountable to the companies that hire them. External auditors are the eyes and ears of all current and future investors in, and lenders to, the companies they audit. Auditors audit for our benefit and on our behalf. They are the independent experts making sure the financial statements and disclosures a company publishes in its annual report fairly portray the company's financial condition and results of operations. Moreover, they are to make sure the company is in compliance with all applicable financial reporting guidelines and that it has a well-functioning system of financial controls that safeguards the company's assets and fosters the recording of accurate financial data. In short and in the extreme, external auditors are the public's assurance that the financial stories published by companies are works of nonfiction, not fiction. It is the presumed reliability of audited corporate financial statements that undergirds the fair and open marketplace in which companies raise capital for fueling corporate growth and renewal.

Ethical Conduct

Even though the number and magnitude of audit failures around the turn of the millennium was shocking, we must insist on and, more importantly, we must assume that auditors are intent on fulfilling their fiduciary role. If current and future shareholders cannot count on the professionalism, good intentions, moral integrity, thoughtful reflection, and bulldog tenacity of external auditors, the part of their audit report that begins . . . *in our opinion* . . . is meaningless. If we cannot rely on their opinion because their commitment to ethical conduct is suspect, their audit conclusions are meaningless.

Historically, the audit profession is based on trust. Corporate owners and lenders often do not have the access or the ability to measure a company's performance and observe the use of their money. External auditors play a key role in making sure owners and lenders receive a clear picture of corporate performance. Owners and lenders trust external auditors to represent their views.

Collection and Evaluation of Evidence

It is possible to do an entire audit of a company's financial statements by simply asking corporate management to explain how they measured various financial items and why they included some things and not others. For sure, the financial statements are the responsibility of management and they do craft them every year. But simply asking management to explain what and why they did certain things does not mean that that is actually what they did, or that they did it correctly, or that there weren't more appropriate ways to do it. Auditors must bring to bear, as much as they can, independently obtained evidence in support of how management crafted their financial statements.

So, on one front, external auditors must know what sort of evidence is needed in specific situations to buttress what is and is not included in the financial statements. Second, once pertinent and useful evidence is obtained, external auditors must be able to evaluate whether it does or does not support the financial story crafted by the company. If upon evaluation the evidence does not support what the company chose to report, external auditors must insist that the financial statements be adjusted and brought in line with what their judgment believes is the required (or better) presentation. To do all this well, external auditors must be rigorously trained, serve a multiyear apprenticeship, pass a multiday certification exam, and regularly participate in continuing education throughout their professional lives.

In Anticipation of the Next Secret

At the Academy Awards® extravaganza, the women wear some beautiful gowns. Bet you never thought about how important that unseen, nonglamorous, widely relied on, double-sided, sticky tape is. It's a bit like financial reporting and annual reports—very important.

Secret #11

It's Important

Perfect? No! Useful? Yes!

The questions behind Secret #11:

- How can financial statement data be used to garner important corporate performance insights?
- Do the DuPont ratios apply to companies other than DuPont?
- Besides performance analysis, are financial statements used for other purposes?
- What cautions and caveats should be kept in mind when analyzing financial statements?

Unlike the educator who asserted that "nobody grew taller by being measured" or the one who opined that evaluating students is "like the gardener who constantly pulls his plants up by the roots to see if they are growing," corporate annual reports can and do foster improved corporate performance.[1] Just as no employee wants to be ranked in the bottom echelon of peers, no company wants its financial performance ranked in the bottom tier of its peers.

The requirement to publicly present their company's financial performance story is one of the factors that inspires corporate executives to strive to present world-class results. Countless times I have heard CEOs challenge their executive teams to achieve top quartile or top decile financial performance in their industries on various specific financial measures.

Naturally that battle cry also applies to product quality, service excellence, and environmental stewardship. For most shareholders and lenders, though, corporate financial performance is critically important. The financial indicators determinable from annual reports help illuminate how well a company has done and is likely to do. What are some of those indicators?

Starting a Financial Statement Analysis

It is important to acknowledge that a financial statement analysis involves a couple of initial, quick assessments. First, is the external auditor's audit opinion favorable—that is, did the company receive an unqualified report? Second, are revenues and profits increasing at a steady, attractive rate? If yes, that is good. If not, that is bad, especially if that is the case several years in a row. Third, does the annual report narrative present a favorable, optimistic, strong image and desirable future or does it dwell on troubles, shortfalls, and a pessimistic future? After considering these initial, general indicators, some basic financial ratio and cash flow analysis is an informative next step in assessing corporate financial performance.

Insider's Note

A basic financial statement analysis task involves trend analysis, ratio analysis, and cash flow pattern analysis.

DuPont Financial Ratio Analysis

When our favorite sports team wins a championship, that is exciting news. Once the celebrations are over, though, a thoughtful coach will spend hours analyzing a wide array of data to ascertain what the team did really well and what aspects of its performance need improvement for next season. The same is true for a company. Your favorite company may have had a great year in terms of stock price appreciation, but the question arises: what did the company do really well and not so well? There are a host of financial metrics, mostly referred to as financial ratios, that are frequently calculated in the pursuit of detailed insights regarding particular aspects of a company's performance. Let's focus on five of those, comprising what is commonly referred to as the DuPont model (named in honor of the company first popularizing them for performance management). Those ratios are highlighted in Figure 11.1.

> **Return on sales (ROS)= Net income / Sales**
> **Asset turnover= Sales / Average total assets**
> **Return on assets (ROA)= Net income / Average total assets**
> **Financial leverage= Average total assets / Average total owners' equity**
> **Return on equity (ROE)= Net income / Average total owners' equity**

Figure 11.1 The DuPont Ratios

Pause for just a moment and look at the elements of each ratio. Where do the data come from for those calculations? Answer: The income statement and the balance sheet.[2] Second, how might each ratio be explained to Grandma, who has never had the opportunity to study financial reporting? The straightforward explanations, for any given year, are:

- If the ROS ratio for the year is 3%, that means the company earned 3 cents in profit from every $1 of sales it generated. ROS is sometimes referred to as profit margin. Managers seek to maximize the value of this metric.
- If the asset turnover ratio is 2, that means every $1 invested in assets generated $2 of sales. This metric is often used as an indicator of efficient (or inefficient) use of company assets. The higher the number, the more efficiently a company is using its assets.
- If ROA is 6%, that means the company earned 6 cents of profit from every $1 invested in assets. ROA is often a synonym for ROI—return on investment. A higher ROA is better than a lower ROA.
- If the financial leverage ratio is 2.5, that means for every $1 the owners contributed to the business, the company acquired and put in place $2.50 of assets. One additional insight is key in this regard. If the company owned $2.50 of assets for every $1 of owners' money in the business, who financed the other $1.50 of assets? Remember A = L + OE? The answer must be creditors. Managers seek to optimize the value of this ratio. Too high a ratio value indicates heavy reliance on debtors. Too low a ratio value indicates overly conservative financing strategies not taking advantage of more credit financing.

- And finally, if the ROE ratio is 15%, that means the company earned 15 cents on every $1 the owners invested in the business. Generally, the higher the ROE, the better.

Now, let's go one step further. Resurrecting what we learned in school about multiplying fractions, recall that:

$$\frac{A}{B} \times \frac{B}{C} = \frac{A}{C}$$

Note that the "B" cancels out in this multiplication. Applying that same process to the DuPont ratios we first see that:

$$\text{ROS} \times \text{Asset Turnover} = \text{ROA}$$

because the "sales" component of the ROS and the Asset Turnover ratios cancel out. Indeed,

$$\frac{\text{Net Income}}{\text{Sales}} \times \frac{\text{Sales}}{\text{Avg. Total Assets}} = \frac{\text{Net Income}}{\text{Avg. Total Assets}}$$

Then we can do it again and see that:

$$\text{ROA} \times \text{Financial Leverage} = \text{ROE}$$

because the "average total assets" figures cancel out in the ROA and Financial Leverage ratios. The details are shown as:

$$\frac{\text{Net Income}}{\text{Avg. Total Assets}} \times \frac{\text{Avg. Total Assets}}{\text{Avg. Total Owners' Equity}} = \frac{\text{Net Income}}{\text{Avg. Total Owners' Equity}}$$

So what does that highlight, and why bother? Let's focus on the last DuPont ratio first—the ROE metric. In many respects, it is a key corporate performance indicator for shareholders. It depicts what the company has earned on their behalf. How might a company management team increase its ROE?

It's time to use some numbers to answer that question. In the previous example where the ratios were interpreted for Grandma, the Figure 11.2 amounts were presented. Let's check the math in Figure 11.2. Three percent×2 does equal 6%. Then, 6%×2.5 does equal 15% . . . the arithmetic works. Clearly, I made up these numbers so that they *would* work, but the truth is, the DuPont ratios' multiplicative relationship works when using real data from real companies. From some computer company financial statements, the Figure 11.3 values for these ratios attest to the multiplicative DuPont relationships.

Here's the important point. The DuPont model depicts the fact that ROE is a function of: (1) the profit margin earned on the company's sales (ROS), (2) the efficient, productive use of company assets (asset turnover), and (3) the extent to which owners' money has been leveraged by using creditors' money (financial leverage). Just as in the cockpit of an airplane where there are various buttons, levers, and dials that the pilot can push, pull,

> **Insider's Note**
>
> *There are three ways to increase return on equity (ROE):*
>
> - *Increase ROS*
> - *Improve asset turnover*
> - *Increase financial leverage*

ROS	Asset Turnover	ROA	Financial Leverage	ROE
3%	2	6%	2.5	15%
		(3%×2=6%)		(6%×2.5=15%)

Figure 11.2 Hypothetical Values for DuPont Ratios

	ROS	Asset Turnover	ROA	Financial Leverage	ROE
Dell	6.2%	2.31	14.3%	3.33	47.6%
HP	4.4%	1.06	4.6%	2.00	9.2%
IBM	8.8%	0.90	7.9%	3.71	29.3%

Figure 11.3 Some Historical Computer Company Values for DuPont Ratios

and turn to make the plane fly higher, faster, and smoother, those who lead a company have these three basic means (margin, productivity, and leverage) at their disposal to make their plane, that is, their company, deliver better ROE for owners.

As a simple illustration of interpreting these ratios in the context of corporate managers proactively seeking to achieve a desired return for shareholders, consider the two companies in Figure 11.4 and their respective DuPont ratio amounts.

Interestingly, Figure 11.4 shows that both companies delivered the same ROE to their shareholders, albeit by two very different paths. To explore this, assume the two companies are direct competitors. Your Company's profit margin (4%) was double what My Company earned on its sales (2%). Since the two company's prices are probably similar because they serve the same customers with similar products, Your Company must have managed costs to a lower level than My Company. But Your Company used assets much less efficiently than My Company did (Your Company's asset turnover was 2 and My Company's was 5)[3]. Consequently, Your Company earned less on its assets (ROA=8%) than My Company (ROA=10%) even though Your Company had a higher ROS.

My Company looks like it might be the winner in the shareholders' eyes. Ah, not so fast. Your Company financed more of its assets with borrowed money, as indicated by its financial leverage factor of 3, than My Company did. So, with every dollar owners put into the business, Your Company was able to obtain $3 of assets (which means the other $2 came from creditors). In contrast, My Company cautiously relied on owners for proportionately more of its asset financing. This is depicted by the financial leverage factor of 2.4, retaining every $1 of owners' money resulted in only $2.40 of assets. Your Company's strategy was riskier than the My Company strategy since debt comes with contractual obligations for inter-

	ROS	Asset Turnover	ROA	Financial Leverage	ROE
My Company	2%	5	10%	2.4	24%
Your Company	4%	2	8%	3	24%

Figure 11.4 Example of Different DuPont Ratios Resulting in the Same ROE

est and principal repayments, whereas there are generally no contractual obligations to pay shareholders anything. But, Your Company's use of borrowed funds enabled it to deliver an ROE exactly equal to that presented by My Company even though My Company's ROA exceeded Your Company's.

The DuPont ratios enable annual report readers to construct similar interpretations. The key point to remember is that corporate executives strive to satisfy shareholders with ever-higher and more sustainable ROEs. To do that simply involves three factors—margin, efficient asset use, and financial leverage. The metrics for each of these are easily calculated from financial statement data.

Periodically, *Business Week, Fortune, Forbes,* and the *Financial Times* publish rank orderings of hundreds of companies using various subsets of the DuPont ratios. Yearly, and without fail, I obtain copies of one or more of these rankings and keep them nearby. They provide a very useful means for making quick and easy comparisons of companies within and across industries.[4]

Statement of Cash Flows Pattern Analysis

As mentioned in earlier chapters, the statement of cash flows (SCF) has three distinct sections, each with their own monetary subtotal. Those sections pertain to net cash flows from operations (CFFO), net cash flows from investing activities (CFFI), and net cash flows from financing events (CFFF). With just a quick, but keen eye, it is useful to note the pattern of net inflows or outflows for these three SCF sections. Such a cash flow analysis contributes to an overall sense of a company's strengths, weaknesses, challenges, and direction.

> ### Insider's Note
>
> *The statement of cash flows presents three very important subtotals. Each depicts either a net cash inflow or outflow condition.*

Let's assume the magnitude of the monetary amounts reported for these three SCF subtotals is significant. That permits us to simply focus on whether or not the SCF section subtotal is a net cash inflow (+) or a net cash outflow (−). Since there are three subtotals, each with a net inflow and a net outflow possibility, that means there are eight different combinations potentially displayed in a single SCF. Those combinations are shown in Figure 11.5.[5]

	#1	#2	#3	#4	#5	#6	#7	#8
CFFO	+	+	+	+	−	−	−	−
CFFI	+	+	−	−	−	−	+	+
CFFF	+	−	+	−	+	−	+	−

Figure 11.5 Statement of Cash Flow Patterns

No one of these patterns is particularly damning or praiseworthy for a company if it occurs for only one year. It is the continued existence of a pattern over time that lends itself to generalized interpretations regarding a company's financial performance. As an example, assume that a company has exhibited pattern #4 for the past several years. The interpretation is that this company's core operations have been generating net cash inflows (a very good thing) that, hopefully, have been increasing each year. Moreover, the net cash outflows for CFFI depict recurring investments in infrastructure, either by acquiring new companies or new property, buildings, land, and equipment. This too is a positive sign, indicative of the company's commitment to modernization and/or putting in place a foundation for future growth. Another positive sign is manifested in a net cash outflow for CFFF. Such a situation signals a net repayment of amounts owed to lenders and/or sizable payments to shareholders. Pattern #4 is the pattern that PepsiCo has displayed for several recent years.

> **Insider's Note**
>
> *Each of the eight possible cash flow patterns depicted in a statement of cash flows conveys an important, distinct message about corporate performance.*

Pattern #5 would not be an attractive pattern for a company like PepsiCo to display. A net cash outflow for CFFO indicates that a company's core business is not able to generate positive net cash flows—this is not a good thing for a mature company. On the other hand, it might not be a bad situation for a start-up company, since lenders and investors appear to be optimistic about the company. Their optimism is signaled by the net cash inflows displayed by a positive CFFF. The additional good news is that the company has used the money provided by lenders and owners to invest in productive assets that should serve it for many years. This is depicted by the net cash outflows for CFFI.

The worst recurring pattern of corporate cash flows might be pattern #8. Here, the core business operations are a net user, rather than net provider of cash, as depicted by a negative CFFO. In addition, the net negative CFFF suggests the company is not raising any further funds from owners or lenders and in fact, the company is disbursing funds to them to meet their requirements and expectations. If the core business is not generating discretionary cash for the company's use and the lenders and owners are requiring payment, where is the cash coming from to do that? From the positive CFFI, it appears that the company may be selling its crown jewels (e.g., a building, a division, a fleet of planes) to generate the cash it needs to satisfy owners and lenders. That is not a sustainable pattern. It is a pattern that investors and lenders want to note as early as possible and view as an early sign of possible financial distress.

Other Uses for Annual Reports

Financial statement analysis is a key use for published annual reports. In concert with that use, annual reports serve a number of other purposes.

Meeting Regulatory Requirements

Generally, whenever there is a public benefit to be garnered and a public harm to be avoided, regulations arise. Take for example the governmental approval process for a new pharmaceutical drug or the test all newly licensed drivers must pass. These requirements are designed to validate whether or not a new product or new driver can enter into our daily world. Similarly, airline pilots are subject to ongoing duty-hour limits and physicians, lawyers, and CPAs must obtain a stipulated amount of annual continuing education in order to maintain their licenses to practice. These mandates are designed to govern the continued functioning of a group already meeting the entrance level requirements.

Financially speaking, both scenarios—the entrance requirements and the ongoing requirements—apply to publicly held companies. In order to initially access the public debt or stock markets to raise money, companies must publish an initial set of financial statements prepared in accordance with GAAP. In order to continue to be listed on a stock exchange, companies must regularly publish GAAP-based financial statements. The privilege of gaining and maintaining access to the public financial markets carries with it the obligation to provide a minimal level of sunshine on company finances. That sunshine comes from publishing GAAP-based financial statements. The information contained in those financial statements should be useful to the public for making performance-oriented, cross-company, and multiyear comparisons. Publicly traded companies do not have a choice—they must file periodic financial reports. Failure to do so in the form, content, and timing stipulated by law can lead to denied access to, or delisting from, the public stock exchanges.

Investor-Oriented Decisions

Visualize a large corporate conference room. Seated inside are a number of individuals, many with laptops open and screens ablaze with spreadsheets. Two people are not poised over a laptop, and it is clear they are in charge—the CEO and CFO. Their staff is poised to provide them with just the right detail should they need it during the cross-examination underway. There is no prosecuting attorney pacing in front of them, firing questions with a machine gun–style staccato, but there are voices coming from a speakerphone. The CEO and CFO are engaged in a conference call. On the other end of the phone line are a number of Wall Street financial analysts sitting in distant offices, asking a variety of financial, operational, and strategic questions concerning the company's latest financial results and plans for the future.

The analysts on the call make a career out of studying the company and its industry. They have, in front of them, the company's most recent financial statements as well as a number of prior years'. The purpose of the call is for the analysts to update their views about the company. From their own financial analysis, as well as via these periodic conference calls with company executives, analysts ultimately render one of three words regarding a company—buy, sell, or hold. Buy, sell, or hold what? The company's stock. To whom will they utter these words? Their investor clients and the public at large. Which word does the company hope gets spoken? "Buy" because it depicts robust optimism and positive prospects. "Hold" would be okay too, as it connotes a positive outlook, perhaps not quite so positive as "buy." On the other hand, in our simple scenario, "sell" is the four-letter word the CEO and CFO do not want to hear.

In addition to the investment banking firms that primarily serve large institutional investors and wealthy individuals, other financial firms sift through reams of corporate financial statements to render observations and opinions. Advisory companies such as Standard & Poor's and Value Line are prominent in this regard. Subscribers to these firms' publications, people like you and me, receive useful company-specific and industry-specific reports intended to help in making our own buy, sell, and hold stock decisions.

Financial statements and their analysis have also been used for even more varied investor purposes. For example, data from financial statements has been used to identify companies that are prime candidates for being acquired by other companies.[6] Similarly, financial statement data has been used for nearly 50 years, with amazing accuracy, to predict corporate bankruptcies.[7] Not to be overlooked is the usefulness of financial statement data in assessing farm viability in Spain.[8] Now, I cannot vouch for the latter use but such varied purposes convey a spectrum of analytical uses to which financial statement data contribute.

Basis for Extra Compensation

Many corporate employees, not just executives and managers, are participants in company-sponsored plans that award extra compensation for attaining targeted levels of financial performance. Like a rock star's stage wardrobe, such plans come in many varieties. Regardless of their nuances and differences, most, if not all, are anchored to one or more profitability measures (e.g., net income, ROA, ROE, earnings before taxes).

As you might anticipate, the metric used to determine such extra compensation is of great importance to the people subject to a particular plan. Might there be a temptation to artificially boost the value of that metric? If my bonus jumps to the next pay level with an additional $50,000 of June revenue, might I look for ways to record an early July delivery as if it were a June sale? If earnings are on target for the awarding of maximum bonuses this quarter, might I delay a major facilities repair till next quarter so the repair expense won't hurt this month's profits? Yes, people might do either of these when the stakes are high and the opportunity is at hand. That is why financial reporting must embrace and rest on a strong system of internal financial controls (discussed in the last chapter) and a set of shared ethical values.

Financial Performance with Ethics

Professional athletes are frequently honored for their record-setting feats. When that happens we assume they have accomplished those feats without performance-enhancing drugs. Their accomplishments are only meaningful if achieved within the rules they are expected to honor. Similarly, we assume their records do not involve collusive behavior. When a soccer goalie doesn't try very hard to stop a goal so that the goal-maker sets a new record, the legitimacy of that scoring feat is undermined. Quite simply, we honor accomplishments that are the true result of effort and talent, achieved in the open arena of fair competition. In the same way, we assume the financial results reported by corporate managers are honestly achieved.

> **Insider's Note**
>
> *For corporate annual reports to be useful, we must be able to presume ethical behavior by those responsible for a company's financial performance.*

There are at least five ethical foundations on which the usefulness of financial statements rest. We must be able to assume corporate managers and executives:

- behave lawfully and with integrity
- are conscientious stewards of the owners', employees', and consumers' interests
- treat all stakeholders with respect
- make timely financial disclosures
- always communicate the full truth

Think of the chaos that would prevail in the financial markets were these cornerstones not the norm. Did, and does, every person who has ever occupied a corporate position of financial responsibility possess these attributes? No, of course not. Many more have than haven't.

We must be able to assume that corporate executives do not use company resources for personal purposes. We must be able to assume that a company's reported sales are to legitimate customers and not simply the result of loading delivery trucks and moving them across town to sit in an empty parking lot. We must be able to assume there is not collusion amongst executives to hide things from external auditors and regulators. As long as investors insist on high standards of ethical conduct and regulators punish those executives who fail to live up to them, we can and must assume that these ethical cornerstones are in place. And just like President Ronald Reagan said when dealing with the former Soviet Union's disarmament, "trust but verify." Indeed, we need to continue to empower external auditors to verify the trust we have placed in corporate executives.

There is a quid pro quo to this ethical expectation, however. Yes, corporate managers should honor the level of ethical conduct that we expect. And investors must not expect unrealistic returns on the money they invested. What is unrealistic? Well, 15 consecutive years of 30% growth in corporate profits is probably unrealistic. Fifteen consecutive years of 2% profit growth is not great but it is not unrealistically high. There is a point somewhere in between where realistic expectations become unrealistic. That point is management-specific, company-specific, industry specific, economy-specific, and time-period specific. Such conditionality puts a burden on investors to be informed and savvy in formulating expectations.

A Financial Statement Analysis Epilogue

Financial statement analysis is the in-depth study of the content, relationships, and signals conveyed in a set of financial statements. The DuPont model and SCF pattern discussions above present a glimpse into that world. It is important to remember that financial statements are imprecise, reliant on management estimates and accounting choices, and they will never be totally comprehensive. Why? Because the evolutionary forces at play are fundamentally political in nature, rife with compromise, open to experimentation, and reliant on people as opposed to provable postulates and theorems.

Understanding the format, content, and conventions used to craft the communications in an annual report is an important, beginning step in becoming adept at financial statement analysis. The next step is learning, using, inventing, and interpreting other financial performance metrics.

Insider's Note

Don't forget the 10 commandments of financial statement analysis.

There are a number of excellent books on the market solely devoted to the art and practice of applying analytical techniques to a company's financial statements. Regardless of whether or not you do use more techniques, remember these "commandments" for using financial statements in assessing the financial performance of a company.[9]

1. Thou shalt not use financial statements in isolation.
2. Thou shalt not use financial statements as the only source of firm-specific information.
3. Thou shalt not avoid reading [financial statement] footnotes.
4. Thou shalt not focus on a single number.
5. Thou shalt not overlook the implications of what is read.
6. Thou shalt not ignore events subsequent to the financial statements.
7. Thou shalt not overlook the limitations of financial statements.
8. Thou shalt not use financial statements without adequate knowledge.
9. Thou shalt not shun professional help.
10. Thou shalt not take unnecessary risks.

The Inside Scoop

Just in case you have any lingering hesitation to undertake a basic analysis of real-world corporate annual reports, please remember:

1. There is *one* basic financial truth → A = L + OE.
2. Annual reports strive to answer *two* basic questions → What did the company do this year, and how well did they do it?
3. There are *three* interconnected financial statements at the heart of the company's performance story → the balance sheet, the income statement, and the statement of cash flows.
4. Annual reports are intended *for* prepared readers like you.

The DuPont model is a great starting point for assessing corporate performance. The five ratios comprising the DuPont model are: return on sales (ROS), asset turnover, return on assets (ROA), financial leverage, and return on owners' equity (ROE). These ratios are closely connected. Specifically, multiplying the values for the ROS, asset turnover, and financial leverage metrics equals the value of the ROE metric. Thus, as corporate executives seek to raise their company's ROE for the benefit of shareholders, it is a process of increasing profit margins (ROS), improving the efficient use of assets (asset turnover), and using borrowed funds to a larger, but carefully managed, extent (financial leverage). Those are the three levers available to corporate managers to raise the ROE accruing to shareholders.

Interpreting financial patterns and trends is another important aspect of financial statement analysis. Clearly, the historical trends in a company's revenues, expenses, and liabilities can illuminate key aspects of the company. Is the company growing or shrinking? Do expenses appear under control? Has it taken on more and more debt? Such foci are useful starting points for gaining an overall sense of the company's direction and performance. In addition, a review of the pattern of cash inflows and outflows as depicted in a company's statement of cash flows is very useful. Specifically, this chapter highlighted eight different pattern combinations for net cash flows from operations (CFFO), net cash flows from investing activities (CFFI), and net cash flows from financing (CFFF). Each of those patterns conveys something different and important about a company's financial strength and direction.

In sum, financial statement information is important. It is the primary scorekeeping, performance-assessing, future-predicting data that the financial markets receive. As such, there is a great deal of temptation placed in front of corporate executives to engineer the data to create a financial picture that may be rosier than warranted. Thus, the ethical climate permeating a company's financial reporting process is a critical component in assuring regulatory compliance and full, fair, and timely financial disclosures.

Practical Application

Consider the following DuPont ratio median data pertaining to several industries (see Figure 11.6).

Note the ROS figures for the aerospace and telecommunications industries—they are both 6%. Note also their respective ROEs—they are very different—22% and 6%, respectively. What explains the aerospace in-

Industry	ROS*	Asset Turnover†	ROA*	Financial Leverage†	ROE*
Aerospace and defense	6%	1.0	6%	3.67	22%
Beverages	7	.57	4	4.5	18
Chemicals	7	1.0	7	3.0	21
Energy	3	1.0	3	5.0	15
General merchandisers	3	2.67	8	2.13	17
Internet services & retailing	11	.45	5	1.8	9
Mining, oil production	27	.30	8	2.75	22
Railroads	13	.46	6	1.67	15
Specialty retailers	4	2.0	8	2.8	19
Telecommunications	6	.5	3	2.0	6
Utilities	7	.43	3	3.67	11

*Source: *Fortune*, April 30, 2007. These amounts are industry medians and rounded.
†These amounts were calculated by the author.

Figure 11.6 Selected Industry Dupont Ratio Medians

dustry's leap to such a high ROE versus that of telecommunications when they both started with 6% profit margins? Two reasons. First, the aerospace industry's median asset utilization, as represented by an asset turnover metric of 1.0, was twice as productive as that experienced by the telecommunications industry. There may be legitimate reasons for that but on the surface, aerospace was twice as efficient with its assets as telecommunications was. Second, the median aerospace company used debt money more extensively to fuel its business than telecommunications. This can be seen in aerospace's financial leverage factor of 3.67 versus telecommunications' 2.0.

Drawing on another industry pairing from the table above, energy and railroads delivered similar median ROEs for shareholders even though their starting profit margins were quite different. Energy's ROS (3%) was less than a quarter than that of railroads (13%). How did energy close the gap to equal railroads' ROE? Again the answer involves different asset utilizations and financial leverage. Railroads' median asset turnover and financial leverage metrics are substantially less than energy's, suggesting that energy is able to leverage its assets and owners' money to a greater extent than railroads.

Turn your attention back to the eight statement-of-cash-flow patterns depicted earlier in this chapter. Specifically, focus for a moment on patterns #1 and #7. What is the basic financial story conveyed by a recurring pattern for each of those? Pattern #1 displays a company with net cash inflows for each of the CFFO, CFFI, and CFFF subtotals. This suggests healthy operations (a positive CFFO), the ability and choice to raise funds from lenders and/or shareholders (a positive CFFF), and the net selling of investments in various assets (a positive CFFI) to raise even more funds. With healthy CFFO and optimistic lenders and shareholders (CFFF), the company's net cash inflow from CFFI may point to a corporate restructuring or business unit divestiture. Either of those events may be undertaken in anticipation of redirecting the company's focus to other businesses through future acquisitions. Or they may simply point to the company wanting to rid itself of underperforming assets. An important step in corroborating either possibility is reading the narrative parts of the annual report prepared by the company executives.

Pattern #7 is different. Here, the company displays net cash inflows only for the CFFI and CFFF subtotals. This is a mixed story. First, the net cash outflows for CFFO suggest the core business may not be healthy, as it uses more cash than it generates. Second, the net cash inflows from lenders and owners (CFFF) suggest that these outside parties have reason to remain optimistic about the company, as they are net contributors of cash to the company. Third, the net cash inflows from CFFI activities point to the fact that sales of assets exceed the investment in new assets. Is the company downsizing? Realigning? Tapping outside third parties to sustain it through a difficult time? In the long term it is not viable for a company to have net cash outflows for CFFO or net cash inflows for CFFI. Such a pattern analysis should prompt us to seek additional information about the company from the business press, financial advisory services, and investment banking reports.

In Anticipation of the Next Secret

What may be revealed on a Greek beach may not be permitted on Virginia Beach.

Secret #12

It's a Global Challenge

Can't we all just get along?

The questions behind Secret #12:

- Are annual reports the same the world over?
- Is there such a thing as a body of international financial reporting guidelines? If they exist, who issues them? What standing do they have in the financial community? How different are they from FASB's?
- What contextual factors must readers of annual reports published by companies from around the world bear in mind?
- What is a 20-f?

Satellite-based communications bring live television pictures from China into our living rooms. The Internet allows us to easily search numerous Web sites for the best tourist destinations in Thailand. E-mail permits real-time discussions with almost anyone around the world at any time. Today's instant, inexpensive, widespread flow of information is unprecedented. For anyone older than 40, this phenomenon is truly amazing, and for everyone else, it should be.

The increased information accessibility that technology has made possible has also had a huge impact on the global financial markets. Banks transfer cash from a U.S. account to one in Moscow in a matter of seconds. Investors in Nevada call stockbrokers in New York and get instantaneous information on potential Hong Kong investments. Likewise, German and Israeli investors can call their stockbrokers and get information on a company in St. Louis. Such easy communication has created massive amounts of corporate information flowing across the globe. Much of that information involves annual reports, more specifically financial statements. Historically, global financial statement information has not been equally useful, reliable, and comparable. Why not? We will explore some of the reasons in this chapter along with what is being done at an international level to ameliorate global financial reporting disparities.

Going Global

Only recently has there been a significant push towards a global set of financial reporting standards. Historically, nations have had their own rules and regulations governing the creation, dissemination, and content of annual reports pertaining to their domestic, publicly owned companies. Needless to say, most of the resulting corporate annual reports contained financial statements that were not very comparable. Annual reports and their financial statements often differed in format, terminology, accounting principles used, line items reported, frequency of publication, currencies, measurement conventions applied, footnote explanations, supplementary data, the degree to which they mirrored tax laws, and the levels of assurance provided by external auditors. Other than that, they were identical!

> ### Insider's Note
>
> *Historically, financial statements from around the world were not comparable on a variety of dimensions.*

In the not-too-distant past, if you wanted to compare the financial statements of the following five airlines—British Airways (United Kingdom), Varig (Brazil), JAL (Japan), SAS (Sweden), and United Airlines (United States)—it was very difficult to ascertain which one was the healthier, which one performed the best in a given year, and whose financial prospects appeared most favorable. Sure, they all reported something akin to "net income," but those figures were not comparable. It was as if you and I reported a number between 1 and 10 to indicate our level of job satisfaction this past week. We could both do that, and indeed we could pick a number. But both of us bring different mind sets and foci to that task. If I picked 6 and you picked 8, were you really more satisfied? Were you actually 33% more satisfied? It would be impossible to render a conclusion on such a comparison unless we had developed beforehand: (1) an extensive, shared, equally weighted list of job satisfaction factors, (2) a set of guidelines as to what each numerical rating meant, and (3) a common means to narratively elaborate on our chosen number.

With just such a task in mind, an international financial reporting organization was created in 1973 to develop an internationally accepted body of financial reporting standards. That organization was the London-based International Accounting Standards Committee (IASC). Pause for just a second . . . envision the task of bringing about the international convergence of financial reporting standards as an endeavor with all the attributes of the United Nations' deliberative decision-making process. For over 20 years, the IASC made little substantive progress. Nationalistic vested interests led to heated debates. Those debates sparked a vast array of compromises. Those compromises resulted in many different approved financial reporting methods to account for a specific financial statement item. As you might surmise, espousing many different acceptable financial reporting approaches undermined the very purpose—cross-country financial statement comparability—of the IASC's existence.

Around the turn of the millennium, momentum for a narrowed, more broadly embraced, set of international financial reporting standards accelerated for several reasons. First, multinational companies, listed on multiple stock exchanges around the world, tired of the effort and cost to prepare multiple sets of financial statements using different financial reporting conventions. Second, the International Organization of Securities Commissions (IOSCO) endorsed an IASC project to eliminate a number of the alternatives it had previously issued. Third, in order to seize the opportune moment for change it had been presented, the IASC reconstituted itself as the International Accounting Standards Board (IASB). It became staffed with 12 full-time members and it officially appointed liaisons to some of the most prominent financial reporting boards around the world, such as the FASB in the United States and similar groups in Japan, the United Kingdom, Canada, France, Germany, Australia, and New Zealand. Fourth, Enron, WorldCom, and the ensuing wave of other U.S. financial reporting fiascos made it clear to all that the U.S. financial reporting system was not without its own shortcomings, thus opening the door to the possibility that the rest of the world might not have to simply agree to the U.S. standards as either the prototype or the default for the international standards. Last, the European Union (EU) abandoned its efforts to develop financial reporting standards for companies in its member countries, instead mandating the adoption of IASB standards.

Considering Country Context

The work of the IASB is to develop high quality financial reporting standards for use around the world. Think about that task. One set of international financial reporting standards (IFRS), narrowly construed, adoptable by and useful for assessing the financial performance, position, and prospects of a Romanian power company, a Brazilian shipping company, a Korean car manufacturer, and an American consumer goods retailer. To date, the IASB has done a remarkable job on a very difficult task. Commingled with the IASB's work, however, is a significant responsibility on the part of the users of IASB-based financial statements to be contextually savvy.

What should we conclude, for example, if the shareholders' equity of a Japanese steelmaking firm's balance sheet is only 10% of its total capital and its current ratio (current assets ÷ current liabilities) is 0.75 as compared with 40% and 1.2, respectively, for a United States steelmaker? Is that cause for alarm or applause? Were managers in these two countries striving for the same results, bringing to bear similar purposes, perspectives, and priorities? Digging deeply into these sorts of contextual concerns is beyond the scope of this book. It is important, however, to highlight three overarching contextual dimensions pertaining to annual reports from around the world.

Culture

Geert Hofstede, the former director of the Institute for Research on Intercultural Cooperation in the Netherlands, defined culture as a kind of "collective mental programming" that affects the way people perceive and act in the world. In his classic book, *Cultures and Organizations: Software of the Mind,* Hofstede discusses several important cultural dimensions that are important to keep in mind when reading the annual reports of companies from other countries. This is true even if the companies are using one set of financial reporting standards such as those promulgated by the IASB. Those cultural dimensions are what Hofstede labels as power distance, individualism, and uncertainty avoidance.[1] He asserts that these cultural dimensions shed light on some of the most substantive similarities and differences in societal core values around the world.

The concept of *power distance* (PD) refers to the extent to which the members of a society expect and accept that power is distributed unequally. High PD countries (e.g., Mexico, Arab countries[2]) have a relatively high tolerance for inequality among their citizens. In contrast, people from low PD countries (e.g., Switzerland, Sweden) strive for power equalization and demand justification for power inequalities. In general, companies from high-PD societies are more likely to harbor a preference for providing fewer, more terse financial disclosures than companies from low-PD societies, in order to preserve secrecy, power, and/or role inequalities.[3] Thus, annual reports from high-PD countries are likely to present the bare minimum required.

> ### Insider's Note
>
> *Geert Hofstede's cultural concepts of power distance, individualism, and uncertainty avoidance are useful constructs to appreciate when reading annual reports from around the world.*

Societies that exemplify high *individualism* (IDV) (e.g., the United States, the Netherlands) tend to be those with loose ties between individuals. In contrast, low-IDV countries (e.g., Korea, Venezuela) have more collectivist populations—that is, people are more integrated in strong, cohesive groups. In more collectivist societies, financial information may be more closely held by the companies domiciled there, and thus there may be a tendency not to share and/or to obfuscate the insights provided to those outside their closely knit group.[4] When studying annual reports from companies located in more collectivist cultures, readers have a heightened challenge to complement those reports with other sources of information.

The concept of *uncertainty avoidance* (UAV) is another important cultural dimension. It can be thought of as the extent to which the members of a society feel threatened by uncertain situations. This feeling is usually expressed through a need for predictability—a need for rules. Uncertainty-avoiding cultures (e.g., Greece, Japan) have historically maintained explicit codes of belief and behavior. In contrast, low-UAV cultures (e.g., the United States, Denmark) tend to be flexible, prefer less guidance, and are willing to entertain different ideas. From a financial reporting perspective, it has been posited that relatively higher-UAV societies exhibit greater tendencies toward limited- or no-choice financial reporting conventions than lower-UAV societies.[5]

Legal and Political Environment

Companies operate within their home country's tax and legal systems. The influence of those systems on corporate performance differs around the world. In the United States and the United Kingdom, for example, the influence of tax laws on the calculation of financial statement net income is minimal. Indeed, as we have already discussed in an earlier chapter, U.S. companies may report one set of earnings figures in their external financial statements and a substantially different set on their corporate tax returns. In many other countries, however, tax reporting and financial reporting are legally linked. Historically in Japanese GAAP, for example, expenses had to be recorded in a company's financial statements in order to qualify as deductible on its tax return. In general, such a requirement prompts companies to report financial statement net income as conservatively as is legally possible in order to minimize tax payments. As a consequence, financial statements are more focused on legal compliance than with a fair presentation of a company's business performance. It is interesting to note that because tax laws are formulated by governmental bodies in response to political and economic agendas, whenever they are closely linked to financial reporting rules such a linkage can be a substantial impediment to accepting any sort of international GAAP.

It is also true that the litigious nature of societies and the relative rights of individuals vis-à-vis corporations differ around the world. The United States has a very extensive body of laws that establish and protect the rights of individuals in their relationships with companies. For example, employment laws, product liability laws, and environmental laws all serve to place a burden on companies to perform in certain ways. Moreover, U.S. companies

Insider's Note

In many countries, the legal rights and duties of corporations to shareholders and other constituencies differ from those in the United States, as does the linkage of financial reporting and tax rules.

must disclose in their annual reports information pertaining to the potential financial exposure springing from lawsuits and concerns in those arenas. In countries without similar legal bases for various aspects of corporate behavior, readers of annual reports may not assume that all pertinent information pertaining to such financial exposures is divulged. And even at a more fundamental financial reporting level, U.S. laws explicitly put a high burden on U.S. companies to provide full and fair disclosures. It is not clear that similar laws and attitudes exist around the world. Thus, different tendencies to disclose and discuss information, rooted in legally mandated corporate duties and individual rights, differ around the world.

Business Environment

Modern financial reporting springs from the development of the publicly held corporation, with its separation of ownership and management and its limitation of owners' liability. Therefore, another contextual factor affecting the financial reporting predilections of companies in various countries is the state of a country's capital markets (i.e., its stock and bond markets). The fundamental purpose of a country's financial reporting system depends on customary sources of capital. In such countries as Germany and Japan, where banks have long played a very powerful role in stoking economic growth, extensive public financial disclosure has historically tended to be deemphasized because lenders generally had ready access to internal, pertinent corporate information. In countries where

Insider's Note

The role, size, and influence of both a country's capital markets and accounting profession influence the financial reporting practices of a country.

share ownership has historically not been a part of the general public's experience, widespread financial disclosures have generally not been needed or practiced.

There is another important business environment factor easily overlooked. A sophisticated and modern system of financial reporting requires an accounting profession that is well educated and numerous enough to ensure the system's proper functioning. One certainly sees this in countries such as the United Kingdom and the United States, where the accounting professions share responsibility for creating financial reporting standards and making sure that companies adhere to the form and substance of the financial reporting standards in effect. But even in nations where financial reporting standards are largely a matter of central governmental legislation, the sophistication and training of the accounting profession noticeably affects the quality of financial reporting. For example, historically Swedish multinationals, under the guidance of an accounting professional elite, have published some of the world's most comprehensive corporate annual reports, even though Swedish accounting standards have their historical roots in commercial law.

Who Will Be the Enforcers?

Assume that all of the previously mentioned differences can be either set aside or fully embraced in conjunction with the IASB's push towards a universal set of financial reporting conventions. Currently, the IASB has no enforcement staff. The IASB has no sanctioning-of-companies capability. The IASB does not have any investigative body. All the positive prospects of a globally embraced set of IASB financial reporting standards are null and void without some enforcement means. Most experts do not envision anything like a financial reporting world court, even though that has been proposed from time to time. I do not envision a globe-trotting SWAT team of accountants descending unannounced on companies to check whether or not they have properly implemented IASB standards. If there is to be a required body of international financial reporting standards, that presupposes there are consequences if they are not followed by a company. In turn,

Insider's Note

The enforcement of global financial reporting standards presents a challenge. Who will enforce them and how?

those consequences presuppose international agreement on who decides when consequences are warranted, what the consequences are, and how they will be implemented.

There are three potential enforcement mechanisms in the international financial community. First, there is IOSCO, introduced earlier in this chapter. That collective body, and its individual members (there are more than 100 of them, including the U.S. Securities and Exchange Commission) have a huge potential enforcement role to play. IOSCO has stated that two of its key objectives are protecting investors and ensuring that securities markets are fair, efficient, and transparent. To a large extent, meeting those objectives requires the implementation of mechanisms to ensure that "there is full, timely and accurate disclosure of financial results and other information that is material to investors' decisions . . . and [that] accounting and auditing standards should be of a high and internationally acceptable quality."[6] If IOSCO members put their full weight behind the IASB as the authoritative, global financial reporting standards-setting body, companies would have to adhere to those standards or run the risk of sanctions from IOSCO and/or their home-country securities commissions. A second group that potentially has a significant role to play in the enforcement of the IASB's standards is the global auditing firms. Those firms can insist on accurate compliance or exercise their responsibility of publicly declaring that a set of corporate financial statements they have just reviewed are *not* in compliance with the appropriate financial reporting standards. Such a declaration is tantamount to branding Nathaniel Hawthorne's character, Hester Prynne, with the infamous scarlet letter for all to see. And last, the investing public can insist that companies comply with IASB standards by avoiding the purchase of securities from those that do not.

The U.S. Form 20-f

The United States is a key player in the effort to have one generally accepted set of global financial reporting standards. In furthering that effort, the U.S.'s SEC and FASB have publicly endorsed the merits of, and the move to, a global set of financial reporting standards. But such a view comes with a caveat—the resultant standards must be at least as beneficial to investors as existing U.S. GAAP standards. That is a big caveat. It is not an insurmountable caveat, however. It will require much discussion, deliberation, and debate on many joint FASB/IASB projects. Until IASB standards are fully embraced by the United States, there is the 20-f.

As of the writing of this chapter, and as has been true for many years, non–U.S. companies seeking to have their securities (stocks or bonds) traded on a U.S. stock exchange must either: (1) file a U.S. GAAP set of financial statements with the SEC or, (2) provide a reconciliation (on Form 20-f) of net income and shareholders' equity derived from the GAAP they did use to what those items would have been had they used U.S. GAAP. In reviewing a random set of 20-f filings, it is obvious that the financial figures can be quite different when two different GAAPs are applied. In fact, just perusing a recent 20-f filed by the French cement company Lafarge,

its IASB GAAP net income morphs into a 22% lower U.S. GAAP figure even though both figures pertain to the very same set of business events and transactions. The magnitude and direction of the difference in net income is not always like this—it may be more, it may be less. The point is, GAAP-based differences can be sizable and are not uncommon.[7] Such differences fuel the flames of the debate about whether the United States should or should not allow IASB GAAP in lieu of U.S. GAAP.[8]

The IASB and the FASB: Dating, Engaged, Married, or Just Fooling Around?

September 18 is a notable day for several reasons. On that date in 1793, George Washington laid the cornerstone for the U.S. Capitol. In 1851, the *New York Times* published its first issue on that date. In 1947, the U.S. Air Force was established as a separate branch of the U.S. military on that date. And on September 18, 2002, the Norwalk Agreement was reached by the IASB and the FASB. Chances are you didn't catch that event on the nightly news, but that agreement registered an 8.0 on the financial-reporting Richter scale. As an outgrowth of that meeting, the IASB and the FASB agreed to work to make their respective GAAPs "fully compatible as soon as is practicable."[9] Five years later the commitment was turbo charged when . . .

> As part of an agreed framework for advancing transatlantic economic integration, President Bush, Angela Merkel (the German Chancellor who doubles as President of the European Union's council of ministers) and Jose Manuel Barroso, European Commission President, agreed to "promote and seek to ensure conditions for U.S. GAAP and IFRS to be recognized in both jurisdictions without the need for reconciliation by 2009 or possibly sooner."[10]

The move toward an internationally accepted, single body of GAAP has taken on a serious, diligent, purposeful tone. It is not clear how intense the FASB and IASB engagement will be, but the two bodies have definitely announced their lifelong intentions. Stay tuned. It will be a rocky road, as there are many GAAP differences between the two organizations, but financial markets and multinational companies want and are expecting GAAP convergence. When (not if) a globally acceptable body of international financial reporting standards does emerge, the need for readers of the subsequent annual reports to acquire contextual literacy will remain.

> **Insider's Note**
>
> *IASB and U.S. GAAP will converge. It is a question of when, at what cost, and with what compromises.*

The Inside Scoop

Henry Ford is reputed to have said that you could have any color Ford you wanted as long as it was black. A hallmark of the auto industry's more modern history is a move toward more varied customer offerings. The historical trend in the global market for financial statements portrays just the opposite trajectory. Until the late twentieth century, most countries had their own version of GAAP. As a result, there was a great deal of variety in the content, form, and conventions embedded in the financial statements from around the world. Of late, however, there is less variety in the financial reporting practices used across the globe. The International Accounting

Standards Board (IASB) has emerged as a key player in developing a single, globally acceptable body of GAAP. To date, over 90 countries have embraced the IASB's financial reporting standards—the United States has not. Of note, however, is the publicly stated commitment of the FASB and SEC to work with the IASB toward an eventual convergence of standards. It will be a pleasure to one day read three annual reports, from three different companies, based in three different countries, and know that the financial reporting conventions used in each are the same.

Even when such a world becomes a reality, it will be important for financial statement readers to have a sense of the unique environmental factors affecting a German company versus a Korean company versus an American company. Those business environments will remain unique, and thus different. Just because you and I might meet a person from each of those countries dressed in Brooks Brothers suits and eating dinner at an Olive Garden restaurant, that does not make those individuals totally comparable. In seeking a deeper understanding of those individuals, it would be informative to see them in their native dress and to learn of their native cuisine. Likewise, even though financial statements from around the world may one day all use IASB GAAP, readers will still find it necessary to become savvy about the local contexts within which companies operate.

For example, most European companies have historically operated with a more substantive and overt societal role than American companies. Many Latin American companies have historically operated in hyperinflationary environments, which gives rise to a different managerial mindset than that where inflation has not been an issue. For these, and many other similar factors, contextual insights must remain an important part of understanding a company. This is true even when, and perhaps especially when, a uniform set of financial reporting standards is overlaid on the financial circumstances of companies from different countries.

Practical Application

Consider this real-world scenario. First, residents of a particular, nonwestern country view free electricity as a basic human right. They steal it from the utility company's substations whenever it is turned off to their apartment building. Would this situation impact the financial results presented by the utility in its financial statements? Yes it would. In what general way(s) would its financial statements be impacted?

First, the electric utility company spent millions to install thousands of new residential electric meters in order to obtain accurate billing information. Those were destroyed by many residents who also refused to pay the electric bills they received. Thus, there was a worthless fixed asset—equipment (i.e., the investment in buying and installing the meters)—that surely had to be written off the books along with thousands of accounts receivable. Second, when people tried to steal electricity by splicing wires to those in the utility's substations, the substations were often damaged and people electrocuted. As a consequence, the normal flow of electricity was interrupted for days and costly repairs were incurred at critical distribution points. Third, when people died as a result of their attempted thefts, the company had to undertake lengthy investigations and endure negative press. Fourth, this perspective—electricity should be free—necessitated that the utility embark on an education campaign for the people of the region.

Virtually none of these phenomena are faced by a utility doing business in the United States. Thus, the financial performance and the management foci of two such companies would be quite different. Given the events noted for the utility operating in the non–United States environment, would its financial picture be different depending on whether it used IASB or U.S. GAAP? No, it would not make a difference. We can say this quite definitively without knowing the intricacies of either GAAP, because the financial reporting for uncollectible receivables, stolen/destroyed equipment, and repairs to facilities is mostly universal. Thus, the real differences to be considered in understanding the financial results presented by the utility operating in the non–U.S. context are those that pertain to the contextual challenges it faces and the cultural root causes of those challenges.

Pertinent to the other major theme of this chapter, envision being responsible for admitting non–U.S. students to the MBA program of a well-regarded U.S. university. Naturally, your objectives include selecting the best applicants. How do you pursue that objective? In short, you do that with a set of standardized tests that measure applicants' ability on the school's key success factors. In order to do that on a comparative basis across a pool of applicants with different backgrounds, most MBA programs require the GMAT (Graduate Management Admissions Test). This is a standardized exam that all applicants take no matter where they live, what their background is, or what their career aspirations are. The exam scores are used, in large part, to assess an applicant's academic capabilities. The higher the score, the more likely the applicant is to be accepted.

Second, for many U.S. MBA programs, an applicant's ability to communicate in English is a critical success factor. Thus, the TOEFL (Test Of English as a Foreign Language) exam must be taken by non–U.S. applicants. The exam is the same whether you learned English from a set of cassette tapes you listened to while growing up in Laos, or from an expatriate teaching in a German school, or from missionaries working in your native Ecuador. The TOEFL exam is a standardized means for measuring English competence. Applicant scores are comparable. School admissions decision makers need not worry about differing measurement scales undergirding the TOEFL scores they review. The higher the score, the greater the applicant's English proficiency.

What would happen if other major business schools ceased requiring the GMAT and or the TOEFL exam and your school retained them? Chances are, applications to those other schools would increase while those to your school would decrease.

The MBA admissions example is similar to the issue faced by U.S. financial markets regulators. Since their aim is to provide investors with the best possible, most comparable financial data from overseas companies listed on the U.S. stock exchanges, how do they do that? The obvious and historical answer is to require overseas companies to use U.S. GAAP or to reconcile their home-country GAAP net income and owners' equity to U.S. GAAP equivalents. Historically, U.S. financial market regulators have used U.S. GAAP as the standardized lens through which all companies are best viewed no matter the company's business, domicile, or history. What would happen if competitor stock markets from around the world started accepting financial statements based on IASB standards and the United States did not? The answer is, in part, what has happened. More and more overseas companies are choosing not to list on the U.S. exchanges. Pressure is mounting for the United States to allow IASB-based financial statements from non–U.S. companies. U.S. companies are also beginning to lobby for the IASB GAAP option. In the future, if these forces and directions fully run their course, there may not be a U.S. GAAP separate and apart from IASB GAAP.

In Anticipation of the Next Secret

Financial reporting guidelines and annual report conventions are the result of a political process. In the political arena, it's bare knuckles time . . . let's get physical!

Secret #13

It's Political

Let's make a deal

The questions behind Secret #13:

- Are financial reporting rules discovered, mathematically derived, or politically determined?
- Do debate and compromise play a role in establishing annual report conventions? If so, what are some recent examples? If so, isn't that wrong . . . isn't there a search for truth that must take place?
- What happens when the rules change?

In an earlier chapter, the Accounting 101 process of capturing, codifying, and communicating financial data was presented. There is another process germane to a robust understanding and appreciation of corporate annual reports. In this chapter, the process by which annual report conventions and financial reporting rules are established is highlighted. Be prepared, it is not necessarily pretty nor is it always a search for the truth. Mostly, it is a process that seeks to serve the investing public, not anger the corporate community, and result in conceptually consistent guidelines.

Blood in the Street?

In 1972, the military draft was real, as was the Vietnam War. A lottery dictated who would be drafted. In one tense, televised event, markers representing each day of the year were drawn from a big lottolike machine. The order in which the dates were drawn dictated every 19-year-old male's position in the coming year's draft sequence. In 1972, I "won" the lottery—my number was 4! This was during a time when campus ROTC buildings were set ablaze, war protest marches were rampant, and student college deferments had been abolished. One hot summer's day before my sophomore year of college, I received notice to report for a military physical. "Follow the red line on the floor. Drop your pants. Bend over. Follow the yellow line. Open your mouth." And so it went all day. It was clear that I would be drafted in early 1973. But by the end of January 1973, the Paris Peace Treaty had been signed and there would be no 1973 draftees! A war that had dragged on for a decade was over. Protests, political pressure, public dissatisfaction, and powerful lobbying all combined to expedite its end.

In battles of a different kind, a former chief accountant for the Securities and Exchange Commission (SEC) once observed, "When faced with accounting changes, people always say. 'Blood will run in the streets!'"[1] Unlike the Vietnam-era protests that hastened the ending of our involvement there, financial reporting protests are not matters of life and death. For sure, no blood has ever run in the streets over financial reporting issues, but some financial reporting constituencies have vigorously lobbied for or against changes to the financial reporting status quo. Like the Vietnam-era protests that dominated my youth, financial reporting rule-making outcomes are affected by the voices raised in protest.

Before chronicling some of the very real ways protests and political pressure have shaped financial reporting and annual reports, let's ask: how is the financial reporting rule-making process suppose to work?

GAAP Overview

Recall that financial reporting rules comprise what is called the body of "generally accepted accounting principles" (GAAP). As you may have deduced from from the words "generally accepted," the principles outlined in GAAP are not absolute truths as are common in the arenas of physics and mathematics. Rather, they are principles that have legitimacy because they have broad support from the financial community. In some sense, they are akin to the rules a group of youngsters devises to govern a game they have created and play—the rules work because they all agree to abide by them.

Moreover, like all such rules, GAAP evolves over time as annual report readers' demands for information change and as companies' willingness to supply information also changes. Since GAAP ultimately depends on a consensus of the parties involved, its establishment is frequently a process of negotiation and compromise.

Some Perspective on GAAP

At the beginning of the twentieth century, the U.S. financial community was relatively small.[2] When local businesses borrowed from local banks, personal reputations and relationships were more important than formalized financial reports in the granting of a loan. In addition, stocks and bonds were investment vehicles only for a small, wealthy, well-acquainted group of people. To the extent that investments were made outside that group, they were predominantly based on personal recommendations from investment bankers. Because communications between creditors and borrowers, or between investors and investees, could be direct and personal, financial reporting tended to be idiosyncratic and even informal. Such an approach served the business community well for many years. But as the business community grew and became more diverse, and as lenders and owners no longer had personal relationships with those they were lending to or investing in, the need for a more rigorous financial reporting system became apparent.

The need for more formal regulation over the form and content of financial reporting became dramatically apparent with the stock market crash of 1929. The global, decade-long depression triggered by the crash made it clear that a reporting system that relied on personal contacts was no longer appropriate. As in prior market failures, many investors were hurt. But this time there were many more investors in the market, and the ones who were hurt most were the first-time players in the market—the "little investors." Because the public was now seen as a sizable party to the country's financial system and, more particularly, a party dependent on the financial reporting system, the U.S. Congress passed the Securities Act of 1933 and The Securities Exchange Act of 1934, which created the SEC. The responsibilities given the SEC included and remain: (1) the regulation of the various U.S. stock exchanges and the broker-dealers who buy and sell stocks and bonds on those exchanges, and (2) the establishment of the "form and content" of the financial reports required of publicly held companies.

The SEC has authorized the FASB to issue specific financial reporting rules. But the SEC does retain full authority to reclaim that role and the FASB, in essence, serves at the pleasure of the SEC. This latter point was again demonstrated with the passage of the Sarbanes-Oxley Act of 2002 (SOX) wherein the SEC was instructed, by the U.S. Congress, to designate a body to establish financial reporting rules. A year later the SEC reiterated its support for the FASB as that rule-making body. The SEC could have created a new body or chosen a different existing body—for now, the SEC has chosen the FASB.

How Does the FASB Choose to Do What It Does?

It is worth repeating—financial reporting rules are an ever-evolving result of the convergence of annual report readers' information demands and annual report issuers' willingness to supply information. In between these two parties, and these two forces, is the FASB. Envision the FASB as the

Solomon-like mediator that must decide which issues will be dealt with, in what ways, and at what times. Indeed, the FASB receives requests for action on scores of financial reporting issues from every conceivable constituency. Vocal constituencies include the SEC, investors, U.S. companies, stock exchanges, overseas regulators, industry trade associations, the accounting profession, stockbrokers, and investment bankers.

According to the FASB Web site (www.fasb.org), it considers seven factors in prioritizing the array of potential topics it could devote its resources to. Is the issue *pervasive*—that is, is it likely to affect many parties, in diverse ways, for an extended period of time? Are there *alternative solutions* that vary in their level of financial reporting improvement provided? Is there a *technically feasible* solution to the issue? Is the solution likely to provide positive *practical consequences* by being widely embraced? Would addressing the issue likely result in the *convergence* of practice between the United States and other countries? Might the issue pose a *cooperative opportunity* for the FASB to jointly tackle it with standard setters from other countries? And finally, are there sufficient *resources* to tackle the issue in a comprehensive, timely fashion?

If all of the questions above are answered yes, the financial reporting issue is likely to be put on the FASB's agenda. At any given time, that agenda is quite lengthy and varied. That fact alone attests to a host of significant financial reporting issues for which feasible alternative solutions exist. For our purposes, the specific issues aren't important. What is important is an appreciation for the fact that financial reporting is like a pot of stew on a stove—always simmering, consisting of many items, with portions being continuously taken out or added, and with a debate raging, boiling over, and settling back down every so often. It is a dynamic context from which financial reporting rules emanate and annual report conventions evolve.

What Steps Does the FASB Take Next?

Once a financial reporting issue is on the FASB's agenda, work begins. All meetings of the seven-member FASB are open to the public and eventually the board prepares an Exposure Draft (ED) of the proposed new rule. The ED is published and comments are solicited from interested parties. You and I could be respondents to an ED. Once the comment period is over, the board reviews all comments, and decides to either issue a final pronouncement of a financial reporting rule (referred to as a Statement of Financial Accounting Standards (SFAS)), or a revised ED for further comment, or to table the issue. From start to finish, this process can take years.

As we try to grasp the enormity of the FASB's task, consider this simple analogy. Assume you are applying for a federal tuition assistance loan to send a child to college and that I am doing the same. In either instance, and in others like them, there is a set of standardized forms that you and I must complete, all soliciting a predetermined array of information. It does not matter if you are a car mechanic and I am a schoolteacher, the forms are the same. It does not matter if the college your child is applying to is well known or obscure, large or small, in Indiana or Idaho, the forms are the same. It does not matter if you live on a farm and I live in a big city, the forms are the same.

Now consider this: a single version of GAAP must also apply in multiple contexts. GAAP must make sense for small companies as well as large ones, for auto manufacturers as well as advertising agencies, for California companies as well as Tennessee companies, and for prosperous companies as well as not-so-prosperous companies. It must accommodate the information needs of Wall Street money managers, kitchen-table investors, and hometown bankers. In addition, the challenge is also to create a set of GAAP that works for a Greek shipping company and a U.S. auto manufacturer.

> **Insider's Note**
>
> *GAAP must be useful for companies from a host of different settings. FASB is not interested in creating industry-, geographic-, or size-specific GAAP.*

So, as the FASB deliberates on a specific financial reporting topic, it must consider an outcome that works in a number of different corporate contexts and for a number of different constituencies. The FASB has no interest in promulgating financial reporting rules that are industry-, geography-, size-, condition-, and/or reader-specific. Now, there are financial reporting issues that are so industry-specific that tailored rules are needed and are created (the motion picture industry is an example). Such contextual specificity is the exception, not the norm, for GAAP.

Lobbying, Compromise, and Reversals

Just this morning, a search of our university library database using the terms "accounting" and "lobby" revealed a large number of hits. I was mildly surprised by the variety of organizations that unabashedly lobby the FASB and the SEC for various actions on various financial reporting rules. The actions requested range from rescinding a particular rule to pass a new one on this or that topic. In a few instances, organizations voice wholehearted support for a FASB proposal. The array of lobbying organizations that surfaced from my quick search included the Financial Executives Institute (FEI), the European Union (EU), the Institute of Chartered Accountants in England and Wales, the Pennsylvania Institute of CPAs, the Mechanical Contractors Association of America, the food service industry, the National Credit Union Administration, America's Community Bankers association, numerous *Fortune* 500 companies, and a host of accounting firms.

Clearly, with so many interested parties, the FASB's final pronouncements seldom please everyone. But, the FASB's role is not to necessarily please everyone. The FASB's role is to establish rules that address substantive concerns and that enhance the usefulness, to the investing public, of an annual report's financial story. Consider the following two examples, each suitable for a TV soap opera, of highly visible financial reporting issues, debates, proposals, compromises, delays, and ultimately new rules.

The Stock Option Soap Opera

Scenes of protest marches, complete with chants, placards, and caricatures of the "bad guys" are not uncommon—just turn on the nightly news. Believe it or not, there was such a march a few years back—directed against FASB. The "Rally in the Valley" (i.e., Silicon Valley), as the press called it, was against a FASB proposal that required companies to report, as compensation expense on their income statements, an amount approximating the market value of the stock options granted to employees. At the time, the recording of such an expense was not required and thus, millions of dollars of potential compensation expense did not appear in corporate income statements.

The rally primarily sprang from the high-tech glamour companies of the era. It was not a benign, token protest. It was a well-orchestrated endeavor intended, along with a well-financed lobbying effort, to garner the attention of Capitol Hill—and it did. Indeed, some prominent U.S. senators seized the opportunity to oppose the proposed financial-reporting rule. In the end, this opposition was codified in the passage of a nonbinding Senate resolution calling on the FASB to drop the proposed new rule—the vote was 88 to 9. (Don't senators have more important things to do?)

> ### Insider's Note
>
> *Envision protest marches and Washington D.C. flip-flops in response to actions taken by the FASB. It happens.*

Later that year, what sounded like a massive cave-in reverberated across the financial reporting landscape. The FASB withdrew its proposal in order to "reconsider" the issue. Eventually, the FASB published a new rule that gave companies the choice to either: (1) report millions of dollars of expense pertaining to the value of the stock options granted (i.e., their original proposal), or (2) omit those millions of dollars in expense from the income statement but disclose the amount in the recesses of the financial statement footnotes. If you ran a company that granted huge blocks of stock options, valued at millions of dollars, to keep your best people, which choice would you make? For a number of years, and as you might have anticipated, only a couple of companies opted to expense the stock options they granted to employees.

Then came a host of headline-making financial reporting fiascos like Enron and WorldCom. Many blamed corporate management's earnings manipulation in these disasters on a desire to boost the company's stock price, which would increase the value of the stock options they had been liberally granted. In the midst of the political rhetoric to reform financial reporting governance to avoid future Enrons, various members of Congress again seized the opportunity to opine on the problematic nature of the financial reporting rules for stock options. This time, however, those voices seemed most loudly raised in favor of expensing the value of the granted stock options. Did anyone hear that big flip-flop in D.C.?

FASB responded. They revised their latest pronouncement that gave companies the choice to expense the value of the stock options granted to employees to reflect their original proposal—required expensing. All seemed on track for that to become the law of the land and then the lobbying began again. Some of the same companies from a decade earlier let it be known that they were still against a required expensing rule. Surprise, surprise—Congress started listening to those voices again and the U. S. House of Representatives voted 312 to 111 to dilute the FASB pronouncement. (Doesn't Congress have more important things to do?) Fortunately, in my opinion, the U.S. Senate did not support the House bill and so the watered-down version never became law. The beginning date for the new stock-option expensing rule was, however, postponed—oh no! FASB! Tell me it ain't so! Finally, the

Insider's Note

Stock options are not a form of compensation expense to be recorded on an income statement. They are. They are not. They are!

new rule came into effect a year or two later. Wow, what a series of twists and turns, loud voices, and flip-flops.

The Mergers Compromise

As we know, corporate shares of stock have a monetary value easily determined by finding the latest price quote on a stock exchange where they are traded. Since shares have such an easily determined, widely accepted value, they are often used as a form of currency by companies and individuals. For example, FISH Company can issue some of its shares to acquire all the shares of BAIT Company from BAIT Company's shareholders. Such a deal would make FISH Company the new owner of BAIT Company (see Figure 13.1). This is a common means for a corporate acquisition—neither BAIT Company as an entity or the FISH Company shareholders is involved in the transaction. The end result is that FISH Company owns all the shares of BAIT Company and the only shares remaining with the public are FISH Company shares.

Assume for the moment that such a deal might involve 10 million shares of FISH Company stock that, at the date the deal is finalized, are worth $100 each. That is a $1 billion purchase of another company—correct? Well, up until a few years ago, this was not considered a purchase at all in an annual report. This corporate takeover was viewed as a marriage of two companies where two financial interests were simply combined and treated as if they had never been separate entities. The reason for this view was that no cash was paid—only shares of stock were exchanged. As a result, FISH Company simply added BAIT Company's pretakeover balance sheet line items and monetary amounts to its own in crafting the combined entities' newly required consolidated balance sheet. As we know from an earlier chapter, those amounts reflect the historical costs BAIT Company reported, not their market prices as of the date of the FISH Company deal. Thus, the BAIT Company balance sheet amounts brought onto the new combined entity's consolidated balance sheet were often drastically less than the value of the shares exchanged in the acquisition.

So if BAIT Company's balance sheet showed net assets (total assets − total liabilities) of $100 million just before the "marriage," $900 million of value given to BAIT Company shareholders by FISH Company would never make it onto FISH Company's consolidated balance sheet for the

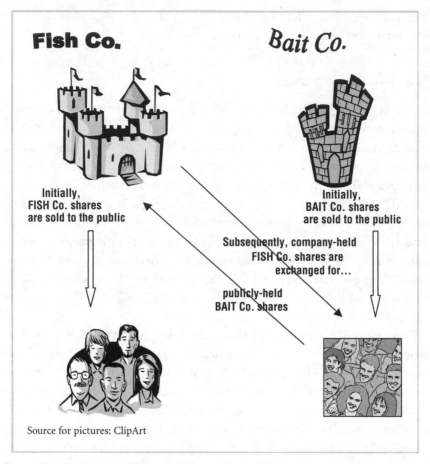

Figure 13.1 Anatomy of a Shares-for-Shares Corporate Takeover

BAIT Company takeover. It doesn't make sense, I know. It was a financial reporting rule that must have made sense to someone at some point in time—indeed it was a generally accepted practice for several decades.

Now, if this very same deal were executed by FISH Company paying cash to BAIT Company's shareholders for their shares in BAIT Company, a different financial reporting method was required. If $1 billion of cash was paid, the deal would be recorded as a $1 billion acquisition and all of BAIT Company's individual assets and liabilities would be added to FISH Company's reported assets and liabilities at an amount reflective of their appraised value (not their BAIT Company recorded historical costs) at the time the deal was done. Chances are that the cumulative appraised value would be much greater than BAIT Company's recorded historical costs for those very same items and yet, still less than the $1 billion FISH Company paid. If BAIT Company's combined net assets are appraised at $400 million, for exam-

ple, what happened to the $600 million difference? It was recorded by FISH Company as an asset called "goodwill" and it appeared in FISH Company's posttakeover consolidated balance sheet as such.

Why would a company pay $600 million over the appraised value of another company's net assets? This is not uncommon and is attributable to the value placed by FISH Company on such non–balance sheet BAIT Company resources as its intellectual property, product reputation, cadre of loyal customers, state-of-the-art distribution channels, product innovation capability, and its talented workforce. Moreover, under the financial reporting rules in force at the time, FISH Company had to depreciate (actually it was called "amortize") the $600 million goodwill asset over time, not to exceed 40 years. Thus, the annual income statement depreciation expense to reflect the "using up" of the goodwill asset would have been at least $15 million ($600 million ÷ 40 years) for each of the next 40 years. What a pain to have 40 years of a recurring $15 million annual expense!

Let's think about these two approaches. You may have gotten stuck on the first example, continuing to wonder why the $900 million never had to be recorded by FISH Company. If you were wondering that, you were not alone. Many in the financial community thought that approach was, quite frankly, without merit. Over time, pressure mounted to have that method eliminated. Finally, the FASB agreed to put the issue on its agenda. After much study, debate, and lobbying, the FASB issued an ED that outlawed it. But loud voices then railed against the fact that companies would now have no choice but to report goodwill in their consolidated balance sheets and drag down income statement earnings for 40 years with a goodwill depreciation expense. To assuage those voices, the FASB then proposed changing the maximum number of years over which the goodwill asset could be depreciated to 20 years.

You would have thought the sky was falling. Companies that had a history of acquiring other companies through the issuance of their own stock raised a ruckus. Quickly, the FASB revised its ED, totally eliminating the requirement to depreciate the goodwill arising from such a transaction. Thus, there would be no future years' "drag-on earnings" just as there had never been under the financial reporting method that had treated the corporate acquisition akin to a marriage. For those who argued that the goodwill item was, in substance, an asset that was "used up" over time, the FASB accommodated them by requiring a periodic review of the balance sheet goodwill amount. The aim of that review is to assess if the recorded goodwill is still as valuable to the business as the amount reported—if it is less valuable, that decrement has to be expensed in that year's income statement. For most companies, there has been no need to reduce their goodwill asset—it just sits on the consolidated balance sheet as an ongoing, untouched intangible asset.

The point here is that the rules for reporting the acquisition of another company changed. One generally accepted method was outlawed and in exchange for eliminating it, a compromise was fashioned to modify the requirements of the remaining method. Such is the reality of the FASB process and the resultant GAAP. As these two examples demonstrate, the derivation of financial reporting rules is a debate-intensive process that often ends with a viable financial-reporting compromise.

When the Rules Change

Rule changes from the FASB are not an uncommon occurrence. Pause for a moment and think about the annual report implications of that fact. If the rules change for a specific financial statement item effective with this year's annual report, that makes last year's annual report noncompliant and not comparable to this year's. Consequently, when the FASB makes a financial reporting rule change one of two actions is prompted. In most instances, a new FASB rule provides very specific transition provisions that permit and instruct companies how to gradually record, over several years, the financial effects of a new rule. In that instance, there is often a requirement instructing companies to discuss in their financial statement footnotes and MD&A the approximate prior year's impact of the change. In other instances, when no transition provisions are provided, companies must actually redo the prior year's financial statements presented in their annual report to comply with the new rule . . . ugh . . . that is a major effort but it is one companies sometimes have no choice but to do.

"Morally Reprehensible" . . . Really?

For many who are learning about financial reporting for the first time, and in spite of the precisionlike patina of an annual report's pie charts, graphs, and columns of numbers, it often comes as a shock to learn that financial reporting is not like mathematics. In mathematics, for example, the area contained in a circle will always equal (π) times (r^2). No amount of special interest group lobbying or constituency compromises will change that—it is a fact. In the financial reporting arena, compromise is alive and well. As a result, it has been argued that the debate and compromise approach to making financial reporting rules is "morally reprehensible" because outcomes end up favoring one group over another.[3]

Wow, I certainly don't buy that verdict nor have I heard many in the business world express that sentiment. Isn't compromise a process intended to provide mutual benefit, not exclusive benefit? Many complex business transactions are not prone to easy, clear methods of financial reporting. The FASB has often found itself having to invent (and I mean that in a positive way) detailed solutions for dealing with novel, complex issues. Historically, the FASB has developed fairly good solutions for the financial reporting challenges laid before it. There is not a scientific-eureka-discovery-like phenomenon it can employ and hone. Financial reporting rulemaking is a human process and therefore prone to the foibles of people—even smart, dedicated people.

Rules versus Principles

One of the current issues in the financial reporting world, probably not to be resolved any time soon, does spring from a legitimate backlash against the FASB's current rule-making process. Many in the financial community believe: (1) there are too many FASB published pronouncements (over 150 Statements of Financial Accounting Standards as of this writing), (2) those pronouncements are too long and too detailed (some are over 100 pages

Insider's Note

Are FASB's financial reporting guide-lines too onerous and too narrow? Some say yes!

long), (3) the process takes too long (often years), and (4) too often those pronouncements spawn numerous, subsequent FASB publications interpreting what was said in the original pronouncement (on some topics, up to 20 or 30 additional clarifications). The issue is: should the FASB publish, and therefore should GAAP consist of, financial reporting guidance limited to short pronouncements that set out the primary objectives to be attained when choosing how best to report a certain business transaction or item? This is a very different approach from the current practice of the FASB, publishing very detailed rules to be followed for a host of specific transactions or a host of specific financial statement items.

The merits of the proposed "principles-based" approach include: (1) it provides leeway for financial managers and accountants to exercise their professional judgment as specific circumstances warrant, (2) official pronouncements would be simpler and shorter than what is currently published, and (3) the approach would lessen the incidence of business events being proactively constructed in certain ways to avoid the precise requirements of existing financial reporting rules. On the other hand, the potential downsides of a principles-based approach to GAAP include: (1) reduced comparability between different companies' financial statements since each would be potentially constructed with more customization, and (2) increased litigation exposure for auditors without the safety of very precise rules against which financial reporting determinations can be made.

Just as we earlier noted the different views expressed on the financial reporting for stock options and corporate takeovers, a range of positions is beginning to develop on the topic of principles-based GAAP. Peruse the excerpts in Figure 13.2, from several financial reporting constituents, reacting to a FASB proposal (titled "Principles-Based Approach to U.S. Standard Setting") to move towards principles-based GAAP.[4]

How would you proceed with such letters from these prominent and varied constituents? It is not clear in which direction the FASB will move. To varying degrees, every issue the FASB tackles prompts parallel reactions. We may see experiments along the way, to explore if a principles-based approach can really work. The International Accounting Standards Board (IASB) uses that approach more frequently than the U.S.-based FASB. The IASB, how-

International Brotherhood of Teamsters (IBT)—a U.S. labor union

The IBT is in support of the FASB's recent proposal . . . The current rules-based system is riddled with exceptions and even exceptions to exceptions. The system is full of loopholes, and frequent rule changes make it necessary for even the most diligent accounting professional to remain current . . . In our view, a principles-based system will correct many, if not all, of the shortcomings of the current rules-based system, and will provide investors with as much direct, reliable, and understandable information about a company as reasonably possible.

Intel Corporation—a U.S.-based multinational corporation

While we support the Board's goal of improving the quality and transparency of U. S. financial accounting and reporting, we do not believe that the Proposal will accomplish that goal. In particular, it is our view that the Proposal's recommendation to eliminate the specificity contained in existing U.S. accounting standards would ultimately have the opposite effect.

U.S. General Accounting Office (GAO)

We have concluded that current accounting guidance is overly rules-based and complex . . . Thus, we strongly support FASB's proposed broad, principles-based approach to high-quality accounting standards.

California Public Employees' Retirement System (CalPERS)

At CalPERS, we believe that many of the issues associated with the recent flood of accounting scandals can be traced to corporate executives who applied the letter of the accounting law rather than the spirit . . . Our current system for GAAP attempts to have a precise rule for every business transaction. Yet, it is impossible for this rules-based system to anticipate every possible accounting situation. Indeed, certain business transactions are created [by companies] to exploit the "gaps" in GAAP.

(continued)

Figure 13.2 Excerpts from Comment Letters Regarding a Rules-based versus a Principles-based Approach by FASB

Figure 13.2 (*continued*)

Goldman Sachs—a U.S.-based investment banking firm
We support the Board's proposal for a principles-based approach to standard setting. We believe such an approach will improve the quality and transparency of U.S. financial accounting and reporting.

America's Community Bankers (ACB)—an industry trade association
While a principles-based accounting framework is attractive in concept, there are numerous practical issues that raise concerns and need to be addressed before adoption. Rather than immediately embracing a new principles-based framework, ACB urges FASB to retain and improve the current system.

Ernst & Young—a U.S.-based multinational accounting firm
We support the Board's efforts to reassess and improve its current approach to standard setting. However, we believe that the Board's proposal for a principles-based approach is ill-defined and, by itself, will not lead to an improvement in the quality of U.S. accounting standards.

---

ever, is relatively new to global financial markets. Its pronouncements are not yet accepted in the United States, where financial litigation is widespread and constitutes a serious contact sport. Nonetheless, the FASB and IASB have committed to GAAP convergence. As they do so, it will be interesting to see whether a principles-based or a rules-based paradigm dominates.

The Inside Scoop

Financial reporting rests on a body of rules primarily promulgated by the Financial Accounting Standards Board (FASB) with the endorsement of the Securities and Exchange Commission (SEC). Those rules evolve over time and the FASB engages in an open-to-the-public discussion process when developing them. This process is often a hotbed of lobbying, debate, compromise, and even reversals of prior positions. The examples of how to report stock options granted to employees, how to account for certain corporate mergers, and a principles-based approach to financial reporting standards were presented as typifying the lobbying, compromise, and diverse views that often exist.

Practical Application

At the most basic level, it is fair to say that the FASB's GAAP-making process, and the official pronouncements resulting from that process, is intended to create annual report information that is useful to a reasonably prudent reader of that report. Early in its existence, the FASB identified several characteristics of what constituted useful financial information. Prominent among the attributes the FASB identified was reliability. Unreliable information is not useful to anyone for any purpose. The conundrum, however, and the focus of much of the debate, negotiation, and compromise throughout the FASB's GAAP-making process, is rooted in the issue of "what constitutes reliable information?"

Can you see how that question was in play in each of the three examples of the FASB process presented in this chapter? Take a moment to reflect on how the issue of reliability was a part of the stock options, corporate takeover, and principles-based approach debates. In regard to stock options, the issue was, in part, that a compensation expense should not be recorded because there was no readily determinable dollar figure to ascribe to the stock options granted. Employees did not pay anything for them. The company did not give up anything to award the options—the company simply printed a piece of paper saying you now had 1,000 options. What monetary figure should a company ascribe to the options it has granted to employees? Well, it is way beyond this book to answer that question. The answer actually ends up being one that requires the use of a mathematical model, drawn from the field of finance, to approximate an option's value. In the end, the FASB said it is more important to use such a measurement approach than to continue to omit the compensation expense from the income statement pertaining to those options.

In regard to the corporate takeover financial reporting issue, the outlawed method was in vogue for so long because, in part, it perpetuated the reporting of the historical costs of the company taken over. The surviving method introduced more judgmentally derived monetary figures into the consolidated financial statements. The tangible net assets of the acquired company had to be appraised—a process replete with judgments, estimates, and lack of precision. Moreover, once those appraisals were made, that figure was deducted from the acquisition purchase price in deriving a catchall, intangible asset category called goodwill. Over what period of time should goodwill be depreciated? Forty years? Twenty years? Not at all? Only when it is judged to be less valuable than its recorded amount? As we know, it is the latter view that FASB ultimately adopted and as you probably can envision, the process of ascertaining whether goodwill's value has decreased is itself fraught with continuous imprecision, estimates, and speculation.

It is not yet clear how debate on a principles-based approach to GAAP will proceed. From the comment letter excerpts presented earlier, it is obvious that some constituencies believe that the precision of very specific financial reporting rules is preferable to only conceptual guidelines. Fundamentally, this too is a debate about more, rather than less, reliability. In the minds of many, more reliable financial statements are those that spring from the execution of narrower rather than broader rules. The reliability achieved is born of the knowledge that the financial statements of two publicly traded companies both adhere to a set of very specific requirements as opposed to each being the product of situation-specific judgments and interpretations.

Under a principles-based approach to GAAP, we'd all have to live with ongoing differences. Human beings are famously not good at this. I, for example, would resent it if my boss rewarded one employee and penalized another, despite similar job performance. (Unless, of course, he rewarded *me*.) My students cry out against any differences they perceive in the grading of exams. In reporting and assessing even minor branches of performance, we tend not to tolerate different scorekeeping methods and interpretations. How much less would we accept this in the financial arena, where our life savings could be at risk?

Whenever you hear a debate pertaining to the creation of new and improved financial reporting, be assured that the issue of reliability has some underlying role in that debate. In such situations, it is useful to ask yourself whether one side of the debate is advocating a position rooted in a desire for more reliable financial information or less, and what are the company insights achieved or lost as a result of those reliability outcomes.

In Anticipation of the Next Secret

Getting dressed and ready for prime time is not quite as simple as the final look might lead you to believe.

Secret #14

It's Not Always as Simple as 1-2-3

Four issues for the experts

The questions behind Secret #14:

- What are some of the recurring and overarching challenges in financial reporting?
- What makes those issues so problematic?
- What, if anything, is being done about them?
- How do companies address these issues in their annual reports?

In Chapter #5, the financial reporting fundamentals behind annual reports were posited to be as simple as 1-2-3. As in all disciplines, however, there are complexities and problematic issues in financial reporting—several of them at the frontiers of the field. As these will shape annual reports to come, it's important to highlight them.

Revisiting the Entity

As defined earlier, the "entity" in an annual report is the corporate body for which that report is prepared, separate and apart from its owners.[1] As further described in Chapter 4, the delineation of a financial reporting entity is subject to important rules, historically tied to the percentage ownership one company has in another. The financial portrayal of an entity has evolved, however, over time and continues to do so.

Not long ago, a company could elect *not* to consolidate in its financial statements a wholly owned subsidiary that focused on a business significantly different from that of the parent company. General Motors, for example, could choose not to consolidate its finance subsidiary, GMAC. This naturally raised concerns about the extensiveness of subsidiary assets and liabilities that were controlled by a parent company but that didn't appear in its financial statements. In response to these concerns, the FASB changed the financial reporting rules to require companies to consolidate all majority-owned entities. Consequently, in its annual report, GM has no choice but to consolidate its core auto manufacturing assets, liabilities, revenues, and expenses with GMAC's more banklike holdings, obligations, and results. And, United Technologies must consolidate its Carrier air conditioning operations with its Sikorsky helicopter business. Such aggregations are the norm.

More recently, in the wake of Enron's collapse, the delineation of the financial-reporting entity has been scrutinized and redefined once again. The reason: Enron's debacle shed a harsh light on companies' creation and use of special purpose entities (SPEs). SPEs are single-purpose organizations created by a parent company and in which the parent holds only a small fraction of the ownership shares. They are used to own and operate assets and liabilities devoted to their specified purpose. Airlines have used SPEs, for example, to own and operate fleets of planes. Banks have created them to own and manage portfolios of mortgage loans or credit card receivables, separate from other banking operations.

Insider's Note

Some believe the rampant use of special purpose entities contributed to the Enron fiasco. Financial reporting rules have since been modified as a result.

Prior to the Enron crash, the financial reporting attraction of SPEs—for the parent company—was straightforward: the parent could record assets and liabilities associated with a specified purpose on the SPE's balance sheet, not its own. Because of detailed financial-reporting rules, the parent at that time did *not* have to consolidate the SPE's financial statements with its own—even though it retained substantive control over the entity's management, and derived both substantial benefits and potential risks from the SPE's operations. Such substantive control was not established through owning large blocks of the SPE's stock but rather, through business contracts and agreements.

When Enron and its SPEs unraveled, the FASB reviewed financial-reporting consolidation rules applicable to SPEs. That review led to a new rule. Now, even if a parent company owns less than 50% of another entity's shares, it must consolidate that entity's financial statements with its own if it, as parent, is the "primary beneficiary" of that entity's activities. These other entities—the candidates for consolidation—are now referred to as variable interest entities (VIEs). Of course, a key issue in implementing this new rule lies in determining when a parent is the "primary beneficiary." We won't go into all the details surrounding guidance on this issue.

For our purposes, it's important simply to recognize a conceptual shift in the delineation of an entity: Under the new rule, the delineation of the entity portrayed in an annual report does not rest only upon the percentage of stock ownership held by a parent company in another entity, but also upon the nature and extent of the benefits received and risks incurred by that parent through that other entity. The new rule brings important, previously excluded data into the parent company's annual report and financial statements. It embraces a broader notion of the "entity" than that which prevailed prior to the demise of Enron.

Insider's Note

The requirement to prepare consolidated financial statements does not rest solely on holding more than 50% of another entity's shares.

In its annual report, a company now must inform readers of any VIEs in its network of affiliated companies. It must further specify whether it consolidated those VIEs in its financial statements. Toward that end, La-Z-Boy, Inc. issued the following in a recent annual report (see Figure 14.1). Please note that La-Z-Boy here defines VIEs for its readers, drawing that definition directly from the FASB.

Looking toward the future, as corporate affiliations evolve, building upon ever more complex and creative contractual arrangements, distribution agreements, and market dependencies, the rules delineating a financial reporting entity may need to evolve, too. The new consolidation rules for VIEs represent a positive step, as they embrace a conceptual approach to the determination of a financial reporting entity, supplementing the percentage ownership approach that's prevailed in the past.

> We adopted [the new FASB rule on VIEs] which
> resulted in the consolidation of several of our
> independently owned La-Z-Boy Furniture Galleries stores . . .
> [Those rules] require the "primary beneficiary" of a VIE to
> include the VIE's assets, liabilities and operating results in its
> consolidated financial statements. In general, a VIE is a corporation,
> partnership, limited-liability corporation, trust or any other legal struc-
> ture used to conduct activities or hold assets that either (a) has an insuf-
> ficient amount of equity to carry out its principal activities without
> additional subordinated financial support, (b) has a group of equity
> owners that are unable to make significant decisions about its activities,
> or (c) has a group of equity owners that do not have the obligation to
> absorb losses or the right to receive returns generated by its
> operations . . . Based on the criteria for consolidation of VIEs . . . we
> consolidated several dealers where we were the primary beneficiary.

Figure 14.1 Excerpt from La-Z-Boy's VIE Disclosure

When Is a Sale a Sale?

After filing financial statements with the SEC, as and when required by law, companies sometimes find they need to correct some of the content presented in those statements. Companies may discover that they've made an error or oversight, that they've misapplied financial-reporting rules, or that a member of their staff has made an intentional misstatement. Under any of these scenarios, companies must correct their financial statements, and refile them with the SEC.

Insider's Note

Aggressive or erroneous revenue recognition practices account for many of the financial statement corrections filed with the SEC.

One of the most common problems necessitating revised filings is inappropriate recording of revenue in a company's income statement. This should not surprise us. Leading financial-reporting interest groups have asserted that revenue recognition guidelines are in desperate need of clarification and strengthening. The chairman of the FASB has noted that there

are more than 180 separate official pronouncements pertaining to revenue
recognition. What a potentially confusing
mess. He's contended that these should be
reviewed, synthesized, and reissued.[2]
Meanwhile, the rise of e-commerce has
generated a profusion of innovative cus-
tomer and supplier arrangements. Under these circumstances, it is perhaps
only to be expected that revenue recognition practices may not be consistent, comparable, and conservatively applied across all corporate settings.

Insider's Note

There are too many revenue recognition financial reporting rules. The SEC has moved to clarify and codify them.

To be fair, however, in today's business environment it's not as easy or
clear-cut as it's historically been to determine when transactions qualify as
sales events. Different companies have applied different guidelines in different ways—sometimes with more creativity than one would hope. The SEC
has been troubled by nonuniform revenue recognition practices used by a
growing number of companies. Anticipating that it might take the FASB
years to study this issue and reformulate rules on it, the SEC issued its own
revenue recognition guidance. This was not out of line. As noted in Chapter
1, Congress has granted the SEC the authority to issue financial reporting
rules and FASB serves at the pleasure of the SEC. That said, the SEC's guidance declared that a sales event must meet all of the following criteria before
a company can report it as revenue in its income statement:

- With regard to the transaction, there is persuasive evidence of a
  vendor/customer agreement (such as a binding contract or pur-
  chase order).
- Product delivery has been made, or services have been rendered.
- The seller's price to the buyer is fixed or determinable.
- Collectability of the sales price is reasonably assured.[3]

These are general rules, of course, open to some interpretation. Recognizing that, the SEC provided additional, more detailed guidance pertaining to specific sales situations. For example, it addressed sales packaged
with seller financing arrangements, layaway programs, nonrefundable up-
front fees, bill-and-hold deals, and those offering various right-of-return
options. Revenue recognition guidance was also issued for the following
scenarios, among others:

- Transactions involving bartered items, as when two companies advertise on each other's Web sites
- Sales over the Internet by companies that do not possess the goods sold
- Sales arrangements that include bundled elements, as when computer hardware is bundled with systems maintenance agreements and/or software licenses[4]

Clearly, while these are all revenue-related events, each is quite different from the others. Likewise, they are quite different from the more traditional sale in which, say, Levi Strauss & Company delivers a truckload of blue jeans to your local department store.

Regardless of their sales arrangements, companies must, in their annual reports, inform readers of their revenue recognition practices. That information is critical because it pinpoints the company's earnings process. And that process, in turn, goes to the heart of the firm's financial results. To put this issue in its most fundamental terms: a company can't report revenue on its income statement until it's been earned, and revenue isn't earned until the firm's earnings process is complete. Because this is such a crucial issue, companies must, in a revenue recognition footnote to their financial statements, highlight the events that signify completion of their earnings process. By way of example, Figure 14.2 is an excerpt, put into bulleted form, from a Walt Disney Company revenue recognition footnote.

Insider's Note

The revenue recognition footnote presented in a corporate annual report is informative and descriptive of a company's basic business model.

Such information is crucial. After all, let's be realistic: Most managers would prefer to report revenue as early in their sales cycle as possible. If I worked for a cable TV channel, for example, and I didn't know the rules governing revenue recognition, I might be tempted to report ad fees the minute I signed a contract with an advertiser. But as Disney notes above, this would be inappropriate. Disney doesn't post ad fees to its income statement until an advertisement airs—even if it must wait a year or more from the date it signs the related contract. Similarly, when the company sells an advance admission ticket to Disney World, it doesn't post revenue until the customer enters the theme park. Until then, it merely recognizes the receipt of

- Broadcast advertising revenues are recognized [in the income statement] when commercials are aired.
- Revenues from television subscription services related to the Company's primary cable programming services are recognized as services are provided.
- Revenues from advance theme park ticket sales are recognized when the tickets are used. For nonexpiring, multiday tickets and tickets sold through bulk distribution channels, we recognize revenue based on estimated usage patterns which are derived from historical usage patterns.
- Revenues from corporate sponsors at the theme parks are generally recognized over the period of the applicable agreements commencing with the opening of the related attraction.
- Revenues from the theatrical distribution of motion pictures are recognized when motion pictures are exhibited.

Figure 14.2 Walt Disney Company Revenue Recognition Disclosure

cash and the incurrence of a liability for the park admittance owed. When the customer enters the park, the company reduces the liability on its balance sheet and recognizes revenue in its income statement.

The recent evolution and elaboration of revenue recognition guidelines has had a generally conservative effect. For multifaceted sales arrangements, the guidelines have tended to delay the reporting of revenue on income statements until most, if not all, aspects of the deal have transpired. This approach provides increased support for the assertion that a sales event is valid and that it won't unravel. What will the future bring in this regard? Stay tuned. The FASB may codify and modify the 180 revenue recognition guidelines. If it does, that's likely to affect some companies' revenue recognition practices—and with them, the earnings declared on their income statements.

Swiss-like Neutrality?

Among other goals, the FASB strives for "information neutrality" in corporate financial statements. That is, it seeks to craft financial reporting rules in such a way that financial statements will not predispose *users* of those statements to behave in a certain way. Most experts agree that the FASB has done a pretty good job in this regard.

A related interest is the effects of financial reporting rules on the behavior of the *issuers* of financial statements. One can make a case, for example, that when new financial reporting rules required companies to start disclosing information on liabilities pertaining to their defined-benefit pension plans, firms began to abandon those plans in favor of defined-contribution and 401k plans that carried no such obligations. Similarly, now that companies must report in their income statements a compensation expense for certain stock options granted to employees, the popularity of such incentive plans appears to be waning. And these are just two examples of powerful shifts in corporate behavior prompted, at least in part, by new financial reporting rules.

This raises an important question: If a proposed new financial reporting rule is likely to affect the behavior of the issuers of annual reports, to what extent should that influence FASB's deliberations on the rule? For example, if a new rule on the disclosure of pension liabilities might lead companies to terminate certain types of retirement plans, is that germane to the decision of whether to promulgate that rule? I think so. But there is much debate on this question. Let it suffice to say that the effects of new rules on the behavior of *issuers* of annual reports are important and should be, in my opinion, a part of rule-making deliberations.

> **Insider's Note**
>
> *Financial reporting rules should not bias annual report readers towards one decision over another. They do seem, however, to influence the actions of companies.*

Gaps in GAAP

Business executives are entrepreneurial and creative. They're always on the lookout for new customers, markets, and products. Many corporate resources are devoted to creating viable innovations in product design, sales arrangements, borrowing agreements, production methods, employee incentives, and many other areas. Moreover, as executives seek to make their mark by finding and seizing new opportunities, they tend to implement creative business ideas on a regular basis.

At the current pace of corporate innovation, financial reporting rules must often play catch-up with business practices. Generally, the FASB or SEC begins to deliberate on the financial reporting rules for a targeted new business practice only after it's been in use for a while, and after they've found an unacceptable level of ambiguity or variance in the way companies report on it in financial statements. Even once those deliberations begin, it may be years before the FASB or SEC issues their final, authoritative guidance.

This introduces a problem: When financial-reporting rules lag business practice, different entities may use different ways of dealing with the issue. This generates variety in the way business arrangements and transactions are handled in annual reports. It makes financial statements less comparable between corporations. Powerful, self-interested parties may exploit the financial reporting ambiguities in such situations for their own benefit. Elements of financial reporting may begin to resemble the lawless Wild West. Frequently, corporate financial executives and external auditors are often the ones who most fervently desire official guidance on how to handle the new business arrangements and transactions in financial reports. Such a desire springs from wanting to do the right thing and wanting to preempt possible shareholder concerns.

> **Insider's Note**
>
> *Financial reporting rules sometimes lag business practice.*

Recognizing the historically long lead times needed to develop financial reporting rules, the FASB has created a SWAT-like team to provide timely and specific guidance. Its Emerging Issues Task Force (EITF) is tasked with responding to the most prevalent and problematic concerns that surface in the field, and to do so in an expeditious manner. The EITF's deliberation and publication process takes much less time than typical FASB procedures. Until the FASB can finish its work on an issue, a published EITF position serves as interim GAAP. A periodic scan of the most recent EITF statements and agenda provides a glimpse into the complex, hot topics before FASB.[5] The EITF has shortened the financial reporting guidance lag time, but not eliminated it.

The Inside Scoop

Financial reports rest upon basic premises and relatively simple processes to capture and codify the effects of business transactions. Nonetheless, the financial reporting field also faces a number of complex and pervasive issues.

In the wake of the Enron scandal, for example, the FASB has reexamined its financial consolidation guidelines and its delineation of the "entity" portrayed in an annual report. It has promulgated new rules, under which, even if a parent company owns less than 50% of the shares of another certain type of enterprise—a Variable Interest Entity—it must consolidate that VIE's financial statements with its own if it, as parent, is the "primary beneficiary" of that enterprise's activities.

A second challenge in financial reporting concerns revenue recognition. Fast-changing technology and entrepreneurial executives have generated many new forms of sales transactions, as well as customer and supplier relationships. This raises questions and variations regarding the point at which a company can be said to have *earned* the revenue on a sale, and can record it on its income statement. The SEC has offered guidance on this issue, asserting that a company could recognize revenue when: (1) its sale was evidenced by a vendor/customer agreement, (2) it had delivered product or rendered services, (3) its price for these was fixed or determinable, and (4) collectability of that price was reasonably assured. Despite these recent guidelines, revenue recognition continues to evolve as a challenging issue, driven by ongoing innovation in transactions, technology, and corporate relations, and by regulatory efforts to keep pace.

In addition to the foundational issues of entity delineation and revenue recognition, the financial reporting world also faces two strategic issues discussed in this chapter. The first of these can best be expressed as a question: in formulating new financial reporting principles, to what extent should financial reporting regulators consider their likely effects on the behavior of companies—the issuers of annual reports? The second issue concerns shortening the time lag between the emergence of new financial reporting challenges—generating variability in financial reports—and the promulgation of official guidance on those challenges.

Practical Application

Let's explore each of these issues a bit further. Regarding the question of entities, please see Figure 14.3, excerpted from a Wendy's International, Inc. annual report.

> The Consolidated Financial Statements include the results
> and balances of the Company, its wholly owned subsidiaries and,
> beginning in 2004, certain franchisees consolidated according to FASB's
> [guidelines] on variable interest entities.

Figure 14.3 Excerpt from Wendy's International, Inc. Entity Disclosure

According to this disclosure, when does Wendy's consolidate the results and holdings of other companies in its own financial statements? Based on this passage, and on our knowledge of the FASB guidelines that it cites, we can answer this question readily. Wendy's consolidates "wholly owned" subsidiaries—those in which it holds all the stock. It also consolidates Variable Interest Entities, in cases in which it's the "primary beneficiary" of the VIEs' activities, even if it holds only a minority interest.

Regarding revenue recognition, Figure 14.4 is an excerpt from a footnote in an annual report issued by Under Armour, Inc., a manufacturer of athletic clothing.

Under Armour has two main sources of revenue—product sales and licensing fees. It makes product sales, in turn, through two primary channels—through its own retail outlets and through those of others, such

> The company recognizes revenue pursuant to applicable
> accounting standards . . . Net revenues consist of both
> net sales and license revenues. Net sales are recognized upon
> transfer of ownership, including passage of title to the customer
> and transfer of risk of loss related to those goods. Transfer of title and
> risk of ownership is based upon shipment under FOB shipping point
> for most goods. In some instances, transfer of title and risk of ownership
> takes place at the point of sale (e.g., at the Company's retail outlet
> stores) . . . License revenues are recognized based upon shipment of li-
> censed products sold by our licensees.

Figure 14.4 Excerpt from Under Armour, Inc. Revenue Recognition Disclosure

as Wal-Mart or Dick's Sporting Goods. Because sales transactions are somewhat different in each of these, Under Armour treats the resulting revenues differently as well. When does the company recognize revenues under each of these scenarios? The answers are all delineated in its footnote. When Under Armour sells goods at one of its own stores, the company recognizes revenue at the point of sale—that is, when you or I take a shirt through the checkout line and pay for it. When the company makes a sale to another retailer, by contrast, it recognizes revenue when it conveys title and the risks of ownership to its corporate customer—that is, generally, when it's loaded goods onto a delivery vehicle for shipment to that other retailer. Finally, the company sometimes grants a license to another company to produce a product bearing the Under Armour logo, for which Under Armour receives a fee. In this business arrangement, Under Armour doesn't recognize revenue until the *licensee* has shipped the resulting goods to *its own* customers.

Regarding the question of information neutrality, Figure 14.5 represents an excerpt from congressional testimony by a vice chairman of the FASB.[6]

Do you agree or disagree with this view? There's no right or wrong answer. Historically, the view espoused in this quote has focused on the behaviors of those *using* annual reports, not on the behaviors of the issuers of those reports. And yet, one might say, the behaviors of the issuers represent the other side of the same coin. If we view the subject this way, we might ask

Unfortunately, it is once again fashionable to suggest that the FASB should abandon the notion that decision-useful information must be neutral and should consider the "economic consequences" of its decisions. Some would even assert that the FASB should try to determine in advance who will be relatively helped or hurt by the result of applying a particular accounting standard, and consider "public policy implications" when it establishes accounting standards . . . The FASB must resist . . .

Figure 14.5 Excerpt from a FASB Official's Speech Regarding Information Neutrality

ourselves a number of questions: Do we want lease accounting rules that incent airlines to fly planes that don't appear on their balance sheets? Do we want companies terminating defined-benefit pension plans because the associated balance sheet liabilities must be disclosed? Do we want employee stock option programs to disappear because companies must report a compensation expense on their income statement equal to the value of options granted?

Do these actions have a public impact? If so, do we want the proverbial chips simply to fall where they may? Or should we try to anticipate the effects of new financial reporting guidelines, and consider those effects in crafting them? Clearly, we can't *order* companies to institute the compensation or benefit plans we want—just because we want them. Financial reporting guidelines, however, have implications in these areas and many others. Those implications, in turn, affect the public. Ignoring them has an effect of its own.

Regarding the lag between innovative business transactions and financial reporting rules, it behooves us to recognize that this dynamic is not unique to the world of financial reporting. Laws and regulations lag new practices and developments in hundreds of fields, including biotechnology, intellectual property, privacy, communications, and even employment. As it applies to financial reporting, therefore, the key question is not Why is there a lag? Or can't it be eliminated? but rather, What must readers of annual reports be prepared to accept? and What can they do to compensate for such a lag?

As new business practices emerge—and they will—readers of annual reports must be prepared for creativity by companies, and variation in the ways they report the financial results of these arrangements. Fortunately, there are many ways to gain a deeper understanding and greater comfort with these variations. As new practices arise, readers can review closely the financial statement footnotes and MD&A sections of annual reports, to examine companies' perspectives on them. Readers can research whether competitors raise similar issues and use similar financial reporting approaches. They can scrutinize auditors' reports to see if these external parties are comfortable with companies' reports. They can also peruse the SEC and FASB websites to learn about new topics under discussion, and ascertain whether these apply to their companies of interest. Also, importantly, readers of annual reports must bring to bear their sense of the integrity of specific management teams.

In Anticipation of the Next Secret

Stay tuned to the business press. Corporate annual reports will continue to evolve. But, you now know the basic "secrets."

Notes

Secret #1

1. Joe Griffith, *Speaker's Library of Business Stories, Anecdotes and Humor* (Englewood Cliffs, NJ: Prentice Hall, 1990), s.v. "Taxes," 347.

2. John Daintith, et al., eds., *The Macmillan Dictionary of Quotations* (Edison, NJ: Chartwell Books, Inc., 2000), s.v. "Taxation," 560.

Secret #2

1. In some instances, the letter is addressed to a variety of stakeholders, not just shareholders, to be more inclusive and multifocused.

Secret #3

1. I first came across this metaphor in Roula Khalaf, "Esperanto for Accountants," *Forbes*, 149, no. 5 (March 1992): 50–51. The history of Esperanto described in this section is from *Encyclopedia Britannica* (1993) 15th ed., s.v. "Esperanto," and from Wikipedia, s.v. "Esperanto."

Secret #4

1. There is a fourth required financial statement—often titled the Statement of Changes in Owners' Equity. For readers of annual reports, this statement generally does not carry the same significance as the other three. It therefore will not be included in the current discussion.

2. The fictitious company Car Seats Inc.'s financial statements presented here are solely for illustrative purposes.

Secret #5

1. By year's end, when the company has received all or some of its 12 months of insurance protection, it will decrease the monetary amount of the prepaid asset account pertaining to the portion of the policy "used up" and make a corresponding increase to the insurance expense account, showing it as a cost of operating the business during the year. Consequently, at year end, the prepaid insurance asset account will show a balance pertaining to that fraction of the 12 months left in force.

2. How might the asset account "vehicles" change during a year? There are at least four ways, assuming it is reported as net of accumulated depreciation. Each of the four ways would be separately detailed in a statement of cash flows. First, vehicles may have been purchased—payments for those will be shown as a line item in the CFFI section. Second, vehicles previously purchased may have been sold during the year—proceeds from such an event are shown as a line item in the CFFI section, too. Third, vehicles owned and used during the year will have been depreciated and that depreciation expense, already embedded in the net income figure as a deduction, will be added back in the cash flow statement in the CFFO section since it was not a cash expense. Fourth, a vehicle asset account may have been reduced due to an impairment of its recorded cost prompted by very negative publicity regarding its safety. That noncash balance sheet reduction would also be reported as a non-cash expense in deriving the period's net income. Consequently, it, too, needs to be added back in the statement of cash flows, converting the accrual-based net income figure to a cash-based CFFO figure.

Secret #6

1. Chapters 6–9 present expanded discussions of issues raised in Mark Haskins and Robert Sack, "Calling All Parties: Now Is the Time to Come to the Aid of the Balance Sheet," *Business Horizons* 48, (2005): 325–335.

2. This chapter's discussion is most easily understood as it pertains to the assets on a corporate balance sheet, and thus we will focus on assets. Amounts reported for liabilities and owners' equity items are also rooted in a historical cost notion, albeit operationalized in terms a bit different from the notion of a purchase price for assets.

3. Unless noted otherwise, all illustrative footnote examples are simple prototypes modified from, and inspired by, a variety of real-world corporate disclosures

from companies such as: Altria Group, Boeing, Campbell Soup, Coca-Cola, FedEx, Ford Motor, General Motors, Harley Davidson, La-Z-Boy, Mattel, Marathon Oil, Microsoft, Molson Coors Brewing, Nike, PepsiCo, Southwest Airlines, Texas Instruments, Wal-Mart, Walt Disney Company, and William Wrigley Jr. Company.

4. Technically, the income statement is only increased (decreased) if the investment asset account's current market value increased (decreased) when that investment is classified by management as a "trading" investment. This designation is assumed to be indicative of management's intent to actively trade that security for the primary purpose of capturing share price movements in a carefully monitored, investor-oriented way. For those passive investments classified as "available for sale" in contrast to "trading," price increases (decreases) at successive balance sheet dates are recorded as gains (losses) in the owners' equity section of the balance sheet, bypassing the company's income statement. Available for sale investments are viewed by management as those not actively traded but rather, those that are likely to be held for a longer time as an investment to be sold when other needs are considered. It is important to note that these two classifications are a bit problematic—in practical terms they are hard to distinguish. They are subject to management's discretion.

5. As of the date of this writing, and in general, the financial reporting rules are beginning to embrace market-value reporting for a wider array of assets. That wider array, however, continues to relate primarily to financial-instrument types of assets as opposed to assets like land or buildings.

6. I first used this analogy in Haskins and Sack, "Calling All Parties," 329.

7. Readers are referred to Alfred King, "Go Figure," *Strategic Finance* 86, no. 1 (2004): 37–40.

Secret #7

1. As we noted in Chapter 1, if the tax books were the focus of our discussion, the preference would be for the largest depreciation expense possible so that the taxable income amount was minimized and thus, the taxes owed also minimized. The IRS recognizes this preference as it applies to depreciation expense calculations and thus sets limits on the maximum allowable amount for a variety of different depreciable assets. GAAP stipulates no such limits.

2. The three additional depreciation methods are the sum-of-the-years digits, the composite, and the 150% declining balance methods. The two long-term contract methods are the "completed-contract" and the "percentage-of-completion" methods. The two oil and gas industry methods are the "full-cost" and the "successful-efforts" methods.

3. It is interesting to note that a change of depreciation methods is considered a "change in estimate" rather than a "change in GAAP." As such, the financial effect of a change in a depreciation method is treated prospectively—no revisions to prior years' financial statements are required. The rules dictating the communications and financial statement adjustments needed when a change is made from one acceptable accounting method to another are beyond the scope of this book. For readers seeking more information on the rules governing the reporting of a change in accounting methods, see FASB's *Statement of Financial Accounting Standards No. 154* (May 2005).

Secret #8

1. It is important to note that this discussion of establishing the useful lives of depreciable assets pertains solely to issues of external constituent financial reporting. As we know from an earlier chapter there is another set of books—the tax books. Suffice it to say for our purposes here that a country's tax code may specify useful-life rules for income tax purposes and those lives may be quite different from the lives used in annual reports.

2. The sale is not reversed because an actual sale was made with all the normal approvals, terms, and deliveries emblematic of the usual mode of conducting business between two companies. The seller shipped goods, the buyer received them, accepted them, and maybe even used them. The sale was a sale. Now, the sale happened to be financed by, perhaps even motivated by, extending credit terms to the buyer. When an uncollectible accounts receivable surfaces, it is the financing aspect of the sale that did not work out. The failure to be paid by the customer is an expense associated with credit financing. It is that expense, not a reduced sales figure, that must be recognized in the seller's financial statements.

Secret #9

1. Recall that chapters 6–9 are expanded discussions of Mark Haskins and Robert Sack, "Calling All Parties: Now is the Time to Come to the Aid of the Balance Sheet," *Business Horizons* 48, no. 4 (2005): 325–335.

2. In the summer of 2006, the FASB put leases on its agenda for review. It is anticipated that any new lease rule that might be forthcoming will not be out before 2009. Many are looking forward to a new rule that will put all lease liabilities on the balance sheet. The SEC has estimated that $1.25 *trillion* of operating lease obligations are "off-balance sheet." See Marie Leone, "FASB Votes to Revamp Lease Accounting," www.cfo.com/fasb (July 19, 2006), accessed August 9, 2006.

3. As this book goes to press, the FASB is still working on its revisions to the financial reporting rules for pensions and other postretirement benefits. The FASB

has decided, however, to require companies to report the over- or underfunded status of their defined benefit pension plans and other postretirement benefit plans on the balance sheet commencing with fiscal years that end after December 15, 2006. This in itself is a huge change as the financial reporting rules prior to this change did not require such a balance sheet depiction.

4. This information is from the 2006 PepsiCo annual report and David Kiley, "Best Global Brands" *Business Week* (August 6, 2007): 60.

Secret #10

1. Much of the discussion presented in this section is reprinted, with permission, from Mark Haskins and Robert Sack, "Of Fiddlers and Tunes: Who Should Pay the Auditors?" *CPA Journal* 73, no. 6 (June 2003): 10–11.

2. Some in the financial arena assert that the SEC would be a better alternative than the stock exchanges.

3. R.K. Mautz and Hussein Sharaf, *Philosophy of Auditing* (Sarasota, FL: American Accounting Association, 1964).

Secret #11

1. The first quote is attributed to Philip Grammage, a noted Australian educator. The second quote is from a very prolific education author and school reformer, John Holt. Both quotes were obtained from www.ontariohomeschool.org (accessed December 17, 2005).

2. Please note that the most straightforward means for calculating the "average" figure for the balance sheet items designated in these ratios is to take the appropriate amount from last year's balance sheet and add it to the same line item's amount from this year's balance sheet and then divide by two. Data for such a calculation are readily obtainable, as all published annual reports present this year's and last year's balance sheets.

3. To gain more specific insights into how efficiently a company used its assets, two additional ratios would usually be calculated. One is the days-of-inventory-on-hand ratio, which equals ending inventory divided by cost of goods sold per day. If this metric were, for example, 22, that would mean that inventory sits in the company's warehouse 22 days before being sold. The lower the value for this metric, the better, assuming there is no danger of product depletion. The second similar ratio is the days-sales-outstanding (DSO) ratio, which is equal to accounts receivable divided by sales per day. Again, the smaller the amount for this ratio, the better as it indicates sooner, rather than later, cash collections from credit customers.

4. *Fortune* magazine publishes the Fortune 500 list around the second week of every April.

5. I first came across the precise articulation of these patterns in Michael Dugan, Benton Gup, and William Samson, "Teaching the Statement of Cash Flows," *Journal of Accounting Education* 9 (1991): 33–52.

6. As an example, see Toddi Gutner, "Who's Ripe for a Takeover?" *Business Week* (May 23, 2005): 122–124.

7. See the review of five bankruptcy models at www.bankruptcyaction.com (accessed December 12, 2005).

8. Josep M. Argilés, "Accounting Information and the Prediction of Farm Viability," (unpublished manuscript, n.d.). Economics working paper 277. Available at SSRN: http://ssrn.com/abstract-76594 (accessed September 5, 2007).

9. William Beaver, "Ten Commandments of Financial Statement Analysis," *Financial Analysts Journal* 47, no. 1 (1991): 9, 18.

Secret #12

1. For an extended discussion of these concepts and two other cultural dimensions, along with the research undergirding each, see Geert Hofstede, *Cultures and Organizations: Software of the Mind* (Berkshire, UK: McGraw-Hill, 1991).

2. See Hofstede for an extensive country listing for each of his culture categories.

3. See Sidney Gray, "Towards a Theory of Cultural Influence in the Development of Accounting Systems Internationally," *Abacus* 24, no. 1 (1988): 1–15 for a discussion of each of the asserted connections between Hofstede's cultural dimensions and the various financial reporting tendencies presented here.

4. Ibid.

5. Ibid.

6. See www.iosco.org (accessed November 18, 2005).

7. Over 100 specific differences between IASB and U.S. GAAP are chronicled, as of August 2005, at www.iasplus.com/USA/ifrsus.htm (accessed May 24, 2007). Two differences of particular pertinence, given the topics discussed in prior chapters, are:

	GAAP	
	IASB	U. S.
LIFO inventory method	not allowed	allowed
Revaluing property, plant and equipment after initial purchase	allowed	not allowed

8. Recent estimates are that 45% and 33% of the world's stock value pertains to companies using IASB and U.S. GAAP, respectively. (See "U.S. GAAP's Decline," *Financial Times* [April 26, 2007]: 18.) This may partly explain why the SEC has recently raised the specter that the IASB/U.S. GAAP 20-f reconciliation requirement may be dropped before complete IASB and U.S. GAAP convergence occurs. (See "SEC and FASB, Convergence, Datatags," *WebCPA* [May 1, 2007].)

9. See www.fasb.org/news/memorandum (accessed November 23, 2005).

10. Robert Bruce, "Giant Step Is Taken Towards a Single Global Standard," *Financial Times* (May 3, 2007): 27.

Secret #13

1. Robert McGough, "Blood Will Run in the Streets," *Financial World* 161, no. 10 (1992): 16.

2. This section is drawn from Darden School reading UVA-C-2216, coauthored by Robert Sack and Mark Haskins.

3. Catherine Gowthorpe and Oriol Amat, "Creative Accounting: Some Ethical Issues of Macro- and Micro-Manipulation," *Journal of Business Ethics* 57, no. 1 (2005): 55–64.

4. The complete letters from which these excerpts were drawn, along with scores of other comment letters on this topic, are available at www.fasb.org/ocl/fasb-getletters.php?project=1125-001 (accessed July 5, 2006).

Secret #14

1. Much of this section is from Mark Haskins and Robert Sack, "Calling All Parties: Now Is the Time to Come to the Aid of the Balance Sheet," *Business Horizons* 48, no. 4 (2005): 325–335.

2. See Ellen Heffes and Jeffrey Marshall, "Updates from FASB, IASB, PCAOB, and the SEC," *Financial Executive* (December 2004): 16. Besides the priority focus revenue recognition issues are receiving from the FASB, the Financial Accounting Standards Advisory Council (FASAC), the Financial Executives Institute (FEI), and the Securities and Exchange Commission (SEC) are all pushing for and supportive of improved guidance on this issue.

3. SEC Staff Accounting Bulletin (SAB) No. 101, "Revenue Recognition in Financial Statements" (December 3, 1999).

4. The specifics of the GAAP guidance published for these latter three scenarios can be found in FASB's Emerging Issues Task Force (EITF) statements No. 99-17, 99-19, 00-3, and 00-21.

5. See http://www.fasb.org/eitf/agenda.shtml for a continuously updated posting of FASB's work agenda.

6. See James Leisenring, "The Meaning of Neutral Financial Reporting," testimony before the Senate Banking Committee September 10, 1990, www.enzi .senate.gov/leisen.htm.

Acronym Appendix

The world of financial reporting has a unique language and set of conventions. This book has sought to unveil some of those. Like many other fields, financial reporting also has its own peculiar array of acronyms—i.e., abbreviations that take on a life of their own and in many instances, become new words themselves. Mark Twain, who was often paid for his articles according to the number of words they contained, is reputed to have said, "I never write *metropolis* for 7 cents, because I can get the same price for *city*. I never write *policeman* because I can get the same money for *cop*." I plead guilty, as are many of my financial reporting colleagues, to perpetuating the use of acronyms as shortened versions of the words from whence they were born. Listed below are many of the acronyms used in this book. They are presented here as a ready reference that I hope is helpful to you when and if needed.

AC   (Audit committee) All public companies must have a board of directors that oversees the company on behalf of the shareholders. The board of directors usually consists of about 10 to 15 people who also organize themselves into various governing committees. One of those committees is the audit committee which, among other things, is responsible for hiring the independent, external audit firm to audit the company's financial records.

A/P   (Accounts payable) Corporate balance sheets report a number of different liabilities owed by the company to various constituencies. Accounts payable represent the year-end monetary amount owed to the company's suppliers for goods and services received before year end but not paid for as of year end.

CEO   (Chief Executive Officer) Just as the military has a hierarchy of people in charge and responsible for ever-larger portions of the organization, companies do, too. The CEO is at the top of the full-time employee corporate hierarchy, responsible only to the company's board of directors. Recent high-profile CEOs include Jack Welch of General Electric, Michael Eisner of Disney, and Bill Gates of Microsoft.

CFFF   (Cash flows from financing) This label applies to the third of three key subtotals displayed in an annual report's required statement of cash flows. The monetary amount associated with this subtotal indicates the net cash inflows (or outflows) pertaining to all of a company's transactions with its shareholders (e.g., selling additional stock to shareholders) and long-term creditors (e.g., borrowing more money from bankers).

CFFI   (Cash flows from investing) This label applies to the second of three key monetary subtotals displayed in an annual report's required statement of cash flows. The monetary amount associated with this subtotal indicates the net cash inflows (or outflows) pertaining to all of a company's purchases and sales of long-term assets such as buildings, equipment, and other companies.

CFFO   (Cash flows from operating) This label applies to the first of three key monetary subtotals displayed in an annual report's required statement of cash flows. The monetary amount associated with this subtotal indicates the net cash inflows (or outflows) pertaining to all of a company's daily, routine, recurring transactions conducted in operating its core business activities.

CFO   (Chief Financial Officer) Amongst the corporate executive hierarchy, the CFO reports to the CEO. The CFO is responsible for the financial affairs, systems, and condition of the company. More specifically, the CFO has the primary responsibility for the company's annual report and all that is communicated therein.

CPA   (Certified Public Accountant) A person trained, apprenticed, and certified in financial reporting, tax, and auditing practices, rules, and conventions. In the United States the external auditor that renders an opinion on the fairness (or lack thereof) of a company's financial statements must be a CPA. In the United Kingdom, a Chartered Accountant is the equivalent of a CPA, and in other countries other terms are used.

ED   (Exposure draft) In the United States, the Financial Accounting Standards Board issues financial reporting rules that companies must follow. Before issuing a rule in final form, an ED of the proposed rule is published along with an invitation to any interested party to comment on its provisions by a certain date. An ED and its related comment letters are accessible by the public.

EITF (Emerging Issues Task Force) Sometimes there is a financial reporting issue/debate so troublesome, so in need of quick resolution or guidance, that the EITF addresses it and renders its guidance prior to the Financial Accounting Standards Board dealing with the issue/debate on a more permanent basis. The EITF is the fast-track path to a financial reporting rule. It issues the interim guidance in effect until such time as the normal Financial Accounting Standards Board deliberative, rule-making, multi-year process is undertaken and concluded on that issue/debate.

FASB   (Financial Accounting Standards Board) The FASB is the primary financial reporting rule-making body in the United States. It is a private, nongovernmental body whose rules and guidelines have the force of law. The FASB serves at the pleasure of the Securities and Exchange Commission.

FIFO   (First in, first out) The costs a company incurs when buying and/or manufacturing the products it sells must flow through the financial records just as the physical goods flow through a company's warehouse, manufacturing plant, showroom floor, and ultimately to customers. Rather than specifically tracking the cost associated with an individual product item manufactured and subsequently sold, FIFO is a simplifying means for flowing product-related costs through the financial records. FIFO simply assumes the first costs incurred to buy or make a product are the first ones associated with the products sold to customers. Thus, the oldest costs incurred are the first assigned to the cost of goods sold expense on a corporate income statement. Indeed, the FIFO nomenclature focuses our attention on which costs are assigned to the cost of goods sold income-statement expense account (i.e., those costs that went "out the door"). By default, and conversely, the latest costs incurred by the company are the ones assigned to the inventory still on hand and depicted on the company's balance sheet as an asset.

GAAP   (Generally accepted accounting principles) The FASB's financial reporting rules, along with those issued by the Securities and Exchange Commission, constitute a body of official pronouncements collectively referred to as GAAP. All companies listed on a United States stock exchange must file financial statements adhering to GAAP.

IASB   (International Accounting Standards Board) The IASB is the international equivalent of the U.S.'s FASB (see above). The IASB is based in London and its financial reporting guidelines/rules are gaining more and more worldwide acceptance. There are many similarities between IASB and FASB rules, but there are some significant differences. As a result, and as this book goes to press, the Securities and Exchange Commission does not accept corporate financial statements filed in accordance with IASB rules as substitutes for (or alternatives to) those required to be filed according to U.S. GAAP.

IDV (Individualism) Geert Hofstede, one of the world's leading researchers and writers on country culture, posited in his classic book, *Culture and Organizations: Software of the Mind,* that countries differ in regards to their peoples' sense of individuality versus collectivism. He depicts the United States as scoring high on valuing individualism whereas in Japan and many Latin American countries individualism is much less valued.

IFRS (International Financial Reporting Standards) The general name given to the financial reporting rules issued by the IASB (see above).

IOSCO (International Organization of Securities Commissions) An international association of over 100 different countries' financial market regulators. The Securities and Exchange Commission (see below) is the U.S. member. In general, the purposes of IOSCO are to promote and share best practices related to high standards of financial markets regulation in order to create and maintain fair, efficient, and transparent global financial markets.

I/P (Interest payable) Corporate balance sheets report a number of different liabilities owed by a company to various constituencies. Interest payable represents the year-end monetary amount owed to the company's lenders for interest accrued on outstanding loans but not paid as of year end.

IRS (Internal Revenue Service) The IRS is the United States' federal-level tax authority. The accounting rules issued by the

IRS govern the filing of corporate tax returns. In many instances, the IRS's accounting rules are different from the accounting rules companies must follow when crafting the financial statements presented in their annual reports to shareholders.

LCM   (Lower of cost or market) From time to time, and due to marketplace factors, a company's inventory on hand may become obsolete, out of fashion, or otherwise less valuable than what it cost the company to acquire or make it. It is that cost figure that is generally reported for the inventory asset on a balance sheet. All companies must subject the inventory monetary amount reported on their balance sheet to an LCM test. If the market value of the inventory is less than what it cost the company, the company must reduce the reported balance sheet amount for that inventory to that lower-market-value monetary figure. Such a requirement is to make sure the inventory asset is not overstated on the balance sheet, vis-à-vis its most likely, subsequent sales price.

LIFO   (Last in, first out) The costs a company incurs when buying and/or manufacturing the products it sells must flow through the financial records just as the physical goods flow through a company's warehouse, manufacturing plant, showroom floor, and ultimately to customers. Rather than specifically tracking the cost associated with an individual product item, LIFO is a simplifying means for flowing product-related costs through the financial records. LIFO simply assumes the latest costs incurred to buy or make a product are the first ones associated with the products sold to customers. Thus, the latest costs incurred are the first assigned to the cost of goods sold expense on a corporate income statement. Indeed, the LIFO nomenclature focuses our attention on which costs are assigned to the cost of goods sold income-statement expense account (i.e., those costs that went "out the door"). By default, and conversely, the oldest costs incurred by the company are the ones assigned to the inventory still on hand and depicted on the company's balance sheet as an asset.

MD&A   (Management's Discussion & Analysis) In their annual reports, companies are required to provide a narrative discussion of their financial performance. That section of the annual report is titled the MD&A. Therein, the company must provide, among other things, explanations of trends in key financial figures, an explanation of the critical accounting estimates it has made, and highlight the important risks it faces.

PCAOB   (Public Companies Accounting Oversight Board) The Sarbanes-Oxley Act of 2002, among other things, created the PCAOB. The PCAOB's mission, according to its Web site, is to "oversee the auditors of public companies in order to protect the interests of investors and further the public interest in the preparation of informative, fair, and independent audit reports."

PD   (Power distance) Geert Hofstede, one of the world's leading researchers and writers on country culture, posited in his classic book, *Culture and Organizations: Software of the Mind,* that countries differ in regard to their peoples' acceptance of hierarchy and the related unequal distribution of power and authority. He reports many of the Scandinavian countries as not accepting of large inequalities in power whereas the populations of many Latin American countries are more accepting of such disparities.

ROA   (Return on assets) ROA is one of the five DuPont financial ratios. It is also one of three common profitability ratios. It is calculated by dividing the monetary amount of a company's net income by its average total assets monetary figure. Generally, the higher the percent calculated, the better the company is performing. If a company's ROA is 7%, that means for every dollar invested in assets the company earned 7 cents that year.

ROE   (Return on owners' equity) ROE is one of the five DuPont financial ratios. It is also one of three common profitability ratios. It is calculated by dividing the monetary amount of a company's net income by its average total owners' equity monetary figure. Generally, the higher the percent calculated, the better the company is performing. If a company's ROE is 10%, that means for every dollar the owners invested in the company that year, the company earned 10 cents.

ROS   (Return on sales) ROS is one of the five DuPont financial ratios. It is also one of three common profitability ratios. It is calculated by dividing the monetary amount of a company's net income by its total sales monetary figure. Generally, the higher the percent calculated, the better the company is performing. If a company's ROS is 4%, that means for every dollar of sales generated that year, the company earned 4 cents.

RV   (Residual value) For financial statement purposes, buildings, vehicles, machinery, and equipment must be depreciated. That is, every year such assets' recorded balance sheet cost must be reduced to reflect a sort of economic "using up" of the asset. In developing a systematic approach to quantifying the annual monetary amount to report for their depreciation, corporate managers must estimate the RV the asset will have at the end of its projected useful life. That RV figure represents the baseline below which that particular asset's cumulative depreciation amount will not go.

SCF   (Statement of cash flows) The SCF is one of the financial statements that must be presented in a company's annual report. SCFs for three consecutive years must be shown side by side in the annual report. The statement depicts the net cash inflows and outflows that a company experienced for the year. It is divided into three sections, each of which was described in

CFFF, CFFO, CFFI. Those sections portray the net cash flows from operating activities (CFFO), investing activities (CFFI), and financing activities (CFFF).

SEC   (Securities and Exchange Commission) The SEC was created in the United States as a result of federal legislation in the 1930s. The primary responsibility of the SEC is to oversee the U.S. financial markets, making sure they are fair, open, and reliable. As part of that responsibility, the SEC has ultimate oversight over corporate financial reporting.

SFAS   (Statement of Financial Accounting Standards) The general name given to the financial reporting rules issued by the FASB (see above).

SOX   (Sarbanes-Oxley Act of 2002) On the heels of the Enron and WorldCom financial disasters, the U.S. Congress passed SOX. Among other things, SOX established the PCAOB (see above), and redefined and increased the financial reporting–related responsibilities of CEOs, CFOs, and ACs. It also placed restrictions on the types of work that external auditors could perform for the companies that they audit, in order to increase the independence of those auditors.

T/P   (Taxes payable) Corporate balance sheets report a number of different liabilities owed by the company to various constituencies. Taxes payable represent the year-end monetary amount owed to the company's tax authorities for taxes due as of year end but not yet paid. There are a number of taxes that a company must deal with, including but not limited to income taxes, real estate taxes, and sales taxes.

UAV   (Uncertainty avoidance) Geert Hofstede, one of the world's leading researchers and writers on country culture, posited in his classic book, *Culture and Organizations: Software of the Mind,* that countries differ with regard to their peoples' sense of being threatened, made uneasy, by uncertainty. He depicts the

United States and the United Kingdom cultures as low UAV whereas many Latin American cultures are high UAV.

W/P   (Wages payable) Corporate balance sheets report a number of different liabilities owed by the company to various constituencies. Wages payable represent the year-end monetary amount owed to the company's employees for employment services rendered to the company before year end but not paid by the company as of year end.

Glossary

In Chapter 3, a limited set of key financial reporting terms was defined, analogized to our personal financial situations, and linked to common corporate examples. Here, a number of additional terms that have surfaced less frequently throughout the book are defined for your intended benefit. As you might expect, there are technical definitions and conversationally friendly definitions—I prefer and present the latter.

Accelerated depreciation A method of reducing the balance sheet–reported monetary amount for a corporate asset such as a building, a piece of equipment, or a vehicle, where it is assumed that the asset depreciates (i.e., is "used up") at a faster rate in the earlier years of its useful life than in its latter years. One popular, systematic mathematical approach for implementing this phenomenon is the double-declining balance method.

Accounting equation The basic accounting equation is Assets $(A) =$ Liabilities (L) + Owners' Equity (OE). The relationship depicted in this equation forms the framework for the construction of a company's balance sheet. At a personal level, if you bought a home for $200,000 by obtaining a $150,000 mortgage and using $50,000 of your savings, the accounting equation would depict the resultant financial picture as $200,000 = $150,000 + $50,000. What is true for the simple depiction of a house we might own is also true for all the assets, liabilities, and owners' equity a company reports on its balance sheet.

Accrual-based accounting   Financial statements published by publicly held corporations must adhere to the accrual-based method of accounting. Accrual-based accounting is a financial measurement and recognition approach that records the financial effects of business transactions without regard to when the cash effects of that transaction occur. For example, accrual-based accounting often dictates the recording of revenues when goods have been delivered to a customer, not when they are paid for by the customer. Likewise, accrual-based accounting requires that expenses be reported in the income statement in the year they are incurred, not the year paid.

Asset turnover ratio   The asset turnover ratio for a company is calculated by dividing total revenue for the year by average total assets for the same year. It is a measure of how efficiently and productively a company used its assets to generate sales. If an asset turnover ratio calculation yields a value of 1.6, that metric is interpreted as: for every dollar invested in assets, the company generated $1.60 of sales. Generally, the higher the calculated value for the ratio, the more productively the company's assets have been used.

Audit failure   An audit failure occurs when a company's financial statements are blessed by their external auditor, published, and then subsequently discovered to have been in error. In such a situation, the audit failed because the auditor did not catch and correct the error prior to the financial statements being disseminated to the public.

Big 4   The Big 4 is a term used to describe the world's four largest public accounting firms that, together, audit most of the world's largest companies. The Big 4 firms are: (1) Ernst & Young, (2) Deloitte Touche & Tohmatsu, (3) PricewaterhouseCoopers, and (d) KPMG International. Besides auditing services, the Big 4 also provide tax and business consulting services to clients.

Capital leases   From a lessee's perspective, a rental agreement (i.e., a lease) qualifies as a capital lease if any one of the following four criteria is met: (1) the agreement contains a bargain purchase option, (2) the agreement transfers title of the leased asset to the lessee at the end of the agreement, (3) the term of the rental agreement is greater than or equal to 75% of the leased asset's useful life, or (4) the present value of the rental agreement's schedule of minimum future payments is greater than or equal to 90% of the asset's purchase price as of the date of the lease. If a rental agreement is classified as a capital lease, a lease liability and leased asset must be recorded on the lessee's balance sheet. Most corporate lessees do not want the leases they sign to qualify as capital leases because they do not want to have to report the lease liability on their balance sheet. The capital lease rules, in essence, require a lessee to report the leased asset as if it had been purchased with borrowed funds.

Cash-based accounting   In contrast to the accrual-based accounting approach (see above), the cash-based approach simply dictates that business events are measured and recorded for financial statement purposes only when cash moves in or out of the company. Cash-based accounting is not acceptable as a means of financial reporting for publicly held companies. For many of us, cash-based accounting is, however, exactly how we measure our personal finances for income tax purposes.

Consolidated financial statements   When one company acquires control of another company (usually through the acquisition of a majority of that other company's outstanding voting shares of stock) the two entities' financial statements must be combined for purposes of meeting Securities and Exchange Commission financial statement filing requirements and for distribution to the public. It is easiest to think of consolidating the two company's financial statements as combining them in a mostly additive way. There are some specific guidelines in GAAP as to what monetary amounts to add together, so it is not merely the process of taking both companies' latest financial statements and adding similar line items together. It is important to note that the process of consolidation frequently gives rise to the consolidated balance sheet recognition of an asset called goodwill (see below).

Contingent liabilities   Sometimes business events arise (voluntarily or involuntarily) for a company where they face the possibility of a future financial obligation. And as of today, it may not be known if that obligation will ever materialize. An example of a voluntary circumstance of this sort is when a company guarantees the debt of another party in case that other party defaults. An example of an involuntary situation is when a company has been sued by a third party. In either instance, the actual financial obligation is contingent on a specific, future event (e.g., default by the other party on the guaranteed loan or a court ruling against the company being sued). If, as of today, it can be reasonably ascertained that the future obligation arising from these situations is *probable* and the monetary amount of that future obligation is *estimable*, a contingent liability must be reported on the company's balance sheet. If that future obligation is not probable or not estimable, the contingent liability need only be discussed in the company's financial statement footnotes.

Current assets   On most corporate balance sheets, all assets likely to be converted to cash through normal business operations within the coming year are classified as current assets. This asset category includes, but is not limited to, cash, accounts receivable, and inventory.

Current liabilities   On most corporate balance sheets, all debts with due dates during the coming year are classified as current liabilities. Examples of current liabilities include, but are not limited to, accounts payable, interest payable, wages payable, and the current portion of long-term debt.

Deferred taxes   Two points are important to understand in regard to deferred taxes. First, corporate managers want to legally postpone paying taxes as long as they can, and they want to pay as little tax as is legally required. Second, the accounting guidelines for determining profit according to the tax code are different from those for determining profit according to GAAP. For example, on IBM's corporate tax return, an accelerated depreciation method (see above) could be used in determining this year's tax deduction for depreciation pertaining to the company's headquarters building, and the straight-line depreciation method (see below) could be used for GAAP purposes for the same building for the same year. Clearly, this year's two depreciation calculations will then differ. It is also clear that over the life span of that building, total depreciation expense under both methods will be the same because the building only had one, actual cost paid for it that can be depreciated no matter which method is used. So, during that building's useful life and for any one year, there will simply be a temporary difference between the tax return depreciation deduction and the GAAP financial statement depreciation expense deduction. As a reconciliation for the tax effects of those temporary differences, a deferred tax account is created and reported on corporate balance sheets. In short, that deferred tax account equals the tax rate times the temporary differences between the revenues and expenses recognized on the tax return versus those on the GAAP-based financial statements.

DuPont ratios Corporate financial statements are useful sources of data for calculating a variety of financial ratios intended to provide insights into a company's financial health and performance. Among the most popular are the five DuPont ratios: return on sales, asset turnover, return on assets, financial leverage, and return on owners' equity. Numerically, and conceptually, the return on assets ratio value multiplied by the asset turnover ratio value equals the return on assets ratio value. Moreover, the return on assets ratio value times the financial leverage ratio value equals the return on owners' equity ratio value. Thus we can see from the DuPont model that the profits a company earns on the owners' investment in the company (i.e., the return on owners' equity ratio amount) is a function of only three things: (1) the profit margins the company earns on goods/services sold (i.e., return on sales), (2) the efficiency with which assets are used to generate sales (i.e., asset turnover), and (3) the extent to which borrowed funds have been used to leverage the owners' money (i.e., financial leverage).

Equity method The equity method of financial reporting pertains to the accounting for an investment in 20% to 50% of the outstanding shares of stock of another company. An ownership interest that falls within this range is assumed to indicate that the investor company has the ability to exert significant influence over the decisions and operations of the investee company. As such, a special means of accounting for that investment is required. In particular, the company purchasing an investment of that size initially records it at the purchase price incurred to obtain it. Then, every year, the investor company will increase (or decrease) the balance-sheet investment asset account by its percentage ownership in the investee company, applied to the investee company's reported net income (or loss). In addition, the amount of any dividends the investor company receives from the investee company as a result of the investor's ownership interest will serve to reduce the investor company's balance-sheet investment asset account.

External audit   All publicly held companies are required to have an annual financial statement audit conducted by professional, non-company-employee auditors. As noted above, the Big 4 firms are the world's leading external auditors in terms of name recognition, number of large publicly held companies audited, and numbers of audit professionals they employ. The objective of an external audit is for the external auditor to render a professional, evidence-based opinion regarding whether or not the financial statements fairly portray the company's financial condition and results of operations in accordance with GAAP. In a corporate annual report, the external auditor's report is published in close, physical proximity to the company's financial statements. In that audit report, the external auditor's opinion is presented for all to read.

Financial leverage ratio   This financial ratio is one of the five DuPont ratios. It is calculated using data from a company's balance sheet, dividing the company's total assets by its total owners' equity. The result of that calculation indicates the extent to which the owners' money has been multiplied (i.e., leveraged) by the company in acquiring its assets. Clearly, and based on $A = L + OE$, any assets not financed by owners' money have been financed by borrowed funds. The higher the numeric value of this ratio, the more a company has relied on borrowed funds, relative to owners' funds, to finance its assets. Generally speaking, borrowed money is not as costly to a company as obtaining money from owners, so financial leverage is good. It is good up until a company has borrowed so much that it is in jeopardy of not being able to repay (pay) the borrowed funds (interest) according to their contracted schedule. Thus, too much debt is not good and zero debt is also not good. Companies are continually striving to ascertain just the right blend of borrowed funds versus owners' funds.

Fiscal year end   This is the term given to the calendar date that companies select as marking the end of their financial year. Companies can pick any date they wish. Most choose to have their fiscal year coincide with the calendar year.

Form 1040 This is the means by which individuals in the United States file their federal tax information with the Internal Revenue Service. The due date for this filing is April 15.

Form 1120 This is the means by which corporations in the United States file their federal tax information with the Internal Revenue Service. The due date for this filing is the fifteenth day of the third month, following a company's fiscal year-end date.

Form 10-k This is the annual means by which U.S. corporations with securities listed on a United States stock exchange file the financial information they are required to file with the Securities and Exchange Commission. A part of that filing must contain audited, GAAP-based financial statements. The due date for such a filing is 60 days after a company's fiscal year-end date.

Form 20-f This is the annual means by which non–United States companies with securities listed on a U.S. stock exchange and who do not publish financial statements using U.S. GAAP, reconcile certain parts of their financial statements to U.S. GAAP. This form is filed with the Securities and Exchange Commission and is thus available to the public.

Goodwill Goodwill is an asset that appears on many corporate balance sheets. It does not pertain to the positive standing a company may have in its community or the charitable good works it has performed. For financial reporting purposes, goodwill only arises when one company buys another. Moreover, it only arises in that instance when the buying company pays a price to acquire the other company that is in excess of the appraised value of the acquired company's net assets (net assets = total assets − total liabilities). Why would a company pay a price in excess of the appraised value of the net assets it is getting from its purchase of another company? The answer is frequently because of the intrinsic worth of the other company's management team, reputation in the marketplace, customer loyalty, track record of innovation, and other such benefits that will accrue to the buying company.

Historical cost One of the fundamental questions in all of financial reporting is: at what monetary amount should those items that are reported in the financial statements be reported? In the United States, and most elsewhere around the world, all financial statement items start out being reported at the original purchase price incurred to obtain them—i.e., their historical cost. In some instances, that recorded cost figure is left unadjusted on the balance sheet no matter how long it continues to exist and be used by a company. An example in this regard is land. On the other hand, there are instances where that historical cost figure is adjusted down over time to reflect the "using up" of the asset. An example in this regard is the depreciation recorded on a building. In still other instances, such as passive investments (see below) in another company's stock, the original historical cost number may be adjusted up or down to reflect changes in the investment's market value.

Intangible assets   Some of the most valuable assets a company might own are those that you cannot drive, push, pull, turn, plug in, spend, or MapQuest® to find. Brand names, trademarks, customer lists, patents, goodwill (see above), and licenses are some examples of intangible assets that might be found on some companies' balance sheets. There are also a number of intangible assets that do not get reported on corporate balance sheets. Those would include intellectual capital, community goodwill, a reputation for quality, and talented personnel. The issue that most often determines if an intangible asset is reported on a company's balance sheet is whether or not it was acquired in an open, marketplace transaction. Generally, it must have been acquired through such a transaction, as opposed to being self-created, to qualify for balance sheet presentation.

Internal financial controls   Companies engage in thousands, if not millions, of business transactions each year. Moreover, the company personnel involved in various aspects of those transactions are often geographically dispersed and operate without a boss looking over their shoulders. Those circumstances, however, do not negate the fact that there are proper ways to identify, record, and report the financial effects of business transactions. The policies and procedures a company establishes to guide and instruct personnel in the required ways to capture all pertinent financial data from the company's business transactions are what is collectively referred to as a system of internal financial controls. The overall purpose of such a system is to ensure the accurate and timely generation of financial data springing from a company's business operations. In compliance with the Sarbanes-Oxley Act of 2002, CEOs and CFOs must certify in their annual reports that their company does or does not have a sound system of internal financial controls in place as of year end.

Life span   When financially depreciating corporate assets such as buildings, vehicles, equipment, and machinery, an estimate must be made of the asset's useful, productive life. That life span is most often estimated in terms of number of years but it can also be estimated in terms of number of operations-oriented measures the asset will deliver. In regards to the latter, a car's life might be denominated in terms of number of miles it will be driven while it is owned rather than the number of years it will be owned. Once a life span is established for a depreciable asset, a depreciation method is chosen in order to systematically calculate the reduction in the asset's reported balance sheet monetary amount each year. That same amount is also recorded as a depreciation expense on that year's income statement.

Noncurrent assets   On most corporate balance sheets, all assets likely to provide the company with a benefit beyond the coming year are classified as noncurrent assets. Such an asset category includes, but is not limited to, land, buildings, vehicles, investments in other companies, and goodwill.

Noncurrent liabilities   On most corporate balance sheets, all debts with due dates beyond the coming year are classified as noncurrent liabilities. Examples of noncurrent liabilities include, but are not limited to, bonds payable, mortgages payable, and certain employee postretirement obligations.

Operating leases   If a rental agreement does not qualify as a capital lease (see above), it is classified as an operating lease. Under an operating lease, neither the asset leased nor the related lease liability is recorded on the lessee's balance sheet. The financial consequences of an operating lease are merely the periodic recording of rent expense as each month's rental payment is made.

Passive investments   A passive investment is when one company purchases less than 20% of the outstanding shares of stock of another company. It is assumed that an investment of such a size is not enough to exert significant influence or control over the company whose shares were purchased. Once the investment is placed on the purchasing company's balance sheet as an asset at the amount paid for it, subsequent balance sheets are adjusted to reflect that investment's market value.

Regulation Fair Disclosure (Reg FD)   In 2000, the Securities and Exchange Commission implemented Reg FD. In short, this regulation prohibits the release of corporate information limited to only selected members of the public (e.g., large institutional shareholders). Under Reg FD, if there is intentional or even unintentional release of significant corporate information (e.g., closing of a plant in China, resignation of the CEO next week, etc.) to a public party, the company must take prompt action to provide that same information to the public at large.

Residual value   For financial statement purposes, buildings, vehicles, machinery, and equipment must be depreciated. That is, every year such assets' recorded balance sheet cost must be reduced to reflect a sort of economic "using up" of the asset. In developing a systematic approach to quantifying the annual monetary amount to report for their depreciation, corporate managers must estimate the residual value the asset will have at the end of its projected useful life. The residual value amount represents the baseline below which that particular asset's cumulative depreciation deductions will not go.

Retained earnings   Within the owners' equity section of a corporate balance sheet, there are two primary sources of funds that a company raises from its owners. The first is from the initial sales of shares of stock to the public. The second is retained earnings. The retained earnings account is indicative of a company's entire history of cumulative net income less the dividends it has paid to shareholders. In essence, every dollar of a company's net income really belongs to the owners. Owners generally do not expect the companies they have invested in to pay dividends equal to 100% of any given year's net income. Owners believe that the company can actually reinvest those profits into the business and generate ever-higher returns for the future benefit of owners. Because those profits have been reinvested in all sorts of business activities, retained earnings is not a figure representing a cash amount sitting in a corporate vault somewhere for safekeeping for shareholders.

Revenue recognition   The central activity of any company is to generate sales of its products and services to its customers. From a financial reporting perspective, an important task is identifying that moment in time when the sales process is completed—i.e., the selling company's contracted responsibilities are fulfilled to the satisfaction of the customer. It is at that moment of completion that the monetary amount related to the sales event can be recognized (i.e., reported) in the company's income statement as having been earned. Companies are required to describe their revenue recognition policies in their financial statement footnotes.

Straight-line method of depreciation   A method of reducing the balance-sheet-reported monetary amount for a corporate asset such as a building, a piece of equipment, or a vehicle, where it is assumed that the asset depreciates (i.e., is "used up") uniformly over its projected useful life.

Tangible assets   This term refers to all those corporate assets that have a physicality that allows them to be seen, touched, held, and kicked. This category would generally include assets as cash, raw materials, finished goods ready for sale, partially completed products in production, buildings, vehicles, equipment, and machinery.

Units-of-production depreciation method   A method of reducing the balance-sheet-reported monetary amount for a corporate asset such as a building, a piece of equipment, or a vehicle, where it is assumed that the asset depreciates (i.e., is "used up") in direct proportion to a measure most indicative of its actual use. For a delivery truck, this might be miles driven this year versus the total number of miles estimated that it will be driven over its useful life. For a jet engine, the measure might be related to flight hours.

Write-off (or write-down)   From time to time, an asset on a company's balance sheet is deemed unusable, obsolete, or not worth the monetary amount depicted for it there. Perhaps a building has been condemned due to its foundation resting on a toxic landfill. Or a factory is mothballed because the products it was designed to make are no longer marketable and it would be too expensive to retrofit the factory for other uses. In situations like these and others, the diminution of that asset's value below what the balance sheet reports for it, if perceived to be permanent and significant, must be subtracted from (i.e., written off) that asset account. The corresponding financial effect is an increase to an income statement expense account. Thus, an asset write-off reduces the amount reported for the asset on the company's balance sheet and it also reduces the company's net income in the year of the write-off. Companies want to avoid finding themselves in a position of having to write off assets.

Index

About the Author

MARK HASKINS has been involved in the financial reporting arena as an auditor, professor, consultant, and writer for more than 30 years. Currently he is Professor of Business Administration at the University of Virginia's highly acclaimed Darden Graduate School of Business Administration. At the Darden School, he teaches in both the MBA and executive education programs. Recently the *Financial Times* rated the Darden School's executive education faculty #1 in the world. In both programs, he unveils the informative world of corporate annual reports to those seeking to know more about such financial stories.

He has designed and delivered financial learning experiences for all levels of employees at such companies as IBM, INTELSAT, Aetna Insurance, Norfolk Southern Railroad, Harris Corporation, United Technologies, AES Corporation, Rolls Royce NA, and the U.S. Navy. Professor Haskins has taught business managers around the world including the United Kingdom, Belgium, Thailand, Germany, Australia, and Hong Kong.

Besides numerous articles in business journals, he is coauthor of three financial reporting textbooks, coeditor of the *CFO Handbook* (McGraw-Hill Publishing), and coauthor of *Teaching Management: A Field Guide for Professors, Consultants and Corporate Trainers* (Cambridge University Press).

Professor Haskins has served on the University of Virginia faculty senate and on the American Accounting Association's executive committee. He earned his Ph.D. degree from Penn State University and currently resides, with his wife, near the Blue Ridge Mountains in Charlottesville, Virginia.